MW01617896

MAKI OPUS

MAKI OPUS

MAKI AND ASSOCIATES

With over 650 illustrations

Table of Contents

Foreword

Gary Kamemoto
Principal, Maki and Associates

Following the calm and peaceful passing of Fumihiko Maki on 6 June 2024, at the remarkable age of ninety-five, Maki and Associates commemorated its sixtieth anniversary in 2025 – a significant milestone for the firm he founded in 1965. In Japanese culture, sixty years mark the completion of a full lunisolar cycle, known as *kanreki*, symbolizing not only reflection on past achievements, but also the promise of renewal and new beginnings. This resonance of continuity and reinvention is a fitting lens through which to celebrate and honour Maki's remarkable legacy.

In Western tradition, a sixtieth anniversary is often celebrated as a diamond jubilee – a metaphor that captures both brilliance and strength. This monograph, *Maki Opus*, seeks to honour this duality: a reflective tribute to six decades of design activity and an inspiring call to explore new horizons. It aims to chronicle the guiding principles, aspirations and evolution of our inquiries concerning architecture, the city and contemporary society.

Chance Encounter: My Voyage with Maki

Fumihiko Maki once said that 'in every person's life there are always a number of encounters. What is thrilling about each one is that it opens up a new reality when we least expect it. We see life's romantic aspects in these unexpected encounters. Every creation of a new reality begins with an encounter, sometimes by chance. I value such encounters and hope to share the joy they bring with people I meet.'

My 'chance encounter' occurred forty-four years ago, in the autumn of 1981, while I was studying at the University of Southern California. My professor, Frank Dimster, had been one of Maki's first students at Washington University in St. Louis in 1962. Amid the flourishing era of post-modernism, I am embarrassed to admit that I had not heard of Fumihiko Maki. Coincidentally, Maki was invited to the school to give a lecture at this time, marking my first encounter with him and his work. Looking back, this was the moment I embarked on my voyage with Fumihiko Maki and with Maki and Associates.

The lecture featured presentations of his latest endeavours which included Iwasaki Art Museum, Keio University Main Library, phase III of Hillside Terrace, Hiroo Bank and a competition entry for Tête Défense. I was instantly captivated by the design approach, a marked departure from the popular

Garden party at Kenzo Tange's residence.
Kenzo Tange (left), Fumihiko Maki (centre),
Yoshio Taniguchi (right).

Maki and Associates Nihonbashi Office, 1967.
Morikazu Shibuya (left), Akira Ozawa (centre),
Fumihiko Maki (right).

Maki and Associates Hillside West Office, 2016.
Gary Kamemoto (left), Fumihiko Maki (right).

4 World Trade Center, fifty-seventh-floor roof terrace construction site.

movement of the time but of a modernism influenced by Japanese sensitivity. This masterful juxtaposition of old and new, Western and Eastern, building and landscape, created an ambience of quiet calm, elegance and serenity. I vividly recall the thrill of listening to Maki's explanation of his work, similar to the feeling of watching the plot of a movie unfold.

Beyond the exhilaration of his lecture, I was left with an indelible impression – not of the Japanese architect I had imagined, but of a gentleman – an intellect, fluent in English, exuding international sophistication, wisdom and charm. Impeccably dressed in a dark blue suit with a striped Burberry tie, Maki embodied a duality that mirrored his work. As a Japanese-American of third descent, bridging two cultures since childhood, this powerful encounter ignited my ambition. Inspired by my instant admiration, I found the courage to seek a summer internship at Maki and Associates, then in Nihonbashi, facilitated by a recommendation from Professor Dimster.

After a brief interview and review of my portfolio, Maki smiled warmly and gave me a chance. This marked the beginning of an unforgettable journey with him. Years later, I learned that Professor Dimster had introduced Maki to tennis during his teaching tenure in Los Angeles, forging a close friendship between them. Maki once joked that if he had never played tennis, Frank would have never sent me.

Since joining Maki and Associates in 1984, my life has been deeply intertwined with Maki's. Most mornings began in his private office, where the surrounding greenery and soft sunlight streaming through clerestory windows created an atmosphere of calm serenity. This idyllic setting became a place for me to report, for him to counsel, and for us to share in heartfelt conversation. Frequently, I found in him a sagacious and paternal presence, tenderly guiding me with care and insight. Our dialogues transcended our projects, nurturing an interdependent relationship that blossomed over the years.

We journeyed across the globe together, expanding our portfolio on an international scale, even as he approached the venerable age of ninety. He took immense pride in his independence and revelled in the freedom our travels afforded. Never once did he permit me to bear the weight of his luggage and bags, typical in Japanese customs of business hierarchy.

I remember an important presentation to His Highness the Aga Khan in Toronto that had been planned months in advance. A week before the meeting, I suffered a cycling accident that left me with a fractured collarbone, my arm immobilized in a sling. Throughout the trip, Maki would help me with my coat and luggage, defying the social norms. This exemplified his level of humility and support. Fumihiko Maki's graciousness finds expression in the elegance and thoughtfulness of his architecture, which reflects his deep respect for humanity and his unwavering commitment to acquire an enduring social value that might be called a 'new humanism'.

Timeless Serenity

Fumihiko Maki, to those who met him, was a gentleman of dignity and quiet elegance. He likened the accumulation of experiences and knowledge over the years to the growth of a tree. Each layer expands outwards around pivotal moments. Much like the seasonal budding of a tree, some lessons or encounters are imperfectly absorbed or shed over time, while others take root and flourish. These buds represent the potential for new life – some wither, others grow into branches, and occasionally, a branch extends in unexpected directions, shaped by external forces.

Through what may appear to be chance occurrences, the essence of the tree remains resolutely clear. Its form transcends mere considerations of size or proportion, embodying deeper principles where ethics and aesthetics converge. Just as the true shape of a tree gradually reveals itself over time so, too, do the contours of a life emerge with clarity. Only through the passage of time can the contours of a life be truly discerned, understood and measured. This moment invites us to reflect on Maki's lasting legacy – a narrative that not only sheds light on the past but also guides us as we navigate the path towards the future.

The Hillside Terrace complex (1967–1992) in Daikanyama, designed in six phases over twenty-five years – and close to our hearts – serves as a vivid narrative of change, capturing a concept that has developed over its journey and holds the promise of further evolution. A close 600 metres (1,969 ft) away on Yamanote Boulevard, we designed and relocated our office to Hillside West in 1998. While Fumihiko Maki is celebrated as an international architect, he has been an integral part of this urban village. The office where he created, the cafe where he had his lunches, the bistro where he drank wine and the bar

Maki and Associates alumni party: Fumihiko Maki ninetieth birthday celebration.

Ninetieth birthday postcard designed by Fumihiko Maki: a self-reflection.

Fumihiko Maki at his desk at Hillside West.

where he enjoyed a gin martini, the bakery that made his favourite bagels, the gallery we use for events, the banquet room that hosts our bi-annual parties, or the French restaurant for special occasions, alongside the residence of his family, all form our shared community in Daikanyama – a place we cherish and enjoy. In the spaces he crafted we remain enveloped in the light of his humanity, his love for people and his gentle spirit.

A Quiet Call for a New Humanism

Maki often made an analogy where buildings are like human beings. Both are born and survive to a certain old age but are always hoping to maintain good health. It is about life! Buildings must be appreciated by people who use them and have society's agreement on their life. Architects are entrusted to make buildings that are good to live in so that these buildings are loved and, at the same time, express something for society. Each client, each project and each place have different attitudes towards architecture, towards the life of architecture. There is no recipe that guarantees success. We always learn from what we have done and try to do something better next time. To Fumihiko Maki, architecture provides a tremendous opportunity to think about human beings, cultures and technology, and he never stopped thinking about them for it gave him great joy. On his ninetieth birthday celebration, he produced a collage likening himself to a horse sprinting towards his eternal quest and in pursuit of architectural ideals that constantly motivate but never fully satisfy, always propelling him forward in his search.

Empathy, Collaboration and Innovation

Throughout his extensive career in both professional and academic realms, Fumihiko Maki consistently highlighted one project above all others: Maki and Associates, the firm he founded. For Maki, the practice represented his most significant design endeavour, one that remains, and will always remain, a work in progress. It is, in his view, a continuous evolution driven by intellectual diversity. The environment of the office embodies Maki's expansive vision of architecture and urbanism, where diverse perspectives and voices are freely expressed in an egalitarian and collaborative atmosphere. This open, communicative approach stands in contrast to the traditional top-down hierarchies, instead encouraging an interactive exchange of ideas.

In practices led by a 'Master Architect', a charismatic figure acts as a true master of their trade with an approach that becomes the golden rule, just like the word of god. Fumihiko Maki was completely different. Much like his mentor, Kenzo Tange, with whom Maki worked for six months after graduating from the University of Tokyo, Maki embraced rational methods in addressing artistic challenges. Both Maki and Tange valued open, cross-disciplinary discussions, where the exchange of ideas significantly informed and strengthened the design process. Maki's approach, like Tange's, fosters a collaborative environment where ideas and solutions are generated collectively and critically examined for their viability and relevance. This practice, this discipline, has allowed Fumihiko Maki's work to remain fresh and significant, as many have attested.

Influenced by his career in academia and research, Maki intentionally maintained a mid-size office, typically around fifty people, to preserve a human-scaled environment that facilitates direct, unimpeded communication. Over its sixty-year history, over 180 professionals (at the time of writing) in addition to current staff have provided invaluable contributions to the works we celebrate through this *Opus*.

Endurance of the Written Word

Fumihiko Maki once said that publications are equally vital acts of creation as the buildings we design. Written words often endure beyond the lifespan of the buildings they describe, offering a timeless platform for ideas to transcend their moment, preserve perspectives and illuminate the creative processes shaping architecture's evolution. In the later years of his extraordinary career, Maki envisioned documenting his journey and that of Maki and Associates. Called upon by Maki to succeed the firm in 2021, this is an unexpected privilege and special honour to introduce this oeuvre. It is our hope that this monograph fulfils that vision – a reflection of work and thought. More than a historical record or archive, it is an invocation: a bridge between past achievements and future possibilities. In a rapidly transforming world, it stands as both a culmination of a rich legacy and a call to inspire new approaches and answers to the humanity of architecture.

Formative Years

Journey to the West

Panathinaikos Stadium and Plaza, Athens, Greece, 1959.

The beginning of the 1960s was a period of intense life experiences for me and a time when I finally formed a certain perspective on architecture and the city. I was able to develop this new perspective through my time on the Graham Foundation Fellowship, my friendships with the Metabolism Group and Team Ten, and through the urban design programme at Harvard University.

I spent most of the 1950s and early 60s in the United States, when it was the richest country in the world. I witnessed and experienced firsthand the maturation of a mass society and the rapid growth of capitalism. The two year period from 1958 to 1960, when I was a fellow of the Graham Foundation, was perhaps the most memorable. My only obligation was to spend a week in Chicago, the Foundation's base, and this took place in September of 1958. While there I met other fellows, including the Indian architect B. V. Doshi, the Spanish sculptor Eduardo Chillida, and the Cuban Surrealist painter Frederick Kiesler, who, unlike the rest of us, was already internationally known for his Endless House and other works.

Thanks to the Fellowship, over the next two years I visited many countries in Southeast Asia, India, the Middle East and Europe. My intention was to see countries and regions that I didn't know and experience architecture based on local historical traditions. Throughout these travels – from magnificent baroque cities to mountain villages – I found that each building was like a fossil of human intention, its collective influences strongly present. And I gradually learned that the more magnificent a building is, the more it serves as a testament to the history of various human desires, grudges and even tragedies.

I still remember the excitement I felt upon seeing the Mediterranean Sea for the first time. One morning in 1959, I drove out of Damascus, the ancient capital of Syria. From the hills above Byblos, I finally saw the Mediterranean shining under the blue sky off to the west. By the next afternoon, I was standing on a hill overlooking Beirut, then known as the jewel of the Middle East. Under the azure sky, the wave caps of the sea sparkling in the sunlight were unforgettable.

I was also impressed by the small but coherent groups of community dwellings in this region. The contrast between the dark shadows of the dwelling walls and the gorgeous colours that emerged when the light hit them was striking. A kind of 'group form' appeared as they folded on top of each other along steep slopes. Yet they were created from very simple forms and spaces – for example, a group of

Beirut, Lebanon, c1895.

private rooms arranged toward a small open court. The aggregation of individual pieces created a strong whole, a clear structure that despite its chaotic appearance was a forceful contrast to our modern cities, which are more a product of gigantic faceless systems.

In many regions of the Mediterranean and the Middle East, building architecture and building towns are synonymous. But in Japan at that time, architects and architectural historians had not yet begun to survey similar settlements. Therefore, I was experiencing this accumulated culture and wisdom for the first time. The importance of typology and the function of assemblage as collective social memory were on full display. As I faced a variety of challenges in the field of urbanism, these travels – and the discovery of these foundational urban principles – ultimately became the main focus of my 1964 essays published by Washington University, *Investigations in Collective Form.*

Approach to the town of Assisi, Italy, 1960.

A joint proposal for Shinjuku Terminal Redevelopment Project – formerly the site of a water purification plant – was co-authored by Fumihiko Maki and Masato Otaka as their contribution to the manifesto *Metabolism 1960*. Concurrent with the proposal was the 'Toward a Group Form' essay, drawing on travel observations through Mediterranean and Middle Eastern cities and villages.

City Room, Movement Systems in the City, November 1965 – a transitional space, both defined and fluid, neither inward nor outward, neither closed nor open, where human activities converge, interact and disperse.

The Metabolist Group

In 1965, after a long period of living abroad, I started my architectural design practice in Tokyo. At this time, the other Metabolist members were already established as up-and-coming young architects in Japan. Through the introduction of Koji Kamiya (who I knew from Kenzo Tange's Atelier), I got to know these core figures of Metabolism: Noboru Kawazoe, Kiyonori Kikutake, Kisho Kurokawa and Takashi Asada, their spiritual mentor.

In the Japanese architecture world at that time, Togo Murano and Kunio Maekawa were at the top. Kenzo Tange, Hiroshi Ohe, Takamasa Yoshizaka and other up-and-coming architects were also quite active. The fact that attention and commissions were soon to go to the young Metabolists – who had not yet achieved much beyond their group name – was a great surprise to all. It was a product of the Japanese mentality of the 1960s, and an appreciation of the positivity and creativity they radiated. In contrast to England's Archigram group (a contemporaneous association, but one which had little opportunity to build), Metabolism was a hopeful movement directed to the actual realization of forward-looking, futuristic dreams for the built environment. Luckily, in contrast to contemporary China's fast-moving consolidation of mature international capital markets and architecture, the Metabolists in Japan had adequate time both to reflect on their intentions and still construct actual buildings to evaluate their ideals.

In 1960, the World International Design Conference was held in Tokyo. At that time, I put forth a joint proposal 'Toward a Group Form' with Masato Otaka, published in the pamphlet *Metabolism 1960.* Other Metabolist members were establishing themselves as young architects at the forefront of the Japanese architectural scene, gradually becoming known overseas as well. I was already approaching my forties, so I did not want to be left behind. Japan's economy was booming and this enabled some of my ideas to be realized. One idea was the multi-use building complex known as Hillside Terrace, the starting point of my conceptualization on the relationship between the individual and the whole in architecture and urban design. Another realized project was the only built collaboration among the members of Metabolism, a housing complex for low-income families in the suburbs of Lima, Peru.

Fumihiko Maki and Kiyonori Kikutake, 1969.

In particular, Metabolism's theory of 'metamorphosis' and its relation to sustainable city development came to the forefront in Lima. Our Metabolist Team proposal – one of three selected from across the world – played a pioneering role in establishing a more flexible way of living and used a spatial system that went beyond rigid functionality. Since completion, the buildings have been transformed well beyond our imagination. Some additions that we expected from the beginning were quickly completed and our white exterior walls were soon painted in various colours. But many more elaborate and unexpected transformations were also apparent. In some places, even the space in front of the housing was converted into a restaurant – a metamorphosis of the building programme itself.

Building on similar principles to the vernacular villages encountered on my journeys to the West, the Lima housing is a testament to how the city can only be maintained by the independence of each individual building or community that uses it. In contrast to the other Metabolists, I have always taken the position that our environment cannot easily be governed by rigid forms and systems, and that the domination of the individual will is ultimately stronger. Although these considerations eventually took me down a different path from the other members of Metabolism, for the first decade we shared a certain spirit of the times as we embarked on our respective careers as architects in Japan.

The First Team X Meeting

Tokyo's World Design Conference in May 1960 was a seminal gathering of the world's leading designers, architects and industrial designers. Among the prominent architects invited were Paul Rudolph and Louis Kahn from the United States. I already knew Rudolph very well and spent a memorable evening at the home of Kiyonori Kikutake, one of the central Metabolist figures, serving as an interpreter for Kahn. Among the European architects invited were Alison and Peter Smithson. When I told Peter that I was planning a second trip to the West that summer, he encouraged me to attend a meeting that he was planning to hold in Bagnols-sur-Cèze, near Avignon, in the south of France.

Fumihiko Maki, Balkrishna Doshi, James Stirling, Aldo van Eyck and Hannie van Eyck at the Second International Congress of Architecture, 24–30 September, 1974.

Fumihiko Maki, seated far left, at the meeting of Team X members in Bagnols-sur-Cèze, France, July 1960.

The main attendees of this meeting – the first gathering of Team X – were the Smithsons, John Voelcker and Ralph Erskine from the UK (Erskine was by this time working in Sweden), Aldo van Eyck and Jacob Bakema from the Netherlands, Giancarlo De Carlo from Italy, Shadrach Woods from the United States, Oskar Hansen from Poland, Stefan Wewerka from Germany and Georges Candilis from Greece (working in Paris). Candilis's office was designing a large residential complex nearby, and a tour of the complex was included in the programme. The mayor lent us a room in City Hall and members brought their recent projects to discuss. I remember showing them one theoretical project, entitled 'Group Formation in Shinjuku', as well as my design for Toyoda Auditorium at Nagoya University. Van Eyck's eloquent explanation of his Amsterdam Orphanage – though widely known in Europe at the time – was most impressive for me. He emphasized the need for organic thinking, rather than a one-size-fits-all theory like those promoted by the Congrès Internationaux d'Architecture Moderne (CIAM).

Half of the five days in Bagnols-sur-Cèze were devoted to theoretical discussions in English, which occasionally became quite heated. However, unlike today's international conferences, where everything runs according to a schedule, this first Team X conference was relatively informal. Some participants brought their families and a strong sense of comradeship was clearly felt between all. This solidarity was not so different from what I experienced within the Metabolist movement of the time. However, in contrast to Metabolism – which was connected to a particular Japanese collective consciousness – Team X discussions were strongly driven by the individual consciousness of each person in the group, giving them a great deal of energy and life.

The central topic of the conference was the creation of liveable modern urban housing through a new form of architecture or urbanism that was based on genuine urban principles (for example, as seen in the vernacular assemblages of an African village) rather than the more abstract, conceptual approaches being discussed within CIAM at that time. Many of the members of the group, who had gathered for the first time in several years, were in their late thirties and forties. They were interested in the relationship between architecture and the broader local culture, and how to integrate regional human behaviour into architecture.

In 1961, I returned to Washington University in St. Louis where I had previously taught. For the next year, I channelled my concerns about the future of urbanism into written essays, parts of which were later consolidated into the first chapter of *Investigations in Collective Form*. I sent this to several American architects and urban designers, as well as the members of Team X; the response was surprisingly positive. Walter Gropius, Kevin Lynch and Jacob Bakema took the trouble to send me comments. In this way my chance encounter with the members of Team X had turned into a formative moment of my career, providing important reinforcement to the first drafts of this publication.

Two Inaugural Projects

Steinberg Hall, 1960

In the autumn of 1956, after several years in Cambridge and New York, I joined the School of Architecture at Washington University in St. Louis as a young professor. While teaching, I was fortunate to also get involved professionally with the campus planning office. In early 1958, they offered me the chance to propose a new building between the existing School of Fine Arts in Bixby Hall and the existing School of Architecture in Givens Hall. This new facility was to be built with funds donated by Etta Eiseman Steinberg, a friend of the university and local resident for many years – the programme was an auditorium and gallery for the Schools of Fine Arts and Architecture and facilities for the Department of Art History and Archaeology. The campus planning office gave me great freedom in the design of the building.

Fumihiko Maki and his drawing of Steinberg Hall, 1958.

In the United States during the late 1950s there was a great deal of interest in the new potential for concrete structures and forms. Eero Saarinen's TWA Flight Center Terminal at Idlewild Airport (now John F. Kennedy International Airport) in New York was receiving a lot of attention within the architectural world and enthralling travellers with its dynamic form. Concurrent with advances in concrete engineering and construction technology, folded-plate concrete structures were also becoming increasingly common for long-span, column-free interiors. Given the limited site for Steinberg Hall, I felt that it should be more formally ethereal than the two rectangular buildings flanking it. This desire, along with the restrictions imposed by the site, led me to the cantilevered folded plate parti, rather than any inherent structural necessity. The folded plate was part of the design zeitgeist in the United States at the time and the concrete construction industry had developed sufficiently to support this trend.

Once the parti was finalized, design studies progressed smoothly, and in the spring of 1958 I was able to present my proposal to Steinberg herself. She liked the design very much and agreed to donate all the funds required for the construction with one stipulation: that it be constructed exactly as designed! Follow-up design work and construction took two years. At that time, I also needed to attend to my Graham Foundation Fellowship research and to travel – and therefore I had to leave much of the detailing to local architects. This team did an excellent job and the completed building was well received. After opening, it was featured in a special issue of *Architectural Forum* (August 1962), introducing young architects of the 1960s and their work.

Almost forty years later, in 1997, I was given the opportunity to make a new proposal for the Sam Fox School of Design & Visual Arts, next to Steinberg Hall, via an invited competition. It took around ten years to realize this complex, which also involved a re-planning and renovation of Steinberg. The library, gallery, and Department of Art History and Archaeology were shifted to the new buildings, while Steinberg was freed up to house functions from the Schools of Art and Architecture on either side. Together, these old and new structures now work as a mini campus for the arts at Washington University, almost fifty years after the completion of Steinberg Hall.

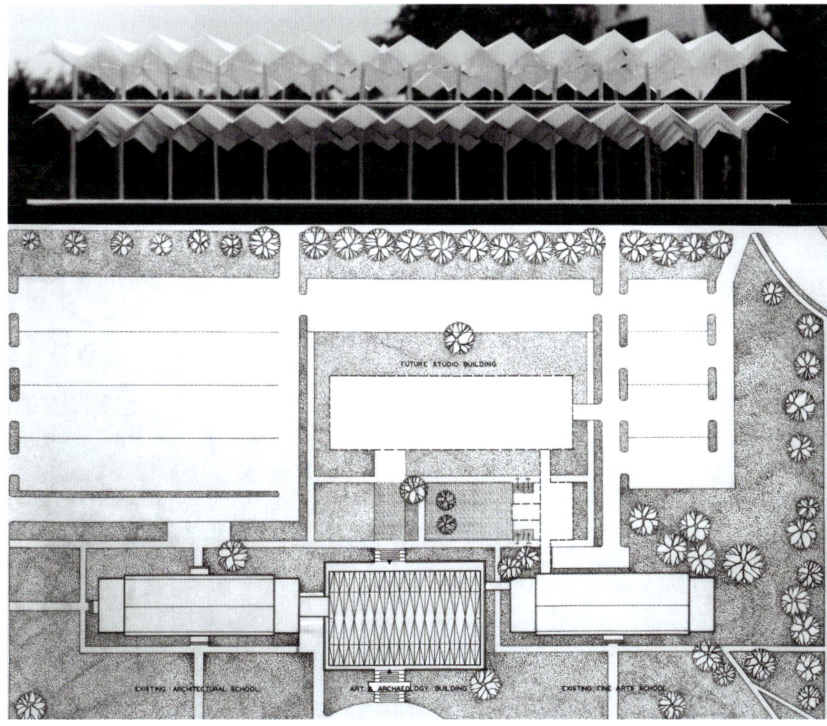

Folded-plate, cantilevered roof parti model of Steinberg Hall against two existing box-shaped buildings flanking it, 1960.

Steinberg Hall Upper Floor Library.

Sketch of south entrance to Steinberg Hall, 1960.

A first commission: Steinberg Hall on Washington University Campus, St. Louis, completed in 1960 and after renovation in 2006–7.

Two Inaugural Projects

Toyoda Memorial Hall, 1960

In 1958, I temporarily returned to Japan from the United States, taking a break from my travels as a Graham Foundation Fellow. It was during this time that I designed Toyoda Memorial Hall at Nagoya University. Construction of Steinberg Hall at Washington University in St. Louis was already in progress around that time, but this was my first project in Japan. Looking back, Steinberg Hall has elements that feel quite American, whereas the Toyoda Memorial Hall is more Japanese. As I had been dividing my time between the United States and Japan, I deliberately designed these buildings differently, reflecting their respective contexts.

When Toyoda Memorial Hall was constructed, the site area fronting the building was completely undeveloped, with unencumbered views to central Nagoya. The building form suggests a gate fronting the site that connects to the small hill at the rear. Massive U-shaped columns made from exposed concrete (bearing the building's seismic forces) ensure the gate's monumentality. Internally, the

A first commission in Japan: Toyoda Memorial Hall, Nagoya University, Nagoya, Aichi, Japan, 1960.

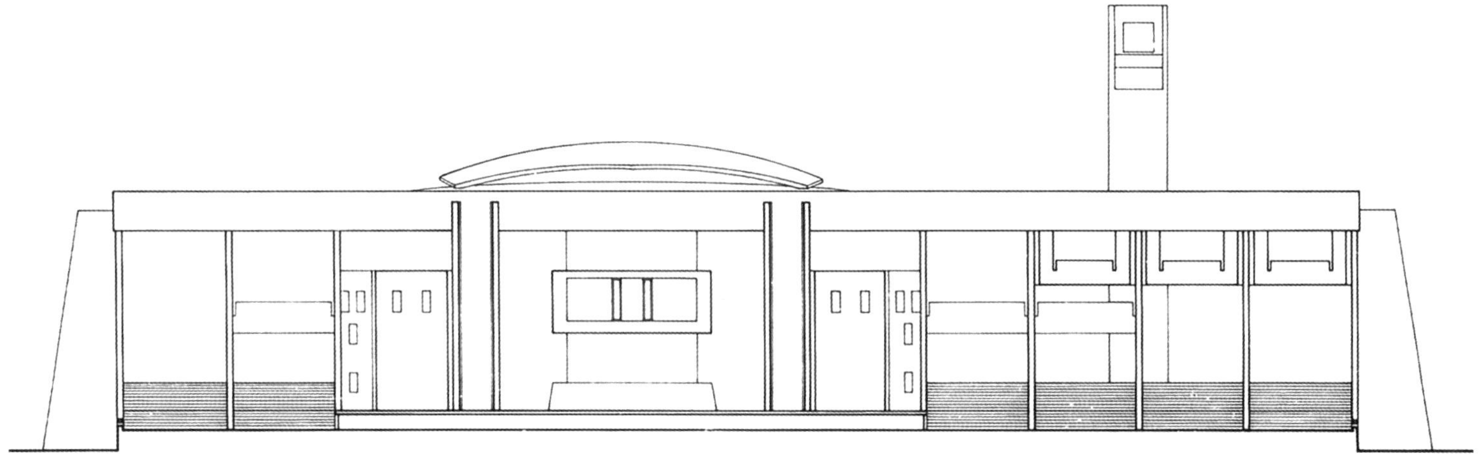

West elevation, Toyoda Memorial Hall.

building houses a 1,400-seat auditorium to serve large gatherings and university graduation exercises, with special box seating for the University President in the upper east corner.

While the design was still in progress, I had the chance to show conceptual drawings and model photographs to Le Corbusier, whom I met in Chandigarh while touring India as part of my Fellowship research. He looked at the drawings in a dimly lit atelier with high ceilings. It may have been just polite flattery, but he said that they were very good. He noticed then that the columns were linked to the wall (necessary for seismic reasons), which apparently bothered him, and suggested that I 'take good care of the column.' I did not venture to contradict him, or to leave him feeling that his few words had not made an impact. They had – although in this case the columns could not be separated from the walls!

Since its completion in 1960, Toyoda Memorial Hall has remained the most symbolic building on the Nagoya University campus, due to both its location and its design. Over time, the facility gradually began to show its age, particularly its exterior finishes and mechanical systems. In 2006, at the request of the university, we began a major renovation with generous financial support from the Toyota Motor Corporation. 3 cm (1³⁄₁₆ in.) of the original concrete were removed from the facade and columns, and 5.5 cm (2³⁄₁₆ in.) of new concrete were added, resulting in an overall increase of 2.5 cm (1 in.). The building was thereby given a brand new appearance and enhanced seismic resistance. The auditorium interior was renovated with new seating and mechanical systems, and a spacious atrium (covering the open court between the original project and a 1992 addition) was also completed at this time.

Opening ceremonies for the renovation took place in the spring of 2008. Together with the newly built Sam Fox School of Design & Visual Arts and the renovation of Steinberg Hall at Washington University, the first two buildings of my career – completed in Japan and the US more than a half century ago – are now fully refurbished, maintaining their enduring legacy at each campus.

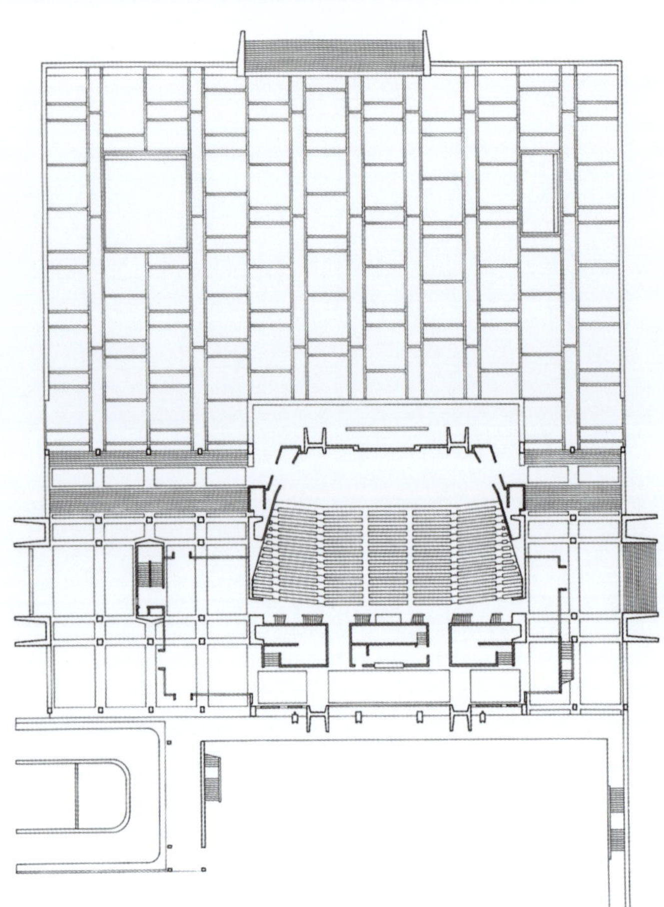

Ground-floor plan, phase I, 1960.

View of main entrance elevation from west, 1960.

Aerial view from south, 1960.

View of Toyoda Memorial Hall from south.

Interior view of 1,400-seat Auditorium Hall after renovation, 2007.

My Tokyo

27

amstyle
+new, amstyle
new, amstyle
60

Hillside Terrace

Location	Shibuya-ku, Tokyo Metropolitan, Japan
Status	Completed
Year(s)	1969–1998 Phase I 1969 Phase II 1973 Phase III 1977 Phase IV 1985 Phase V 1987 Phase VI 1992 Danish Embassy 1979 Cedar Stone Villa 1984 Hillside West 1998
Typology	Urban Design, Residential, Offices, Retail, Restaurants, Exhibition Hall, Multi-purpose Hall, Gallery, Event Space, Library, Member's Club, Parking
Area	18,328 m² (197,281 ft²) Danish Embassy 1,896 m² (20,408 ft²) Cedar Stone Villa 988 m² (10,634 ft²) Hillside West 2,958 m² (31,839 ft²)

(Opposite) Hillside West Building A facade view facing Kyū-Yamate Avenue.

Hillside Terrace is a phased mixed-use development in Tokyo's Daikanyama district, a rare example in the city of contiguous interventions by a single architect along the same street. Daikanyama was originally a wooded, hilly enclave bridging Shibuya and Ebisu Stations, with only a few low-rise structures present. Maki and Associates and landowners Asakura Real Estate approached this sensitive context with an emphasis on exterior space, preservation of existing trees, and a modern but modest design vocabulary. Spanning 1969 to 1998, the project's design strategies have evolved over the years and maintained their vibrancy and relevance.

As it unfolded, each phase of Hillside Terrace addressed unique issues, and offered important lessons for subsequent work. Phase I has a thin plot, so its public spaces are kept along the street. The vocabulary includes a corner plaza, a transparent lobby serving ground-floor shops, a sunken garden, a raised pedestrian deck, and *maisonette* apartments. Phase II has a deeper lot, allowing for a central public plaza with surrounding shops. By phase III, the Daikanyama neighbourhood had progressed. Buildings facing the main street were tile-clad and shops were interiorized to differentiate from the previous phases and mark the passage of time. Phase III also has an inner court, but – unlike phase II – is preserved as greenery, centred on an extant ancient burial mound.

This formal progression from phase to phase was instrumental in making Hillside Terrace a heterogeneous but still coherent complex. The trend continued in phase IV: two small office buildings designed by Makoto Motokura (who opened his own practice after supervising phase III). Motokura's buildings possess a clear geometry and are more closed than earlier phases. The next addition was the Danish Embassy, together with an underground event space, comprising phase V. Both projects preserve the scale and spatial flow of the original three phases, while introducing newer materials and technical innovations.

By the time phase VI began, Daikanyama had become an energetic mixed-use district with increased density and building height limits. Phase VI's three new buildings create a light impression and disguise their larger size through strategic massing and material selection. A prominent eave line at 10 m (33 ft) was introduced, echoing the building height of previous phases. Enhanced public programmes, including an extensive art gallery, signalled Daikanyama's transformation into a bustling cultural hub. Hillside Terrace's influence extended beyond its boundaries, beginning with Cedar Stone Villa in 1984 and continuing with the Hillside West complex in 1998. These projects, located 500 m (1,640 ft) west of phase VI, though not part of Hillside Terrace, shared its DNA and contributed to Daikanyama's broader expansion.

Despite its modest collective footprint, Hillside Terrace is recognized as one of Tokyo's finest examples of award-winning urban design. While its surroundings are now also extensively redeveloped, Hillside Terrace has functioned as the standard for the neighbourhood. The result is a genuine townscape unique in Tokyo, anticipating and adapting to a half-century of continuous growth.

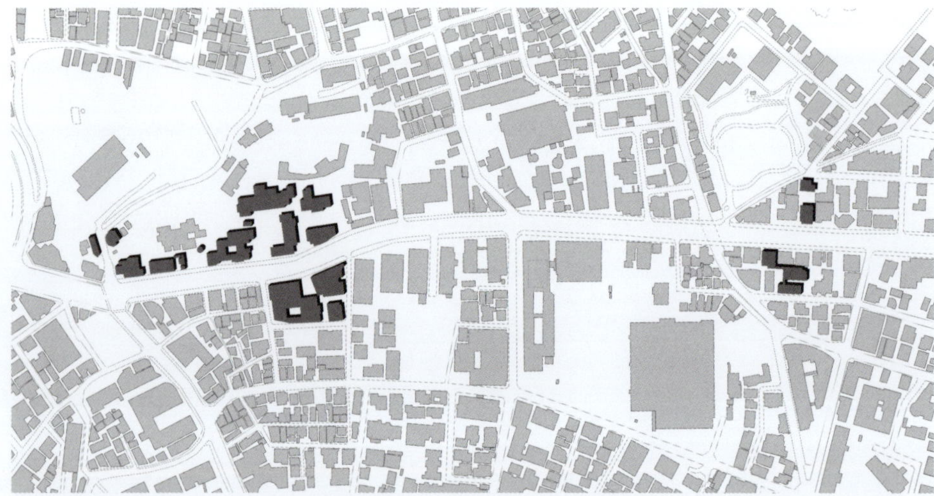

Developed in six phases from 1967 to 1998, Daikanyama's Hillside Terrace shaped the evolution of the surrounding urban fabric, with its influence extending well beyond Kyū-Yamate Avenue. Through its layered composition of permeable spaces, the complex redefined the boundaries of urban and architectural experience in Daikanyama – where architecture is not an isolated object, but part of a larger, evolving whole, nurturing continuity, community and the collective memory of place.

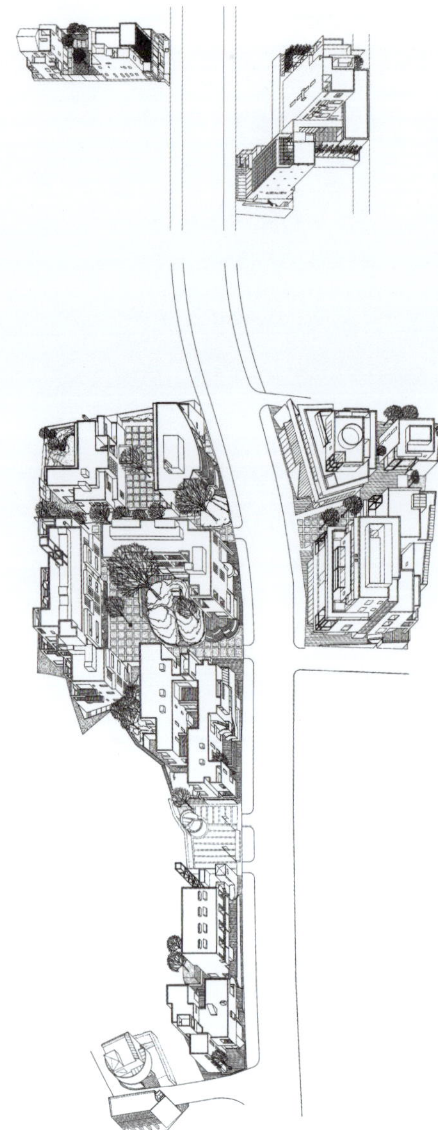

Axonometric site plan of Hillside Terrace complex showing massing.

Hillside Terrace phase I with Building A and Building B, 1969.

Evening view of Hillside Terrace phase I at the intersection of Kyū-Yamate Avenue and Hachiman Avenue, 2024.

Building C with shops at the lower levels and apartments above.

Phase III Building E mediates the sloping topography of Daikanyama via a stepped massing and layered residential programme.

Unit in Building D overlooking the greenery of the Sarugakuzuka burial mound.

Phase III, Building D and the Sarugakuzuka burial mound.

View of Building C phase II from plaza.

The Royal Danish Embassy ambassador residence, 1979.

Cedar Stone Villa courtyard with shops and offices.

Cedar Stone Villa facade view facing Kyū-Yamate Avenue.

The Royal Danish Embassy Chancery defining the street edge.

View of the inner courtyard within the Royal Danish Embassy.

Cedar Stone Villa courtyard with residences.

Hillside Plaza, multi-purpose hall in basement 2.

Phase VI, Building F.

Entry hall and basement of Building F facing street.

Entry hall and basement of Building F facing street.

Plaza seen from forum in Building F.

Courtyard of Building F and G, 2024.

Evening view of Building G facing plaza and sidewalk.

Hillside West Building A, 2024.

Passageway between Hillside West Building A and B.

Connecting stairway inside Hillside West Building A.

Passageway and courtyard connecting Hillside West Building B and C.

View of plaza from Hillside West Building C.

Interior view of residence in Hillside West Building A.

View from passageway of courtyard with Building C in background.

spiral

Spiral

Location	Aoyama, Minato-ku, Tokyo, Japan
Status	Completed
Year(s)	1985
Typology	Gallery, Multi-purpose Hall, Retail
Area	10,560 m^2 (113,667 ft^2)

The Kyoto-based Wacoal Corporation, originally a Japanese kimono fabric concern, is one of Japan's largest manufacturers of lingerie. Wacoal's Spiral Building, completed in 1985, was part of a larger corporate strategy to enhance the company's presence in Tokyo by promoting cultural and commercial programmes in a highly visible locale. Spiral's advanced material palette and sophisticated spatial composition remain fresh and vital today, a cherished landmark in a constantly changing city.

From its basement through to the third level, Spiral is highly public, incorporating both permanent and 'pop-up' retail events, temporary art, fashion and music exhibitions within its open circulation and event zones. The first level houses temporary exhibitions along its perimeter, culminating in a semi-cylindrical skylit atrium at the rear. A gently sloping ramp along the atrium's curving wall – the eponymous 'spiral' – leads to a commercial space for Japanese crafts at the second level. A sunken cafe flanking the temporary exhibition space is the centrepiece of the ground floor, anchoring the circulation and programmes around it.

Visitors can also reach the second floor via the 'esplanade', a gently cascading series of steps and platforms connecting the lobby to the Japanese craft store along the building facade. The esplanade continues up to a 300-seat multi-purpose event space and its foyer on the third level. From the fifth floor, a variety of smaller studios, restaurants and offices complete Spiral's active offering of public, private, open and closed spaces – culminating in an open roof garden overlooking the city.

As with its complex building programme, Spiral's exterior facade is conceived as a collage of overlapping elements and a reflection of its internal functions, building requirements and the urban surroundings. The facade itself has a public character, animated by visitors walking and sitting along the esplanade – making Spiral a symbol of Tokyo's image, fragmented but in constant renewal. As evidenced by its receipt of the Japan Institute of Architects' prestigious twenty-five-year award in 2011, Spiral's unique qualities have been recognized not only by the public, but also by Tokyo's architectural community. It remains a vibrant cultural icon and a lasting benchmark of good design in the city.

(Opposite) Evening facade view facing Aoyama Avenue.

The esplanade unfolds across a cascade of stairway landings overlooking the street.

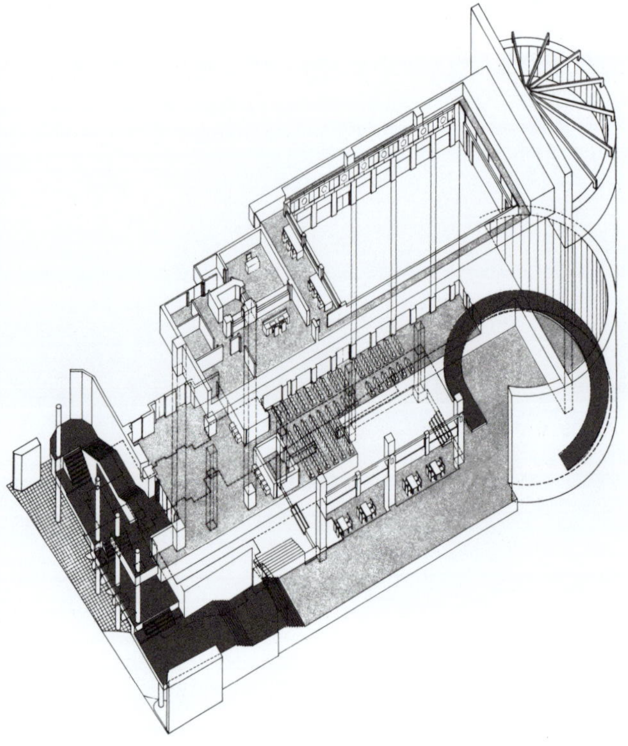
Interior axonometric drawing.

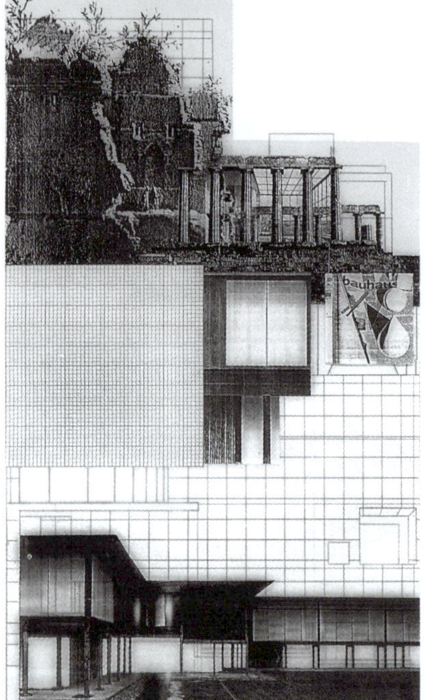

Collage of Spiral, 1985.

Foyer of the Spiral Hall Theatre.

Aerial view showing the roof garden and atrium skylight.

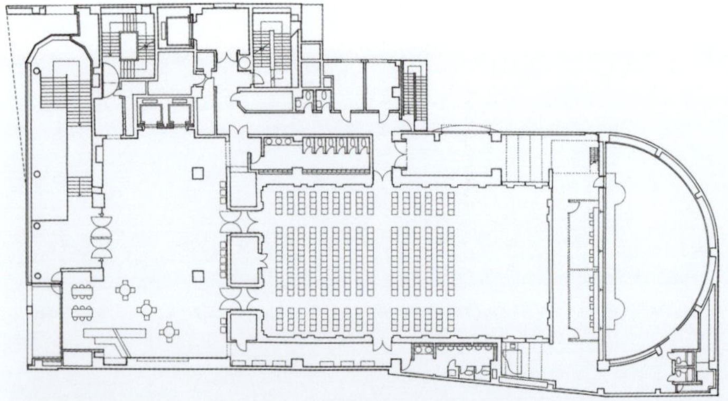

Third-floor plan.

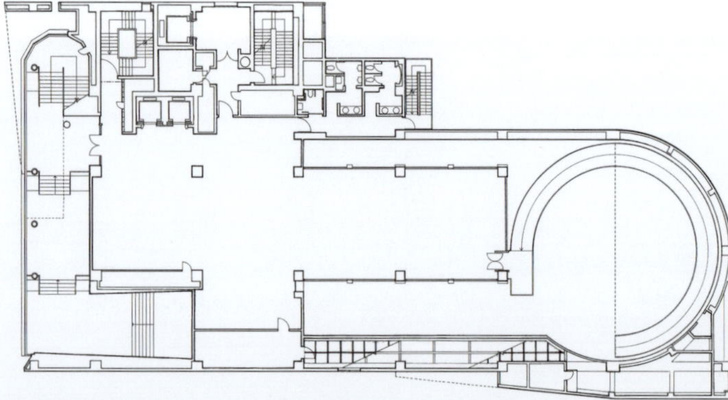

Second-floor plan.

A gentle sloping spiral ramp, cantilevering from the wall, forms an exhibition path within the naturally lit atrium.

Atrium skylight.

Collage of the building facade.

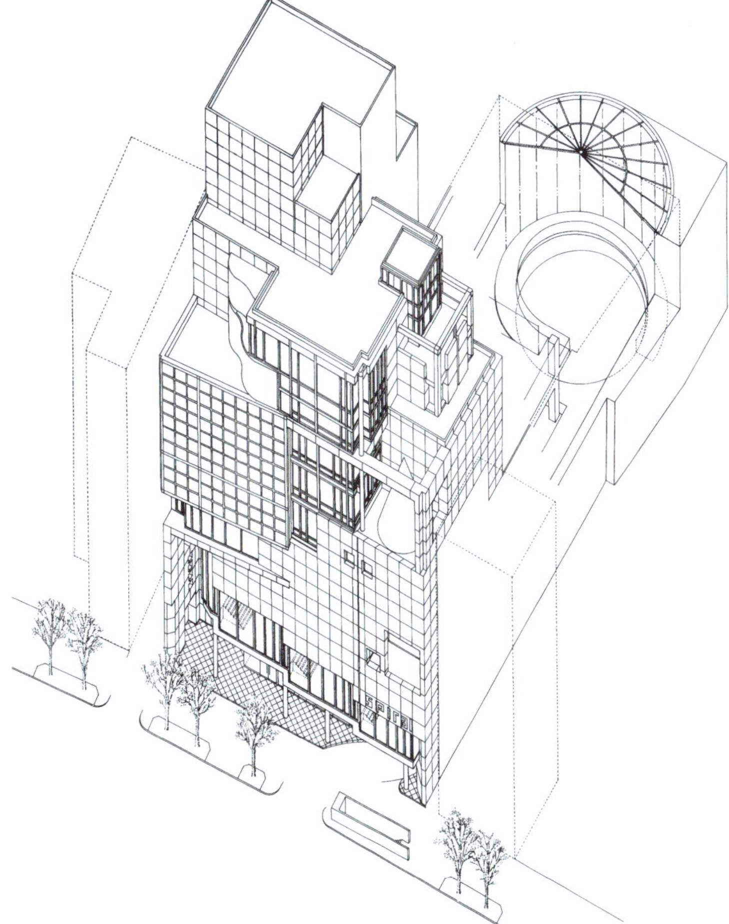

Axonometric drawing of Spiral.

The roof garden on the fifth floor of Spiral. Abstract forms such as a pyramid in the fountain and the conical cypress trees create a calm and surreal space removed from the surrounding city.

Rolex Toyocho

Location	Koto-ku, Tokyo Metropolitan, Japan
Status	Completed
Year(s)	2002
Typology	Office
Area	11,042 m^2 (118,855 ft^2)

The Rolex Toyocho Building is a maintenance and service headquarters for the renowned Swiss watchmaker. Completed in 2002 on a tight rectilinear site in eastern Tokyo, the facility includes maintenance space, offices, staff training areas, a generous winter garden, a cafeteria and a presentation room on its top floor. Its clear planning and highly transparent facade combine to create a generous, light-filled, flexible environment, perfect for the precise work carried out inside.

While essentially modern in expression, the massing of Rolex Toyocho utilizes a classical tripartite composition. Its base is articulated via exposed columns and rich stone finishes, its *piano nobile* via an all-glass curtain wall and its crown via a fully glazed winter garden and deep aluminium overhangs. To maximize transparency at the building's perimeter, the structural design concentrates seismic forces in its central core and horizontal bracing in the floor plates. As a result, the building's peripheral columns accept only gravity loading, enabling their extremely slender proportions.

The curtain wall is a double-skin assembly with overlapping layers of etched glass. This creates varying degrees of transparency and patterning effects when seen from different angles. Supported entirely by structural glass fins, this double skin maximizes natural light penetration to the interior while affording ample acoustic insulation from the major thoroughfare at the front of the site. With its minimal column size and precision-engineered facade, the building's exterior has a light, ethereal presence, in stark contrast to the solidity of its surroundings.

Rolex's own products are known for their elegance, quality and durability – a result of their precise detailing, sophisticated technology and fine artisanship. Rolex Toyocho provides a similar sense of high design and quality for its Tokyo-based staff. The elegant, light-filled facility and its strikingly open facade are a unique but welcome presence within a densely developed downtown district.

(Opposite) Rolex Toyocho workspace looking west.

View of Rolex Toyocho Building from Eitai Street.

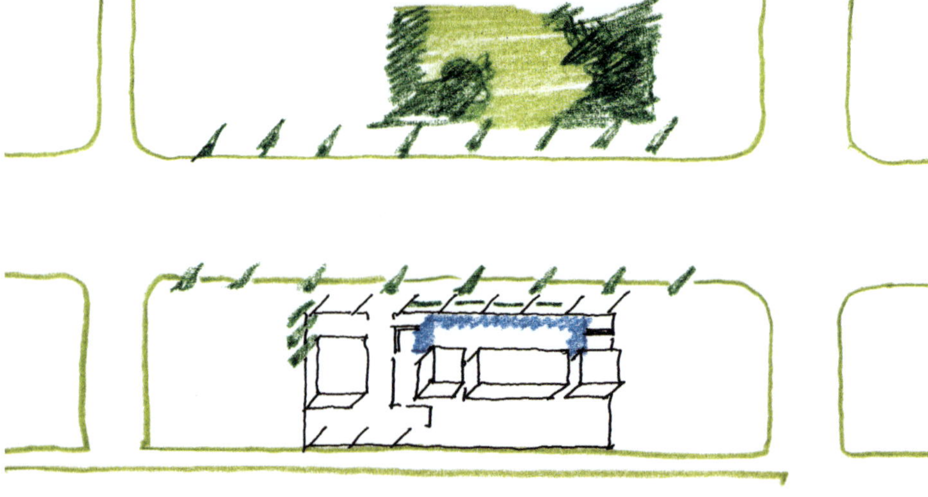

Site concept sketch.

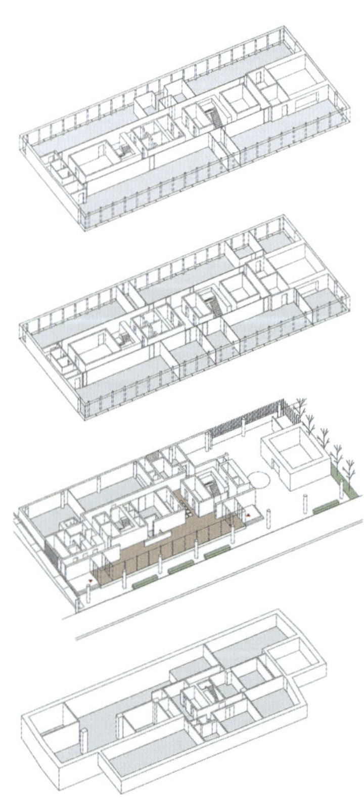

Basement to third-floor plan.

Evening view of entrance lobby.

Evening view of north facade.

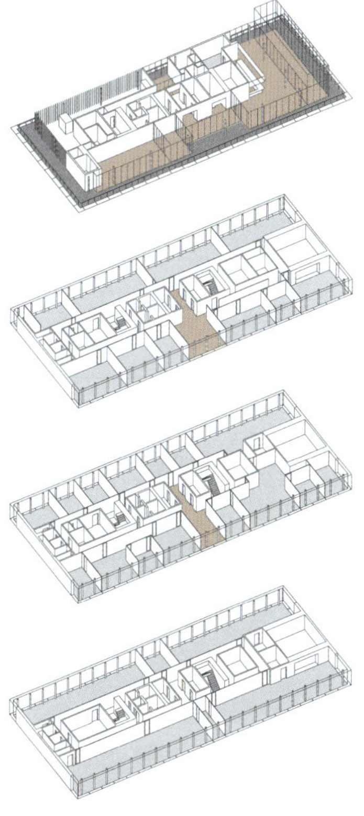
Fourth-floor to seventh-floor plan.

Entrance lobby with Iranian red travertine wall and illuminated glass fibre cloth ceiling.

The Japanese Sword Museum

Location	Sumida-ku, Tokyo Metropolitan, Japan
Status	Completed
Year(s)	2017
Typology	Museum, Conference Hall, Offices, Retail
Area	2,620 m^2 (28,201 ft^2)

The Japanese Sword Museum, completed in 2017, highlights the development of Japanese swords from their origins as weapons to their current status as art objects. In addition to collecting and displaying outstanding examples of this unique craft, the museum operator (the Society for the Preservation of Japanese Art Swords) promotes traditional sword-making techniques and appraises swords for the public. The museum's collection includes several designated national treasures.

The institution's new site is adjacent to Yasuda Garden, originally part of a samurai estate from the eighteenth century. Its exterior form (a cylindrical volume with two wings) follows the outline of the Ryōgoku Kokugikan previously located here. While echoing the massing of the older building, the museum entrance's crisp metallic forms – juxtaposed with its softly rounded concrete garden facade – result in an entirely new composition. The overall effect is reminiscent of traditional sword displays, which contrast silk-covered stands with the sharp metallic swords perched above.

The building's first floor is fully accessible and includes a public cafe, a regional information corner, the museum shop and a multi-purpose event hall. Connected directly to Yasuda Garden and the surrounding streets, the building is an integral part of a larger neighbourhood pedestrian zone connecting cultural points of interest. The main staircase echoes design themes from the exterior, its crisp stainless-steel panels a poetic counterpoint to the rounded geometry and draped-cloth lighting in the museum lobby. The second floor is private, devoted to administrative functions, offices, storage and workshop space.

The climax for all visitors, the public exhibition space, is concentrated on the third floor. The swords are displayed under a light-washed vaulted ceiling that follows the gently curving exterior roof. Low-angle spotlights focus attention on the swords themselves, ensuring optimal viewing of their artistry and craftsmanship. The sequence ends with a generous public exterior terrace, contrasting the subdued lighting of the exhibition space, affording panoramic views of the Japanese garden below and connecting the rarefied sword museum experience back to the surrounding city.

(Opposite) Sword Museum facing Yasuda Garden.

The museum's main entrance is composed of an extended roof eave that shelters a stainless steel-clad wall.

The deformed vaulted roof ceiling creates an immersive experience for visitors in the Exhibition Hall.

Sharp-edge stainless steel panel-clad stairs leading to the Exhibition Hall allude to the craftsmanship celebrated inside the Japanese Sword Museum.

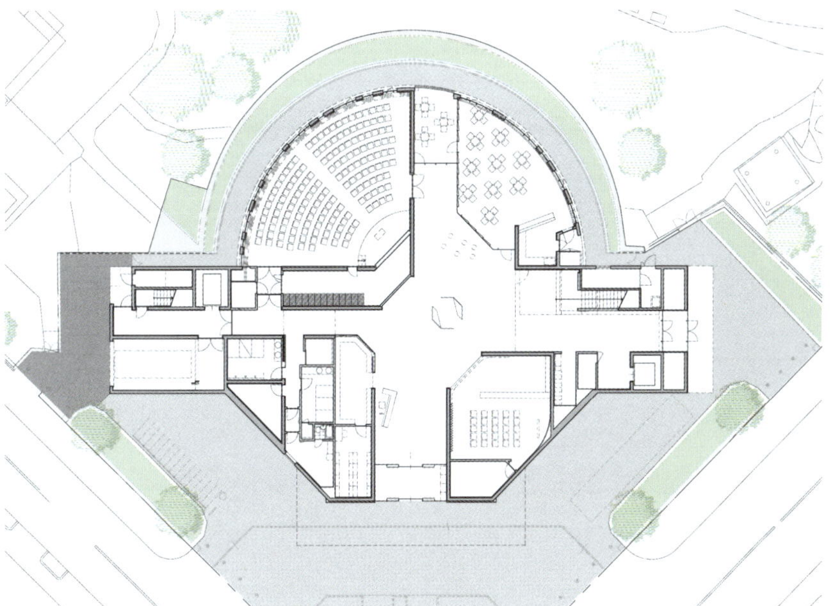

First floor.

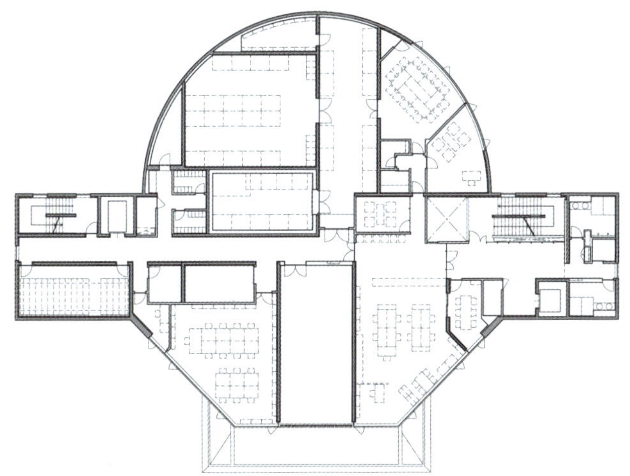

Second floor.

Aerial view of the Japanese Sword Museum nestled within Kyu-Yasuda Garden and Sumida River.

Aerial view of TV Asahi headquarters in Roppongi Hills with Mount Fuji in the background.

TV Asahi

Location	Minato-ku, Tokyo Metropolitan, Japan
Status	Completed
Year(s)	2003
Typology	Broadcasting Studios, Offices, Retail
Area	73,700 m^2 (793,300 ft^2)

TV Asahi's new broadcast headquarters is part of Roppongi Hills, an ambitious central Tokyo urban renewal project encompassing eleven hectares of office, residential, cultural, hotel and commercial space. As one of the original development landowners, TV Asahi worked with Maki and Associates and other stakeholders for over seventeen years, from the project's initial conception to its completion in 2003.

The building's corner site is open on all four sides, surrounded by two major streets, an event plaza and a Japanese garden. Its gently curving shape responds to this geometry and to the natural contours of the site. To the southwest, the building's vehicular entry is marked by *Counter Void*, a luminescent glass wall created by artist Tatsuo Miyajima. Just beyond the vehicular entry, the building's gently curved southern facade shelters a colonnaded sidewalk lined with zelkova trees. Employee and VIP entrances are located to the east, marked by a cascading water terrace, and within sight of the Japanese garden and Martin Puryear's sculpture *Guardian Stone*.

Overlooking the garden, a voluminous north-facing atrium serves as the interface between visitors and TV Asahi. Its multistorey exterior glass screen allows views of the nearby greenery and cityscape while sheltering a series of diverse programmes inside. At the building's interior core, the thick concrete walls enclosing four separate broadcast studios offer superior acoustic isolation and earthquake resistance. Offices surround the studios at the building perimeter, affording employees a comfortable, light-filled work environment. This planning enhances work-flow efficiency internally, while protecting the studios from exterior heat and noise infiltration.

Vertical louvres on the east and west facades and horizontal louvres on the south facade protect the offices from direct sunlight during the day. In the evening, these facades light up like Japanese lanterns, while a bright mural by US artist Sol LeWitt animates the atrium to the north, highlighting the building's twenty-four-

hour operation cycle. In this way, the TV Asahi headquarters takes on a unique role within Roppongi Hills and the larger city, bridging both commercial and cultural worlds. It is the most visited private broadcasting centre in Japan.

North elevation and west elevation.

Atrium with reception desk.

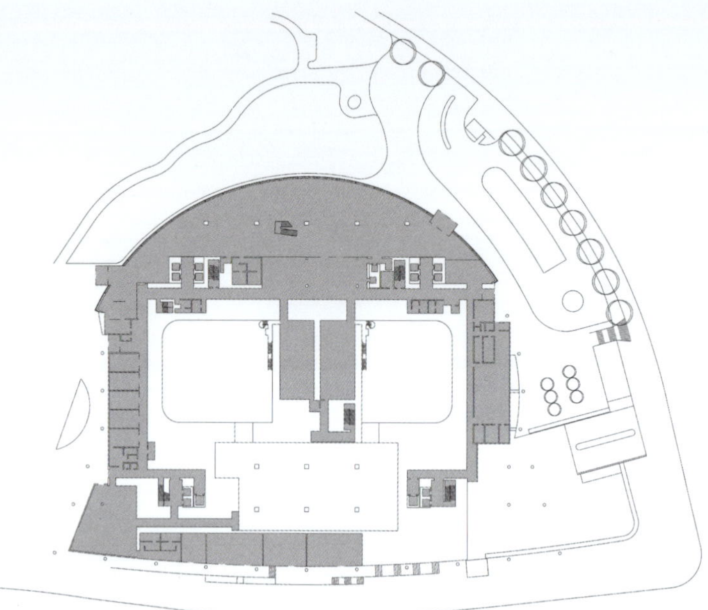

First-floor plan.

Reception lobby with 'wall drawing' mural by Sol LeWitt.

Main conference room overlooking roof garden.

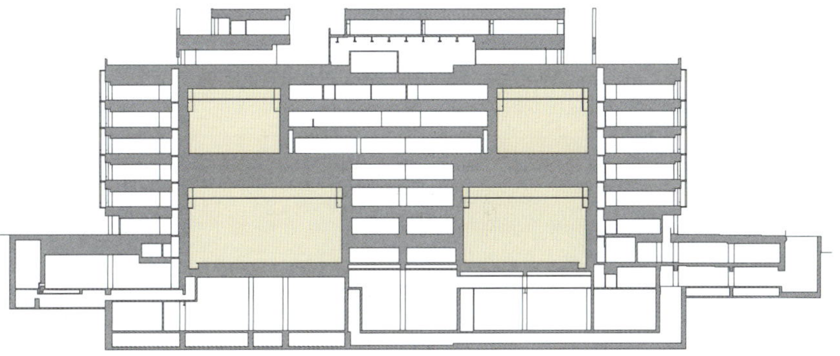

Section showing the studios.

Roof courtyard with *Untitled* sculpture by Abraham David Christian.

(Next spread) Evening view of TV Asahi HQ with roof garden from north.

tv asahi

The Tokyo of Tomorrow and Architects

Fumihiko Maki

City as the Foundation of Culture

Throughout my career, I have had the privilege of visiting major capitals across three continents. This includes New York, Paris and New Delhi. Despite the brevity of these visits, they afforded me a rich visual and tactile experience of each city, as I navigated their streets by foot, car and subway.

After each trip, I resumed my daily routine in Tokyo, and what I sensed at all times was the calmness – one might call it the gentleness – of the Japanese capital.

One evening, I arrived at Delhi Airport and made my way by car to the city centre. Like most large cities at that hour, traffic typically flows outward toward the suburbs. However, in Delhi, the traffic was immense in both directions. Perhaps because the number of traffic lights drops off markedly outside the central district, there was a cacophony of honking horns. The discombobulating sea of vehicles and the sheer number of people made even a simple car ride exhausting.

In Paris, I often stay at the The Westin Paris – Vendôme (formerly the Intercontinental), located near the Louvre. This hotel, once a haven of tranquillity, is now marked by a constant flow of people. While the buildings of Paris may retain their historical appearance, the atmosphere of a place can change significantly. If hotels were rated by their tranquillity, I believe no place rivals the serene lobby of the main building of Hotel Okura Tokyo. The lobby is a superb space worthy of designation as an important cultural asset. Although the historic main wing of Hotel Okura was demolished in 2015, the iconic lobby was meticulously restored and retained in the new building, which will reopen in 2019 as The Okura Tokyo.

Tokyo is also characterized by the scale of its ongoing construction projects. Buildings of various sizes, from the very small to the very large, are being constructed simultaneously. This phenomenon is partly due to Tokyo's historical structure. Edo, which in the eighteenth century became the first capital in the world to reach a population of one million, and Tokyo after the Meiji Restoration, faced the challenge of accommodating a growing population within a limited area. The progressive subdivision of lots toward the city centre, as seen in the pattern of samurai estates and areas for artisans and tradesmen in Edo (Figure 1 and 2), hindered the widening of existing roads and the creation of new ones during Tokyo's modernization.

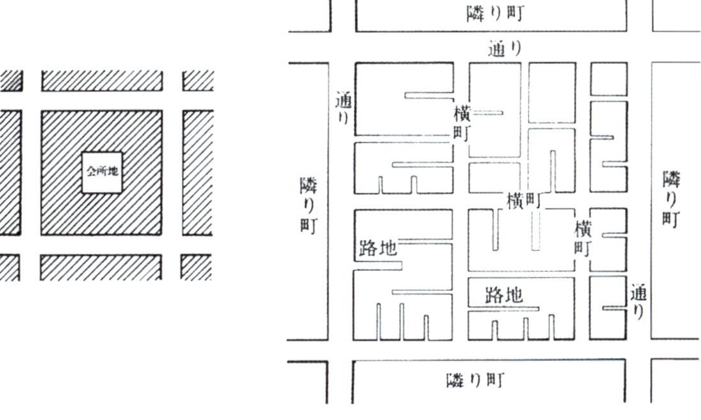

Figure 1: Typical street and block division in a *shitamachi* (下町) area of Tokyo.

The grand Baroque-style proposal for Tokyo's central district, developed by Böckmann & Ende from Berlin, was never realized. The railway lines completed in the 1920s, now known as the Yamanote and Chuo lines, established the framework for modern Tokyo. These lines were routed through valleys where land prices were lower, contrasting with Baron Georges-Eugène Haussmann's approach in Paris, which prioritized sightlines and focal points. The subdivision of land into diverse configurations and sizes, along with city-planning designations, has shaped the three-dimensional forms of present-day Tokyo.

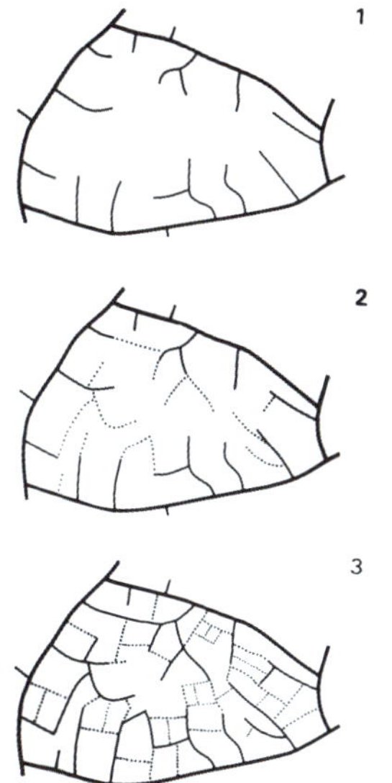

Figure 2: Road development in an uptown neighbourhood of Tokyo.

Fine-Grained City

A public transportation network of unprecedented density has been completed in Tokyo since the establishment of the Yamanote and Chuo lines. Excluding the unpredictable effects of suicides, this network surpasses those of other countries in terms of precision, transportation density, safety, cleanliness, and the availability of information-related services. Naturally, linear concentrations of services such as stores and offices have developed near stations as shown in Figure 3.

Kevin Lynch and Lloyd Rodwin of MIT once predicted a shift in basic urban configuration from a concentric pattern organized around a single centre to a polycentric pattern.[1] However, Japanese metropolises, including Tokyo, have far exceeded such projections and began developing into cities with myriad centres by the 1930s. Besides the central district around Tokyo Station, subcentres have formed around stations where multiple railway lines converge, such as Ueno, Ikebukuro, Shinjuku, Shibuya and Shinagawa. Including clusters of adjacent cities, they form a polycentric urban region with a population of approximately 37 million people.

A recently published book, *Urbanalización, Paisajes comunes, lugares globales*,[2] by Francesc Muñoz, a Spanish geographer, highlights that the traditional urban image of a civic society where people live and work in the same place no longer applies in this age of globalization, especially in metropolises. The development of transportation has led to an increase in people living in distant places and working in the city only five days a week or at multiple locations. Instances of the reverse pattern are also rising. The number of people passing through Tokyo's subcentres each day

Figure 3: Linear concentrations of services developed near stations.

symbolizes this phenomenon. It is not just residents; in international cities, the numbers increase further when including tourists and temporary residents. According to the author, these people are not citizens but 'territoriantes'.[3] Territoriantes tend to concentrate in particular places at specific times, generating a dynamism in people's movement that cannot be explained by past urban theories. Moreover, the dynamism of a fine-grained city like Tokyo undoubtedly has an even more complex aspect.

Today, the twenty-three wards of Tokyo have a combined population of approximately 9.5 million people. Several of these wards have populations exceeding 500,000. Not many people in Tokyo are aware that the largest, Setagaya Ward, already has nearly 900,000 people, and only 100,000 more are needed for it to rival the so-called 'ordinance-designated cities' (cities granted a high level of autonomy) in size.

We are exposed daily to media reports about Japan's declining and aging population. However, these reports often make sweeping generalizations. There remains little specific information about how individual districts in Tokyo will evolve in the coming decades, what challenges may arise, and what countermeasures might be taken. Most news in newspapers and on television has little to do with the realities of everyday life. Instead, it focuses on infrastructure projects, such as the underground redirection of expressways, the designation of special economic zones, or the construction of large-scale developments. There continues to be a near-total absence of projections regarding how the living environment for Tokyo's many residents will change over the next fifteen, twenty or thirty years. This issue must be addressed by both the public and private sectors.

A city as intricate as Tokyo should be examined in finer detail, with its neighbourhoods considered as distinct, compact communities – each comprising approximately 20,000 to 30,000 people. Collecting detailed demographic data within these areas, particularly insights into residents' future settlement intentions and mobility patterns, would provide a clearer picture of urban change. This would, of course, need to include the movement of 'territoriantes' within those communities.

As we all recognize today, statistics have the power not only to capture the present but also to illuminate the past and anticipate the future. Their significance in historical analysis and future projections

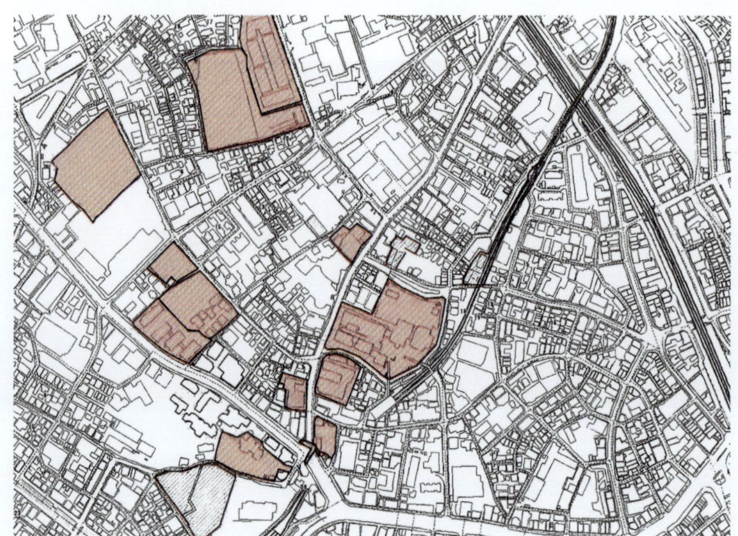

Figure 4: Large-scale developments surrounding Hillside Terrace.

Figure 5: Community activities within Tokyo Denki University.

has grown considerably. However, the ability to interpret and critically engage with statistical data is essential. A good example is the widely discussed bestseller *Defure no Shōtai* (真実のデフレ, *The True Nature of Deflation*).[4] By examining population fluctuations as a key parameter, the author challenges commonly accepted economic assumptions, particularly regarding added value, domestic and external demand, and regional disparities.

The community plan I propose here, however, goes beyond projections based solely on statistical trends in housing and public infrastructure. It takes into account the unique *placeness* – the distinctive character of a community – that cannot be fully captured through numerical data. This includes topographical conditions, which lie outside the realm of statistical analysis, as well as subtler patterns that shape daily life within a given locality.

Toward a New Approach to Community Planning

The community plan proposed here differs fundamentally from conventional city-planning laws and regulations, which are often imposed from above as fixed directives. Instead, this approach seeks to visually and spatially map the challenges and opportunities unique to each neighbourhood, offering a flexible reference point that can adapt to evolving local conditions.

Equally important is the development of this community plan through the active involvement of residents. Unlike government agencies planning efforts that primarily serve to establish regulatory frameworks, this initiative would be a collaborative process between local authorities and the people who live and work in these areas. Its purpose is not simply to dictate urban policies but to foster a deeper, shared understanding of the community as a whole. While professional expertise in statistical analysis remains essential, the broader task of synthesizing spatial relationships and envisioning future possibilities should be a joint effort among architects, planners and residents.

Given Tokyo's rapidly ageing population, it is not difficult to imagine retired educators, administrators and professionals contributing their expertise to this endeavour. Moreover, with the many universities with departments of architecture in the region, there should be no shortage of students to staff the actual survey teams. With such resources available, the role of local government would be primarily to support and facilitate rather than to assume full responsibility for implementation.

The task may seem vague at first glance, and for those people and communities that may not know where to start, a practical first step might be to select a few representative communities of different character in Tokyo – such as a *shitamachi* (下町), a *yamanote* (山の手) and a central business district. Architects, planners, statisticians and engaged residents could collaborate to develop model plans for these areas, making them public to encourage broader discussion and refinement.

These plans would not be rigid blueprints but evolving frameworks that document differing perspectives, acknowledge points of contention and present multiple possibilities for future development.

Furthermore, the data collected through this process could ultimately contribute to a more comprehensive understanding of broader demographic and spatial trends, both at the ward level and across Tokyo as a whole. Taken together, these community-based studies – these mini-community plans – would provide a more nuanced and citizen-driven vision of the city's future, one that better reflects the aspirations and needs of its people.

Reflections on Daikanyama

Nearly three decades have passed since the completion of Hillside Terrace and Hillside West (1969–1998), a project that took shape gradually over multiple phases. Through this extended process, a community of residents and businesses naturally emerged around the project's owners, eventually forming what is now known as the *Daikanyama Suteki na Machizukuri Kyōgikai* (Forum for the Development of a Wonderful Community in Daikanyama – 代官山ステキな街づくり協議会).[5]

Today, the forum has expanded to include more than one hundred members, encompassing not only residents of Sarugakuchō and its surroundings, but also individuals from other parts of Tokyo who share an interest in preserving and enhancing the district's urban character. The forum continues to serve as a platform for diverse initiatives aimed at improving the built environment, particularly in areas surrounding Kyū-Yamate Avenue and Hachiman Avenue. While some of these efforts involve proactive urban enhancement, others take the form of resistance against large-scale developments that threaten the area's existing fabric. Figure 4 shows the cases in this district in which the organization has been involved over the years. Naturally, not all efforts have resulted in outcomes favourable to the forum's goals, but certain initiatives have led to meaningful improvements. Notable examples include:

1. The designation of the former Asakura Residence and its garden as an Important Cultural Property, ensuring their long-term preservation and public access.
2. The removal of the pedestrian overpass at the intersection of Kyū-Yamate Avenue and Hachiman Avenue, restoring the continuity of the streetscape.
3. The preservation of significant trees along the Tsutaya development site where it meets Kyū-Yamate Avenue, maintaining an important green buffer.
4. The reduction of a proposed high-rise residential tower in the nearby Jōsenji district, resulting in a more contextually appropriate low-rise development.

While the forum's successes are outnumbered by instances where its initial objectives were not fully realized, its very presence serves as a psychological counterweight to unchecked development, prompting greater scrutiny and dialogue around proposed changes to the district.

In parallel, a group of architects from Shibuya Ward has established a district chapter of the Japan Institute of Architects (JIA). The group engages in a range of activities beyond periodic meetings, including topographical research, disaster-prevention studies and field investigations across Shibuya Ward. Many of these architects are also active participants in the Daikanyama forum, further strengthening the connection between professional expertise and grassroots urban advocacy.

The extent to which similar initiatives exist across Tokyo is difficult to determine. However, for a metropolis of this scale and complexity to evolve meaningfully, it is crucial for residents – particularly long-term inhabitants – to take an active interest in their surroundings, engage with their communities in diverse ways, and foster the expansion of such efforts.

The Role and Responsibility of Architects

Let us revisit the calmness of Tokyo (and other cities in Japan), a defining characteristic I mentioned earlier, and the intimate scale of spaces that emerge from the fine grain of the urban fabric. In my keynote address at the UIA Congress in Tokyo in 2011, I suggested that this calmness, inherent to Japan's architectural culture, stems from the ongoing interaction between reason and sensibility. This dynamic is shaped by the interplay of kana and kanji in the Japanese language, which spills over not just into spatial design but also the physical actions within it. An Australian scholar of Japanese cities and architecture, in the book *Learning from the Japanese City*,[6] explores this concept, attempting to decode the unique nature of Japanese urban environments through the parallel use of kana and kanji. Much like how Western critics once sought to reframe Japanese architecture, there now seems to be a growing movement to reinterpret Japanese cities not as 'chaotic' but in a more positive way. While the introduction of the Landscape Law (*Keikan-ho,* 景観法)[7] is a welcome development, its true potential will only be realized when applied to community development and individual building designs that reflect a deeper understanding of the characteristics defining Japanese cities. Architects' involvement in the creation of community plans, as I discussed earlier, is crucial in this context.

A major issue facing Japan today, as pointed out by many experts, is the challenge of halting the outflow of young people from both metropolitan areas and rural regions. This mirrors the urgency Japan once faced after the devastation of the Second World War, when rebuilding housing and educational infrastructure was paramount. Today, the challenge is to create cities and residential environments that are attractive and responsive to the diverse needs of people at different stages of their lives.

In my view, the standard of contemporary architecture in Japan is exceptionally high when compared to other nations. I am optimistic that this collective expertise will prove crucial in addressing the challenges currently confronting Japan. We must continuously learn to view architecture from the perspective of the city (or community) and, equally,

Figure 6: Kindergarten teachers often bring their young students to the university square.

Figure 7: The open square encourages play within the university campus.

view the city through the lens of architecture. To illustrate this philosophy, I would like to share a personal experience from my recent work.

When the first phase of the new Tokyo Denki University campus was completed back in 2012, it was located on a former site of a JT factory near Kita-Senju Station. The site is surrounded by an existing residential neighbourhood and retail areas with a public street running through the heart of the campus, directly connecting to the square next to the station. After extensive collaboration with Adachi Ward, we chose to design the campus without barriers – there are no walls or gates preventing local residents from entering or leaving the campus freely. As a result, community members can easily access campus facilities, including restaurants, galleries, libraries and shops located along the main street and side streets. The restaurant located near the station square features a spacious loggia – a 'city room' – where everyone is welcome to relax. This space is often frequented by not only university students but also local residents, including neighbourhood matrons (Figure 5). On occasion, kindergarten teachers bring their young students to the university square (as seen in Figures 6–8). Looking at these photos, I can almost hear the children's laughter, echoing through the square.

In stark contrast, gated communities are becoming increasingly common in US cities, where the affluent isolate themselves from the rest of society. In some places, even entire cities are now being designed with a focus on exclusivity for the wealthy. Tokyo, on the other hand, remains a polar opposite: a city that continues to prioritize public space accessible to all. As long as architects and urban planners continue to design such inclusive, open spaces, Tokyo will maintain its distinctive calmness and vitality.

Figure 8: The circular columns encourage movement – children instinctively orbit around them.

1 Lynch, Kevin, and Rodwin, Lloyd. 'A Theory of Urban Form'. *Journal of the American Planning Association* 24, no. 4, 1958, pp201–14.

2 Muñoz, Francesc. *Urbanalización: paisajes comunes, lugares globales.* Barcelona: Editorial Gustavo Gili, 2008.

3 Muñoz, Francesc. *Urbanalización: paisajes comunes, lugares globales.* Barcelona: Editorial Gustavo Gili, 2008, pp33–50.

4 Kosuke Motani, *Defure no Shōtai* (The True Nature of Deflation). Tokyo: Kadokawa Shoten, 2010.

5 Daikanyama Suteki na Machizukuri Kyōgikai (Forum for the Development of a Wonderful Community in Daikanyama), *Daikanyama Suteki na Machizukuri Kyōgikai*, http://daisukikai.org/.

6 Shelton, Barrie. *Learning from the Japanese City: Looking East in Urban Design*. London: Routledge, 2012.

7 Japan, Landscape Law (Keikan-ho, 景観法), Law No. 110 of 2004, officially enacted on 1 June 2004. https://laws.e-gov.go.jp/law/416CO0000000398.

Making Collective Form

65

Section showing the studios.

Rissho University, Kumagaya Campus

Location	Kumagaya, Saitama Prefecture, Japan
Status	Partially Demolished
Year(s)	1967, 1968 Phase I 1967 Phase II 1968
Typology	Institution (University, Dormitory)
Area	20,148 m^2 (216,871 ft^2)

Rissho University was one of the first master planning projects undertaken by Maki and Associates. Located on an undeveloped site outside of Tokyo, the campus was designed and built in twenty-seven months over two phases and completed in 1968. Its low-density master plan includes classrooms, offices, a gymnasium and dormitory buildings for men and women.

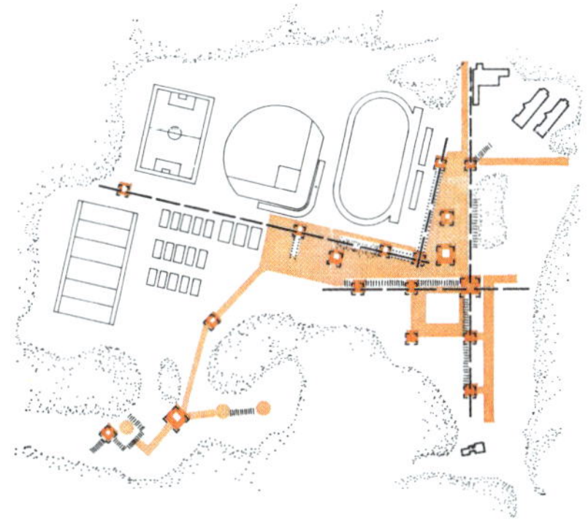

Master plan showing the Stations, their linkages and open spaces.

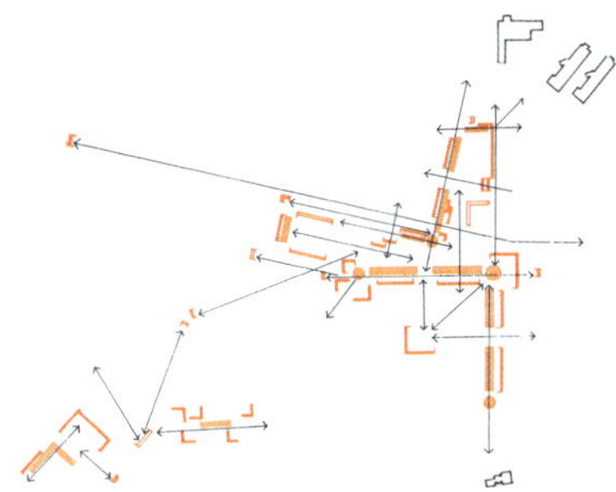

The master plan organizes the campus by arranging buildings, open spaces and pathways via sightlines and colour to guide the experience of the site.

The master plan organizes Rissho's academic programmes primarily along a symbolic spine known as the 'academic axis'. This spine controls all movement through the campus buildings and is bookended by two multi-purpose transition spaces known as 'Stations'. In phase I, the Station was realized as an interiorized outdoor space; in phase II, as an exteriorized indoor space. Both serve as informal communication spots, animated by a wide variety of activity, media and events – de-facto 'living rooms' for the university community at large.

The academic axis is comprised largely of generous circulation zones known as 'Corridors' and 'Malls'. As with the Stations, these spaces are not definitively programmed, but they do much more than directing pedestrian traffic. With controlled vistas, strategic node points and engaging materials and colours, they complement the Stations as informal communication and activity zones between classes and extra-curricular activities.

The master plan also creates a secondary campus axis via its siting of the Gymnasium and its facing Plaza. This secondary spine is used for both outdoor and indoor extracurricular activities, animated by the spillover from the Stations, Corridors and Malls along the academic axis. The Plaza brings various groups and activities together, but also serves as buffer space keeping them physically apart when necessary. It thus maintains Rissho's dynamic balance between academic and extracurricular activities and gives the campus a constant sense of renewal and energy.

With its unique arrangement of urban spatial archetypes, Rissho University's informal and spontaneous campus atmosphere has made it a popular choice for Japanese and international students seeking an inspiring, vibrant campus experience within easy reach of central Tokyo. Elements of phase II and portions of the residential components remain in use today, more than fifty years after completion – a testament to the validity and universality of the planning concepts.

The Plaza at Rissho University Kumagaya Campus is framed by the surrounding campus buildings, serving a dual role: it unifies the diverse facilities along its edge, while simultaneously maintaining their distinct identities. It exists in a state of dynamic balance – at once connective and autonomous.

Station at Rissho University Kumagaya Campus overlooking the landscape.

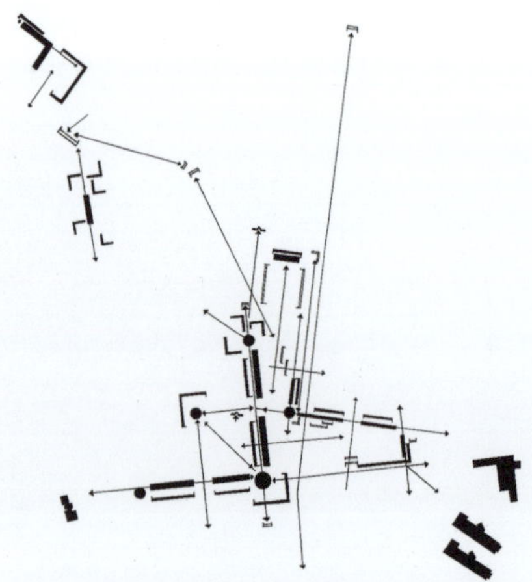

Site plan diagram, showing buildings as solid blocks and pedestrian circulation as vectors.

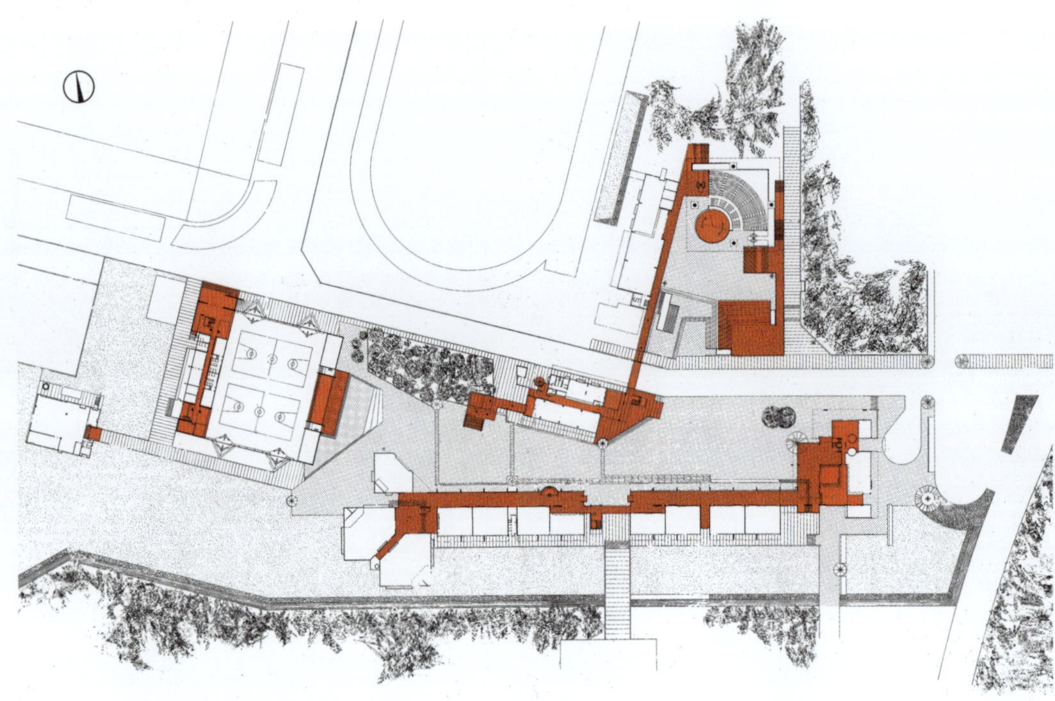

Plot plan of Rissho University Kumagaya Campus. The areas marked in orange on the plot plan represent zones without specified functions.

Aerial view of Rissho University Kumagaya Campus from the north, 1968. From left, the central administration building, classroom buildings, the student union and the Gymnasium.

Exterior, 1968. The Plaza connects the administration building and student union.

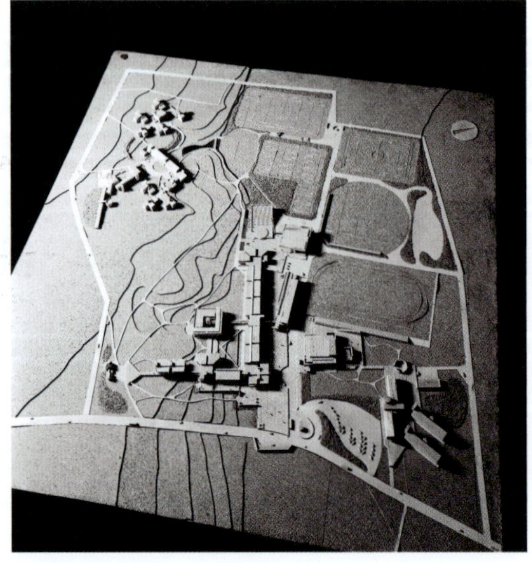

Aerial view of model from east, 1968.

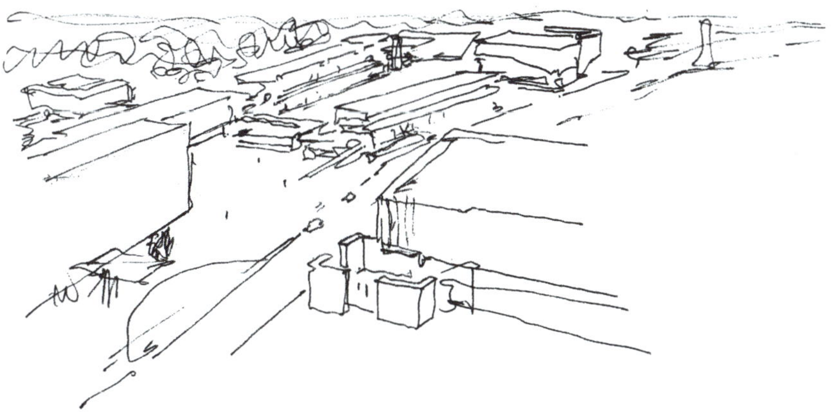

Concept sketch of building group of Kumagaya Campus for Rissho University.

Entrance plaza of the classroom building with view of Plaza and Gymnasium, a built example of Fumihiko Maki's concept of a 'city corridor', a central urban space that is allocated for the interaction and activities of students.

View of the broad corridor in the classroom building, looking toward the administration building. The walls are lined with bulletin boards and punctuated by a balcony projecting from the second-floor corridor. Though primarily a circulation space, the corridor is designed to accommodate multiple functions, including the display of information. Its spatial character is reminiscent of Station spaces.

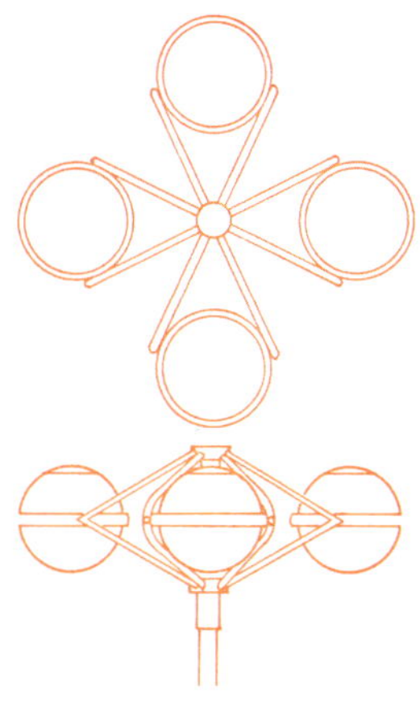

Custom lighting details.

Exterior view of the campus from the south, 1968. From left, the central administration building, the small central plaza and classrooms.

Keio University, Shonan Fujisawa Campus

Location	Fujisawa, Kanagawa Prefecture, Japan
Status	Completed
Year(s)	1990–1994, 2023 Phase I 1990 Phase II 1991 Phase III 1992 Phase IV 1994 Project H Dormitory 2023
Typology	Institution (University), Dormitory
Area	58,701 m^2 (631,852 ft^2)

In the late 1980s, Keio University established a satellite campus in Shonan Fujisawa, supplementing its two older campuses in central Tokyo. Maki and Associates' master plan for the new campus was completed and opened in four stages between 1990 and 1994. As the home for two new academic departments (Policy Management and Environmental Information), Keio's Shonan Fujisawa Campus

View of the large lecture hall and Kamoike Lounge, overlooking Kamoike (Gulliver Pond), as seen from the junior and senior high school sports grounds.

Sketch of Keio University's Shonan Fujisawa Campus.

has become one of the most celebrated institutions of higher learning in post-war Japan and continues to expand today based on the original master-planning concept.

The rural Fujisawa site consisted of four plateaus enveloped by a gentle swale, with interspersed evergreen trees and lower green growth covering the entire plot. The new campus plan preserves the given site conditions as far as possible, its existing contours driving the basic zoning division into a central core and a periphery. At the core, the new buildings are organized via clear geometric patterns; a gently curving loop access road clearly defines the edge. At the periphery, buildings are sited more freely and the campus edge gradually merges into the surrounding pastoral landscape.

The core facilities are designed in accordance with the university's desire to maintain a smaller-scale, village-like atmosphere. Vantage points and view corridors influenced both the building siting and the landscape planning. Public spaces – outdoor plazas, courtyards, indoor malls and corridors – are dropped within this Cartesian building grid. Together, they form an easily navigable but still vibrant network of physical and visual connections between disparate parts of the campus.

The main campus for undergraduates was supplemented in 1994 with the completion of the Graduate School Research Centre and a Guest/Seminar House. The Graduate School terminates a prominent pedestrian axis on the central campus, while the Guest/Seminar House is nestled back among denser greenery, closer to the main entrance but hidden from clear view. In 2023, Miraisozojuku EWH, an international dormitory located south of the main campus, was completed and is the latest contribution by Maki and Associates. Its planning follows the steeper topography of its site, a cascading series of low-rise buildings connected by a central exterior landscape opening back to the older central campus.

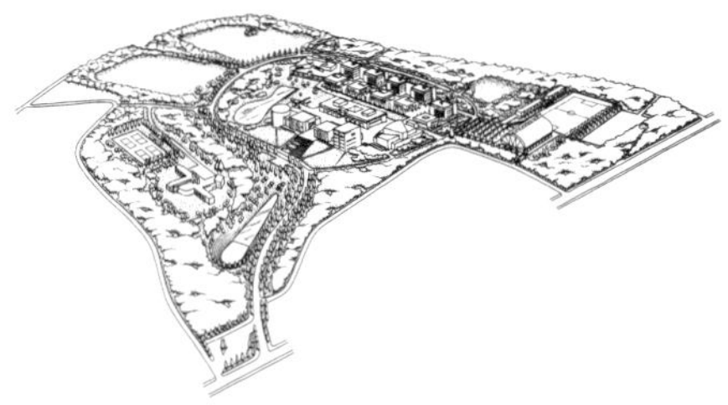

Perspective view of the campus site.

The pedestrianized 'spine' of the campus, seen from the staircase in the Graduate School Research Centre.

Entrance facade of the Shonan Fujisawa Campus with large lecture hall on the left and administration building on the right.

The Graduate School Research Centre building as seen from the pedestrianized zone.

Aerial view of the campus. The Graduate School of Research Centre is located to the north, outside the loop road.

The Media Centre (Library) building as seen from main entrance.

Entrance of the Graduate School Research Centre from the southeast.

Interior view of the gymnasium.

Research & Lecture Room Building B seen from the corner of Research & Lecture Room Building A.

Republic Polytechnic

Location	Woodlands, Singapore
Status	Completed
Year(s)	2007, 2015
Typology	Institution (School), Dormitory
Area	273,503 m^2 (2.9m ft^2)

Republic Polytechnic's new campus, located on a twenty-hectare site in the Woodlands district at the northern tip of Singapore, was chosen as the winning scheme in an invited international competition. First opened in 2007, the two-year technical college houses a total floor area of more than 270,000 square metres (2.9m ft^2) and serves over 17,000 students, faculty and staff.

To accommodate the required density of students on its limited site, Republic Polytechnic's educational programmes are concentrated within a single central nucleus (the Learning Hub), surrounded by lower density satellite buildings for support functions (administration, performing arts, sports, housing and infrastructure). While the Learning Hub and the satellite buildings are formally distinct, common design themes, similar materials and a coherent siting strategy unite to create a singular and functional campus plan.

The Learning Hub's eleven medium-rise classroom buildings (Learning Pods) connect at their lower levels to a contiguous interior space known as the Agora. The Agora houses all group learning programmes and includes a library, research labs, lecture halls, food courts and other gathering spaces. After beginning their day in the Pod classrooms, students spend most of their time within the Agora – individually and collectively researching, completing classroom assignments and socializing – before returning to the Pod classrooms to give reports and share assignments. This pedagogical model, known as problem-based learning, is streamlined by the proximity and design of the Pods and the Agora, enabling a smooth flow of students back and forth.

The Agora is crowned by a gently sloping elliptical green roof (the Lawn), dotted with eight outdoor courtyards that flood its interior with natural light, air and views. A network of covered walkways interacts with these courtyards and reduces the Lawn's enormous scale, while the outdoor spaces and courtyards double as classroom extensions, meeting areas, break and lunch areas. On the interior, despite the Agora's enormous scale (240 × 180 m / 787 × 591 ft), transparent partitioning and terraced floor spaces along its primary axis allow for end-to-end vistas and create the feeling of a gently sloping hill town. It has a variety of comfortable, human-scaled spaces equally suitable for one or two people to talk quietly, or for noisier groups to congregate.

(Opposite) The main circulation spine of the Agora interior space.

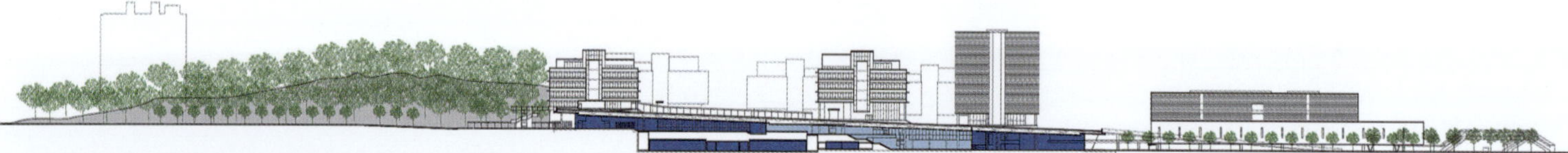

Republic Polytechnic longitudinal section.

Aerial view of the Singapore Republic Polytechnic Campus, including the Singapore Institute of Technology expansion with the regional park beyond, 2015.

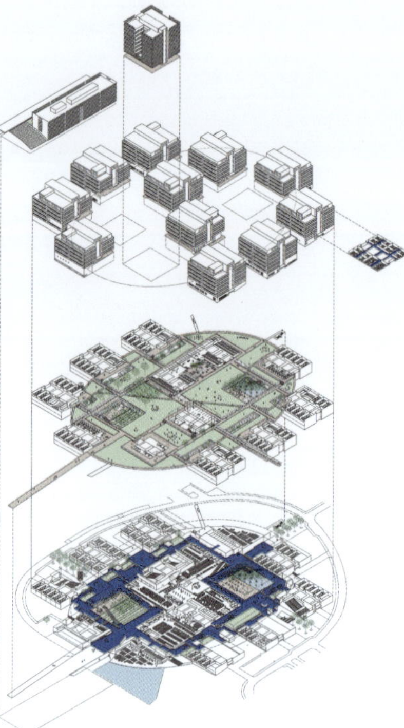

Republic Polytechnic axonometric spatial diagram.

Reflecting pool on the Republic Polytechnic Campus.

The multistorey library on the Republic Polytechnic Campus is partially lit by the adjacent south court.

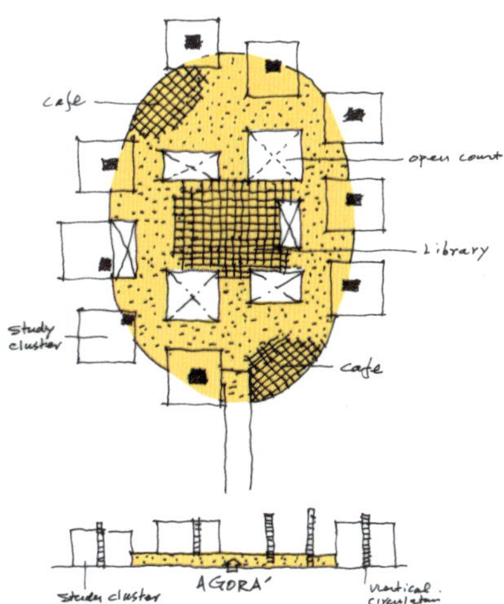

Concept sketch showing the Agora and study cluster.

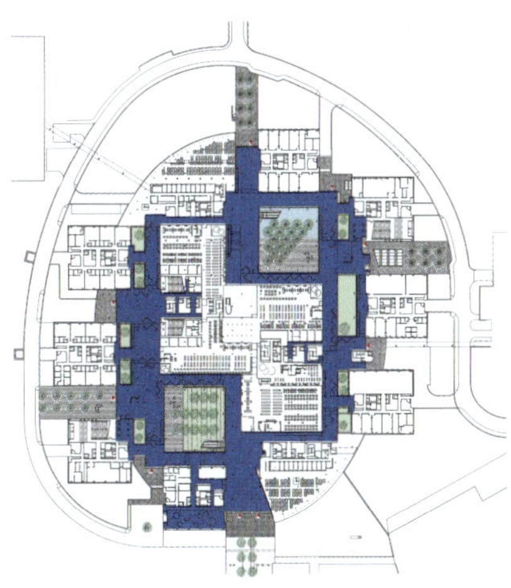

Republic Polytechnic Agora plan.

View of one of the eight sunken courts to create space variation.

Students performing in the Agora.

Looking down on the Lawn and the south court.

Promenade through the Republic Polytechnic Centre.

International College for Postgraduate Buddhist Studies

Location	Bunkyo-ku, Tokyo Metropolitan, Japan
Status	Completed
Year(s)	2010
Typology	Institution (College), Dormitory
Area	6,365 m^2 (68,512 ft^2)

The International College for Postgraduate Buddhist Studies (ICPBS) was founded in 1996 with the establishment of the Reiyukai International Library, a rich collection of Buddhist materials engendering academic exchanges with world-renowned institutions and scholars. A dramatic increase in library acquisitions, steady growth in students and a major redevelopment project at the original location necessitated the college's move to a new site in Kasuga, central Tokyo (on land formerly owned by Yoshinobu Tokugawa, the last Tokugawa Shogun). The new campus opened in 2010.

Consisting of three interconnected and two freestanding structures, the campus plan mobilizes its open site's existing greenery and topography to create a serene atmosphere appropriate for research and learning. The five low-rise buildings have small footprints and connect via courtyards, exterior spaces, walkways and bridges. These generous transition spaces encourage contemplation and innovation for researchers spending long hours on surveys and analyses – the circulation through the building and landscapes aims to inspire new outlooks on stagnant ideas.

Each of the five buildings has a distinct identity, but the campus maintains harmony through its consistent use of warm materials, including masonry and wood. The main library, the largest structure at the southern site edge, houses over 100,000 volumes, with 1,700 periodicals and 800 microfilm sets, together with other audio-visual material. The library joins directly to the central cluster of connected seminar rooms, offices and classrooms, and to Kasuga Hall, a multipurpose lecture room. The dormitory is located at the northern site edge, providing twelve furnished flats for regular students and guest scholars from abroad.

Despite its dense central metropolitan location, the college's strategic siting ensures multiple green vistas and a wide variety of sheltered exterior spaces throughout the complex. With its small enrolment quota, unique setting and open design, the campus offers a rarefied and intense atmosphere for the study and contemplation of Buddhism and its place in the wider world.

(Opposite) Entrance to the second-floor corridor.

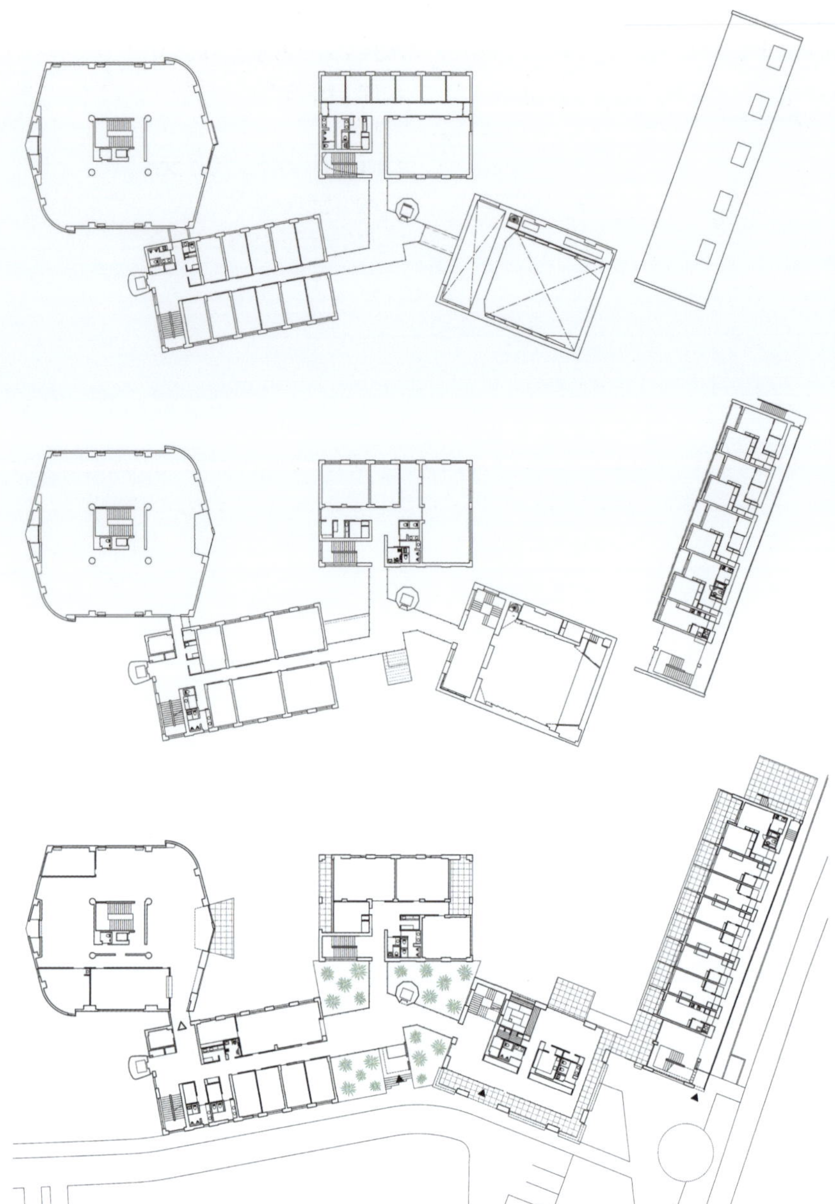

College floor plans.

Kasuga Hall on the second floor.

Entrance view of the college.

Exterior courtyard with garden sculpture.

Stairs with round windows overlooking the Sumeru Lawn to Kasuga Hall.

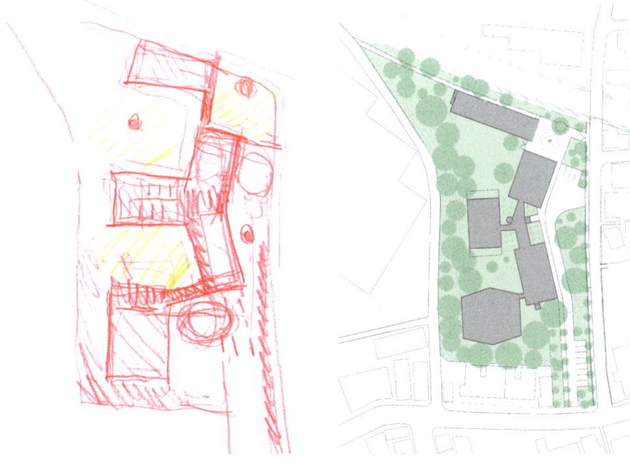

College concept sketch.

College site plan.

Aerial view of model of the college campus.

Entrance and reception area.

Tokyo Denki University, Tokyo Senju Campus

Location	Adachi-ku, Tokyo Metropolitan, Japan
Status	Completed
Year(s)	2012, 2017 Phase I 2012 Phase II 2017
Typology	Institution (University)
Area	106,136 m^2 (1.14m ft^2)

Tokyo Denki University is a renowned engineering school that celebrated its centenary in 2007. Its new campus is the culmination of a ten-year effort begun at the centennial, relocating from a series of dispersed buildings in central Tokyo to a newly consolidated campus to the northeast. The first phase was opened in spring 2012 with the second phase completed in spring 2017.

Prior to this project, the university's new site was privately held and walled off to residents. As a condition for land use, the local government insisted that the university allow public access to lower levels of its new campus and further lobbied for the inclusion of integrated public programmes there. The resulting campus design is free of walls dividing town and gown and integrates restaurants, children's daycare and sports facilities for use by the community. This confluence between students and locals, rare in Japan, has animated and transformed the formerly closed site.

The detailed master plan disperses the university's large programme requirements into four mid and high-rise buildings. This programme concentration allows the campus to maintain a high percentage of exterior public spaces, critical to its open, civic campus atmosphere. Landscaped open areas along the surrounding streets define the campus border without limiting visitor access, while an open-air Campus Plaza integrates the four new buildings around it. Connecting bridges above the Plaza link the academic programmes inside these four structures, while the Event Plaza below is left open for daily activities, special events, performances and festivals.

The facades of all the new buildings utilize white ceramic fritted glass, white spandrel panels, aluminium extruded profiles and pre-cast concrete. The result is a bright silhouette of white towers emerging from the chaotic cityscape around the campus. High-performance glazing and the introduction of air-flow windows minimize perimeter energy loading and ensure that the interiors remain naturally ventilated throughout the year. Overall, the new campus's mix of public programmes, hard and soft landscaped public spaces and the welcoming nature of the architecture itself has resulted in new life for both Denki University and the surrounding community.

(Opposite) Building 5 Atrium in phase II, used as a public corridor and interior events space.

Aerial view of Tokyo Denki University, Tokyo Senju Campus from northwest.

TDU
SINCE 1907

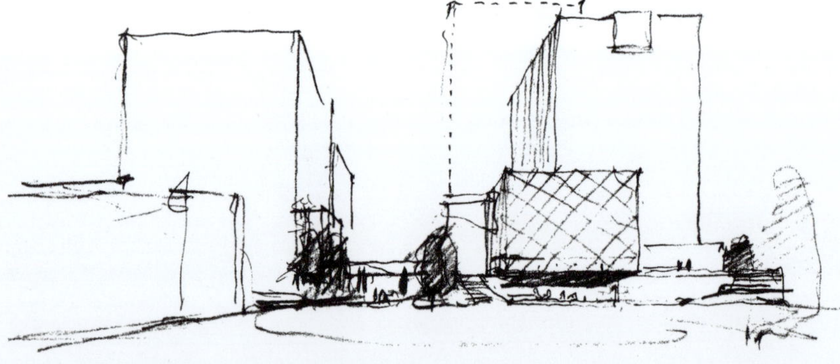

Campus concept sketch.

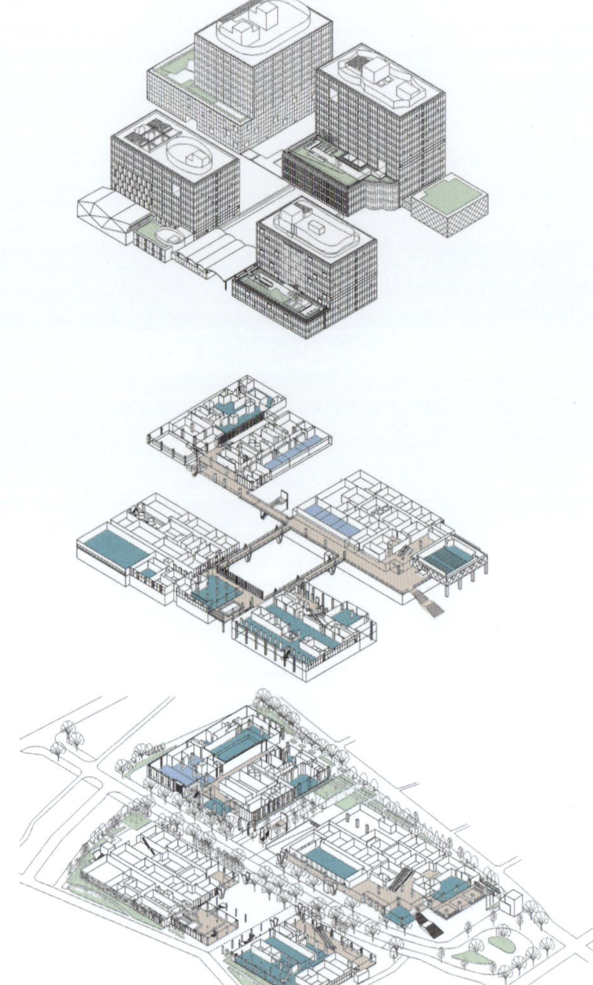

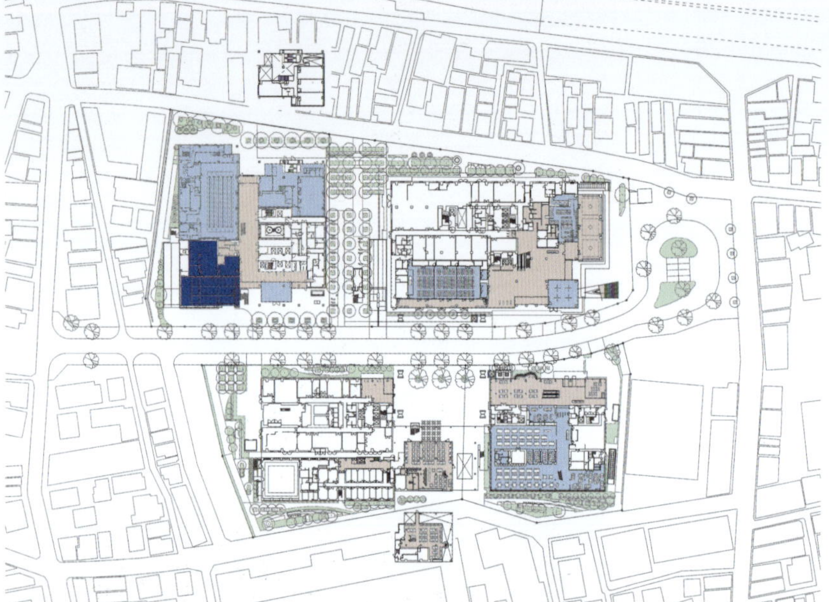

First-floor plan showing the different zones open to the public.

Axonometric spatial diagram.

View of Dendai Street – a central public thoroughfare integrated into the campus layout which serves as a shared space for both students and local residents.

Tokyo Senju Campus, viewed from the north, featuring the central public thoroughfare known as Dendai Street.

Entrance lounge.

Children playing at the forest plaza.

Evening view of the campus plaza.

Exterior view of Haus 5.

Isar Büro Park

Location	Munich, Germany
Status	Completed
Year(s)	1995
Typology	Offices
Area	68,366 m^2 (735,885 ft^2)

Isar Büro Park is Maki and Associates' first built project in Europe. Awarded in an international competition in 1990, the project encompasses the development of a four-hectare office park near Munich's international airport and was completed in 1995. The planning is based on a study of the local landscape, aspiring to create a new type of working environment for high-technology industries that combines the exciting, urbane atmosphere of high-tech office spaces with the contemplative rural qualities extant in the site.

The multiple building siting was based on a study of the relationships between land patterns and natural forces – including the age-old layout of farming fields (according to topography and watercourses) and the contemporary orientation of nearby airport runways (according to predominant winds). The office park landscape weaves together this local meadow ecology with new, increasingly dense, interventions: disperse paving blocks lead to wooden boardwalks and eventually to crystalline office buildings with roofs mirroring the sky. The nearby Isar Forest is recreated within the site via the introduction of dense maple tree *alleen* crossing the complex. All buildings are oriented toward these *alleen*, with footpaths offering alternative routes among the offices to the nearby town of Hallbergmoos and connecting as far away as the forest itself.

The building programme includes eleven office buildings in two types – large buildings for single anchor tenants and smaller buildings for multiple tenants. The larger are designed around a central glazed atrium, creating a sense of internal unity and framing views of surrounding trees, sky and neighbouring buildings. The smaller structures are more closely divided floor by floor, for clearly defined tenant zoning. They connect via exterior arcades to each other and the surrounding landscape.

Both the larger and smaller structures orient their public zones to face one another, increasing visual awareness and communication across the development and activating the park-like setting of the inner blocks. The contrasting roof forms – one circular, one parallelogram – ensure a dynamic skyline silhouette as one walks around the complex and a memorable public image for tenants and passersby alike.

Isar Büro Park site model.

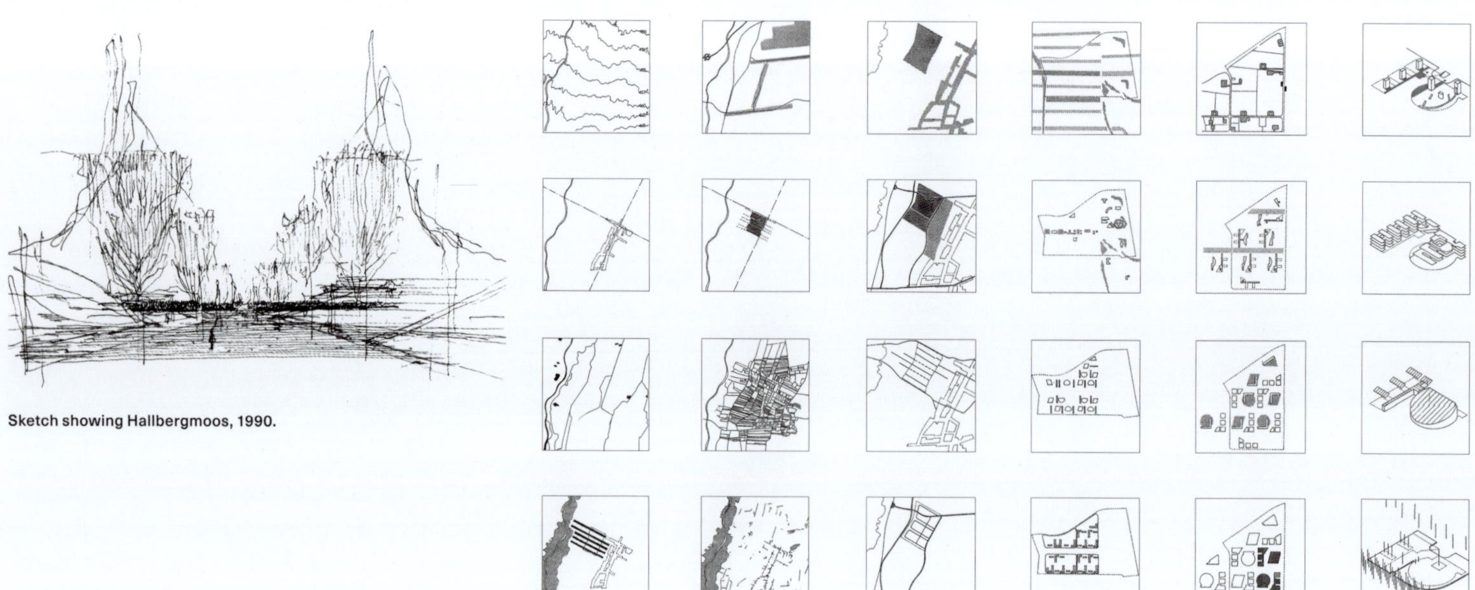

Sketch showing Hallbergmoos, 1990.

Various analysis diagrams.

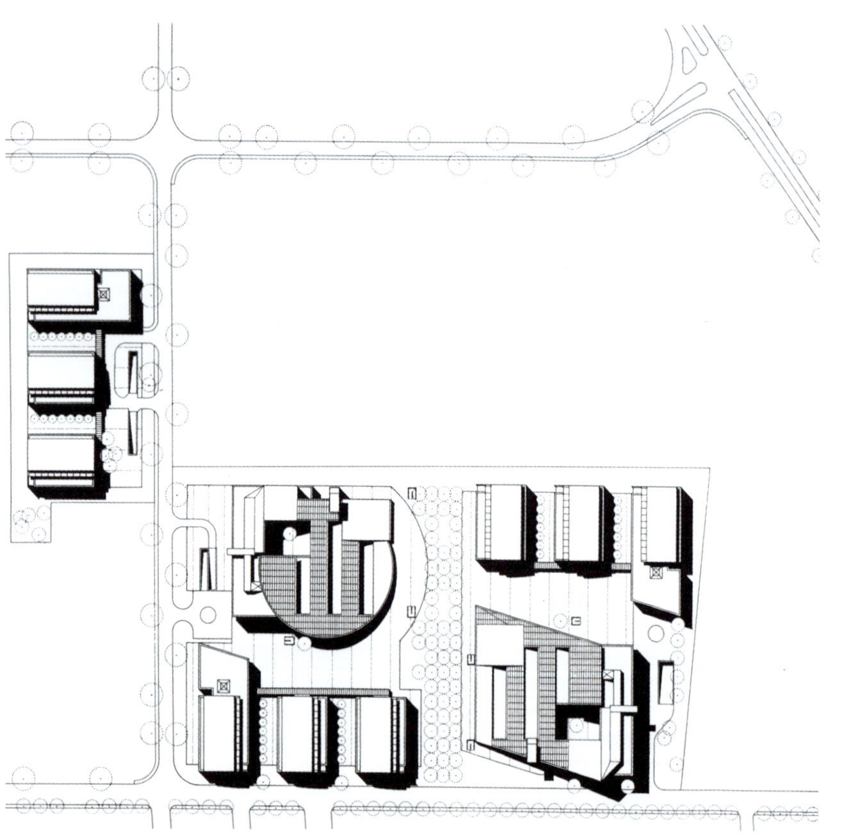

Isar Büro Park site plan.

Open office space within the atrium in Haus 5 in Isar Büro Park.

Site sketch depicting the landscape and the forest beyond.

Overview from the north.

Eye-level view through the landscape.

Participating in Collective Form

World Trade Center Tower 4

Location	New York, New York, USA
Status	Completed
Year(s)	2013
Typology	Offices, Retail
Area	213,700 m^2 (2.3m ft^2)

World Trade Center Tower 4 is a sixty-five-storey office building completed in 2013, the first of four major towers to open following the tragic events of 11 September 2001. Occupying a full city block and fronting prominently onto the National September 11 Memorial & Museum, Tower 4 is the starting point of a cascading spiral following Daniel Libeskind's master plan, including Towers 2 and 3 and culminating in the ninety-four-storey Freedom Tower. Respecting its unique location opposite the memorial, Tower 4's office lobby and facade above are understated and reverent. At the same time, its podium actively mobilizes frontage onto two adjacent streets to foster pedestrian-level activity and bring vitality to this section of downtown Manhattan.

Tower 4's lobby, with its generous forty-six-foot ceiling height, offers panoramic views of the memorial and its surroundings. The inner core wall is clad in polished black granite, reflecting the memorial greenery and supporting a semicircular cantilevered titanium sculpture called *Sky Memory* by the Japanese artist Kozo Nishino. This artwork also reflects in the granite, creating the illusion of a complete circle, symbolic of unity and rebirth. Three 'streets' lead from the lobby to elevator banks, featuring video art installations of skies, trees and water synchronized to music by the composer Philip Glass.

The podium concentrates three floors of retail space (one at street level and two along the pedestrian concourses below grade), its humane scale helping to knit the building into the streetscape. All podium levels are spatially interconnected via a central atrium and connected to twelve subway and commuter lines, filling its retail floors with life throughout the day and evening.

The tower facade is comprised of unitized glazing units, uninterrupted from floor to ceiling. Its reflective coating has a matte metallic quality, giving the tower an ephemeral, luminous sheen that changes in different light and weather conditions. Seen from a distance, Tower 4's angular profile is further chiselled at its crown, strengthening the original spiral concept set out in the master plan. Its state-of-the-art safety systems exceed building codes and its energy efficiency measures have achieved a LEED Gold rating. Tower 4 is therefore both a technical and aesthetic landmark, its quiet beauty underlying a robust, user-friendly and highly secure functional core – equally integrated with its city neighbours, the rarefied surroundings of the memorial and the skyline of lower Manhattan.

(Opposite) West view of World Trade Center Tower 4 from the World Financial Center.

Redevelopment master plan 'Memory Foundations' – 6 September 2006.

Aerial view from the World Financial Center.

North view of midtown Manhattan.

View of Tower 4 overlooking the National September 11 Memorial.

View of Michael Arad and Peter Walker's *Reflecting Absence* memorial and Tower 4 podium in the background.

North–south podium section.

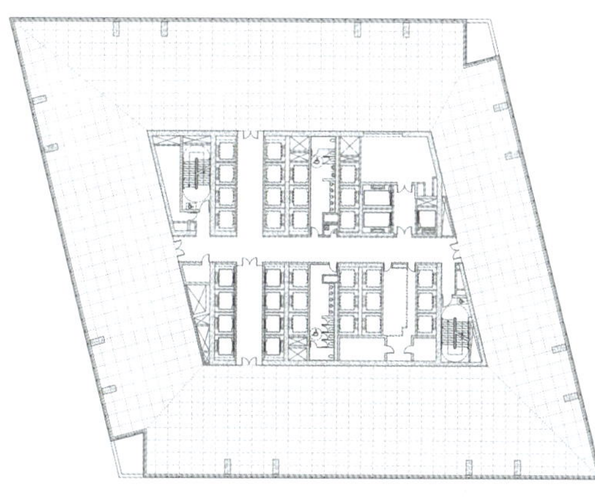

Lower floor plan for the 15th–54th floors.

Tower 4 site plan.

Retail facade and east entrance on Church Street.

Memorial Park reflected in the polished black granite wall.

Video art installation within elevator lobby.

Office lobby in the evening.

MEN
SHOES
Akimoto Asahi
Sushi
212-766-3351
WE ARE NEW YORK'S LAW SCHOOL
CASH 4 GOLD
SHOE REPAIR

View of World Trade Center Tower 4
from Church Street.

Tranquillity in a Place of Torment

David W. Dunlap

At the most troubled, complex, fractious building site in America – the World Trade Center in Lower Manhattan, where 2,753 people were killed by terrorists on 11 September 2001 – Fumihiko Maki, Gary Kamemoto, Osamu Sassa and their colleagues performed a near miracle. They introduced context, order and peace.

Architects typically say they care about context. Often what they mean is that they want to make an idiosyncratic mark with just enough superficial contextual traits to placate city planners, historical preservationists and community activists.

With 4 World Trade Center, by contrast, Maki and Associates fashioned a truly contextual building. It not only sets the tone for its district, it would be largely meaningless elsewhere.

Picture 50 Rockefeller Plaza. Chances are, you can't. Apart from Isamu Noguchi's thrilling News relief, the building blends into the milieu of Rockefeller Center, contributing to the whole without raising its voice above the ensemble.

Like the best of the Rockefeller Center buildings, 4 World Trade Center respects and enhances several contexts simultaneously and subtly. The facade overlooking the National September 11 Memorial is as restrained as an architect could make it. A plane of smooth glass, unbroken by any mechanical louvres or other interventions, descends to within 14 metres (47 feet) of the sidewalk, where it turns into a delicate veil – almost a transparent shoji screen – enclosing a lobby whose spare simplicity is meant as a respectful gesture to the memorial directly across Greenwich Street.

What does it mean to be a Japanese architect at what Americans call 'ground zero'? After all, civilization's first ground zero was Hiroshima, upon which America dropped an atomic bomb on 6 August 1945, that killed at least 100,000 people. That was followed three days later by the second – and, to date, the last – atomic bombing in human history, this time of Nagasaki, where 40,000 people died. The destruction of Tokyo by American incendiary bombs in March 1945 was equally fearsome, if not more so. At least 100,000 people were killed in those air raids. Fumihiko Maki, born and raised in Tokyo, was sixteen years old at the time. Later, as a student in the Kenzo Tange Laboratory at Tokyo University in the early 1950s, Maki was exposed firsthand to the preparation of construction documents for the Hiroshima Peace Center.

One lesson he apparently learned was that architecture can respond quietly to a holocaust. There is no need for bellicosity where moral culpability is ambiguous. There is no need for melodrama when the facts alone are so horrendous.

What Maki has brought to America's ground zero is an imposing sense of calm. The main wall of the lobby at 4 World Trade Center is clad in a Swedish black granite with flecks of feldspar. This reflects the canopy of swamp white oak trees around the memorial pools, in a pointillist diffusion that Kamemoto likens to a Seurat.

Puncturing the monolithic wall are three corridors of luscious anigre veneer coated with highly polished polyester. Though they stretch into the core, they appear to lead back out to nature, thanks to 7-metre-high (24-ft) screens at the end of each spine, on which gracefully kinetic video images of water, trees and sky are shown, set to Philip Glass music. Cheesy as this may sound, the experience is seductively hypnotic. In your tranquil reverie, you may even notice such subtle effects as how the wall planes seem to descend behind and below the floor planes, a building method known as *kabe-gachi* that lends delicacy and depth to the most ordinary junctions.

Hovering over the lobby is Kozo Nishino's *Sky Memory*, a lacy semicircle of lightweight titanium truss, 30 metres (98 ft) across, cantilevered from the wall. Because of the reflection, Mr Nishino's sculpture can be read as a full circle. Or, if you will, as a zero.

Contrasting vibrantly with the Greenwich Street lobby is the entrance at Liberty and Church Streets, cater-corner from Zuccotti Park. This corner of the building is an important portal between the business district of Lower Manhattan and the World Trade Center: its office towers, the Eataly food hall, the Westfield World Trade Center shopping mall (in the Oculus, designed by Santiago Calatrava) and the PATH commuter railroad transit hall (also by Calatrava), through which 60,000 passengers travel every day to and from New Jersey. Befitting its role as a hub, this entrance proclaims itself boldly with a 45-degree V-shaped column, nearly 13 metres high (44 ft), that frames criss-crossing escalators.

In any other setting, the tower's overall form – a sheer fifty-six-storey parallelogram topped by a sheer sixteen-storey trapezoid – might be dull, ponderous, awkward, overbearing. Yet here, the prismatic structure treads lightly. How can that be?

Ever since the completion of 4 World Trade Center in 2013, many writers, including this one, have marvelled at how the tower seems to disappear on the skyline. That's an astonishing design feat, especially given its tremendous height of 298 metres (977 ft), which makes it the tenth tallest building in New York.

To explain the phenomenon, many writers, including this one, have focused almost exclusively on the brilliant curtain wall. Of course, there's a lot to be said for it. The tower is glazed with 11,000 crisply and tightly abutting panels. The vision lights are made of low-iron glass, which yields a more neutral colour than the greenish tint common to many modern skyscrapers. A low-emissivity coating has been applied to the glass to increase its insulating properties, and therefore its reflectivity. The panels are 4 metres high (13.5 ft). They are tall and reflective enough to conceal the spandrel sections between each floor, creating the illusion of a seamless facade. Because the glass is 36.5 mm thick (1 7⁄16 in.), and because each light is framed discretely, the curtain wall is less subject to the deformation known as quilting. From certain angles, at certain times of day, the tower seems to dematerialize, becoming no more than a hairline grid in the sky, behind which nearby buildings appear almost tangible, though they're only reflections.

Far more than a simple mirror, however, the facade is a sophisticated and ever-changing composition. This is due in part to the 76-degree notches at the southwest and northeast corners of the tower, which sharpen its knife-edge profile on the skyline and also create – for tenants who care about such things – a perimeter allowing for six corner offices instead of four.

The notches and cantilevered corners were made possible by an ingenious structural framing. Four World Trade Center sits atop a complex underground structure, 21 metres deep (70 ft), that includes portions of the shopping mall, the transit hub and the National September 11 Memorial & Museum. Column penetrations had to be kept to a minimum and situated strategically. Together, Maki and Leslie E. Robertson Associates devised a system in which only eight pairs of columns carry the entire perimeter. In concert with especially deep girders, these pairings permitted the architects and engineers to span lengths up to 24 metres (80 ft) without any columns, creating unparalleled vistas, especially of the harbour.

The hybrid parallelogram and trapezoid together sound the opening notes of what Studio Daniel Libeskind, master planners for the new World Trade Center, intended as a spiralling crescendo of four skyscrapers enveloping the memorial, ascending from 4 World Trade Center, at the southeast corner of the site, to the 541-metre (1,776-foot) 1 World Trade Center at the northwest corner. The Maki office embraced this concept by effectively twisting the facade of 4 World Trade Center to set Libeskind's spiral in motion.

There is a kinship with several neighbouring towers by Skidmore, Owings & Merrill, where Maki worked from 1954 to 1955 as a junior designer to Gordon Bunshaft. Four World Trade Center shares the prismatic form of SOM's 7 World Trade Center, the taut skin of 140 Broadway and the silvery incandescence of 1 Chase Manhattan Plaza.

There is another SOM connection to the story of 4 World Trade Center, in the person of David M. Childs, an influential and high-profile partner in the firm's New York office. In July 2001, Larry A. Silverstein, the chairman of Silverstein Properties, entered into a ninety-nine-year lease on the World Trade Center site with the Port Authority of New York and New Jersey, builders and owners of the complex. At the time, Mr Silverstein envisioned Mr Childs and SOM updating the twin towers and environs, which were showing their age.

Exactly seven weeks after the lease was signed, however, the entire World Trade Center was destroyed.

In the aftermath, rather than clear ground zero of encumbrances and begin anew, the Port Authority chose to maintain the leasehold. Because Silverstein Properties still had to pay rent on the site, and because it was the insured party, it appeared that Silverstein was likely to have the resources and the incentive to rebuild quickly.

Silverstein picked SOM to design the new Tower 1 and Tower 7. Then he asked Childs if SOM ought to be given the entire World Trade Center project. As the developer tells it, Childs stood in silent shock for a moment before answering: 'This would be the architectural challenge of ten lifetimes. There's nothing that could be greater for an architect than to be asked what you've asked. But I have to tell you, as a friend, that I don't think it would be in your best interest to do that. I think it would in your best interest to hire a group of world-class architects.'

In New York circles, Silverstein was known for sharp elbows, long timeframes and a tenacity at the bargaining table that has worn down many negotiators. He was not known as a patron of 'world-class' architecture. Indeed, his choice for the World Trade Center project of Richard Rogers, Norman Foster and Jean Nouvel might have come right out of the cliché starchitect playbook. The choice of Maki was a surprise.

As it happened, however, Silverstein had been exposed since the 1980s to the work of Maki and Associates, thanks to the friendship that he and his wife, Clara, struck up with Japan's most prolific builder, Minoru Mori, and his wife, Yoshiko, whom they would visit in Tokyo. 'We were hugely taken by how magnificent the detail work was,' Silverstein recalled about Maki's buildings. 'The facades were very plain, simple, almost austere. But the quality of the design was spectacular.'

The developer said he never estimated the premium paid to ensure the quality of execution demanded by Maki and Associates. Suffice it to say that the 213,700 m^2 (2.3m ft^2) building wound up costing more than $2 billion (¥225 billion).

'There comes a time when you put cost considerations aside,' Silverstein said. 'This was one of them. I'm very pleased that we did. Tower 4 had to be a hugely successful building. It had to garner architectural plaudits of major critics from all parts of the globe.' Even so, it took four years until the building was fully leased.

Meanwhile, 4 World Trade Center has served steadily as a deferential complement to the National September 11 Memorial. In that sense, it is a public space; more so than 1 World Trade Center, where casual visitors are greeted by an unwelcoming security apparatus; more so than the Westfield shopping centre, an extravagant showcase for retail brands one finds in every other high-end mall in the world; more so even than the Memorial Museum, which requires a $24 admission fee.

You can simply walk into the lobby of 4 World Trade Center and, provided you don't take photos, stand there quietly as long as you wish. The space invites contemplation, even – or especially – when it hums with business activity while crowds gather just across Greenwich Street to honour the dead. From within this tranquil room, the jumbled trade centre seems more rational and purposeful. Thanks to the work of Maki and Associates, there is a sense of resolution that would have seemed impossible on 12 September 2001; a feeling of peace that once seemed beyond reach.

David W. Dunlap was a reporter on the *New York Times* from 1981 to 2017 where much of his coverage focused on the historical landmarks of New York City, including the redevelopment of the World Trade Center. Now retired, Dunlap is the curator of a small museum housed at the headquarters of the *New York Times* and which tells the story of the newspaper since its founding in 1851.

Building context sketch.

Location	New York, New York, USA
Status	In-Progress
Year(s)	–
Typology	Offices, Conference, Dining Facilities
Area	92,900 m^2 (1m ft^2)

United Nations Consolidation Building

The United Nations Consolidation Building (UNCB) is designed for a tight site on First Avenue between 41st and 42nd streets, immediately south of the original United Nations complex in New York. Currently on hold, the project was awarded via an invited competition in 2003 and will provide 950,000 square feet of expansion space for the consolidation of current UN offices dispersed throughout the city. It is designated to be the fifth building of the UN campus, complementing the original General Assembly, Secretariat, Conference and Library buildings designed by a consortium including Wallace Harrison, Le Corbusier and Oscar Niemeyer and which opened in 1951.

The UNCB programme includes office, conference and dining amenities in a thirty-six-storey tower exactly matching the height of the Secretariat. Its solid podium (floors 1–12) contains conference facilities and large rectangular office floor plates for open office use. The upper floors (13–16) utilize a slimmer office span as in the Secretariat but shaped into a u-configuration, forming a symbolic lightwell at its centre. All offices receive an abundance of natural light and are afforded framed views of the UN headquarters to the north, panoramas of midtown Manhattan to the west and generous outlooks over the East River. At the transition between podium and tower, a cafeteria and private dining rooms encircle a sky garden with open vistas back towards the original UN complex.

Seen from a distance, the UNCB is a simple, abstract white tower anchoring the southern end of the UN campus. From midtown Manhattan, the tower presents an iconic presence along the 42nd Street view corridor. From the north, the new tower's twin vertical slabs rise from the podium to the sky, echoing the slender silhouette of the Secretariat building – creating a harmonious relationship between the new and old structure. The high-performance exterior facade, utilizing white fritted glazing, creates subtle variations in transparency, translucency, light and shadow throughout the day. Set against the blue sky this gleaming white tower will embrace a spirit of peace and tranquillity, capturing the promise of the UN itself.

View of United Nations Consolidation Building from the north with the United Nations Secretariat building in the foreground.

View of UNDC / UN Consolidation Building from the East River.

Yerba Buena Center for the Arts

Location	San Francisco, California, USA
Status	Completed
Year(s)	1993
Typology	Gallery, Multi-purpose Hall
Area	5,388 m^2 (57,996 ft^2)

Yerba Buena Center for the Arts (YBCA) was Maki and Associates' first building to open in the United States since Steinberg Hall in 1960. Completed in 1993 and part of a major mixed-use redevelopment, the Center for the Arts combines with an adjacent theatre designed by James Stewart Polshek to create a new focus for cultural activities in San Francisco's energetic SOMA (South of Market) district. Providing space for art exhibitions, installations and experimental performances, the complex highlights the city's ethnic and cultural diversity in a modern, open atmosphere.

The centre's height and mass were severely restricted by its unusual location. Sited directly above an underground addition to the pre-existing Moscone Convention Center (a long-span concrete waffle structure), the building utilizes a steel ductile moment frame to minimize imposed structural loads and is clad in lightweight corrugated and flat aluminium panels to minimize its weight. The combination of materials, while based primarily in engineering logic, also gives the centre a unique visual weightlessness and recalls the image of an 'elegant factory', akin to the industrial spaces where many of the centre's participating artists reside and work.

The diaphanous metallic building vocabulary further expresses the temporality inherent in the centre's contemporary art programme. These materials and the non-hierarchical, open-ended planning avoid the sense of monumentality found in most museums. Fractional massing and windowed vistas connect the galleries and other interior spaces seamlessly back to the city and to Yerba Buena Gardens itself – a green oasis surrounded by the convention centre, hotels and other cultural facilities.

The centre also aspires to another image rooted in the consciousness of San Francisco and its origins as a port town. Its low-profile horizontality, metallic skin and sculptural steel stairs, handrails and flagpoles all suggest the image of a ship harboured in the Gardens, gleaming in the California sunlight. Equally part of the surrounding city and the park, the YBCA remains a vibrant outpost for San Francisco's thriving art community and a beloved anchor in this still-evolving neighbourhood some thirty years later.

(Opposite) Entry-plaza view from Yerba Buena Gardens.

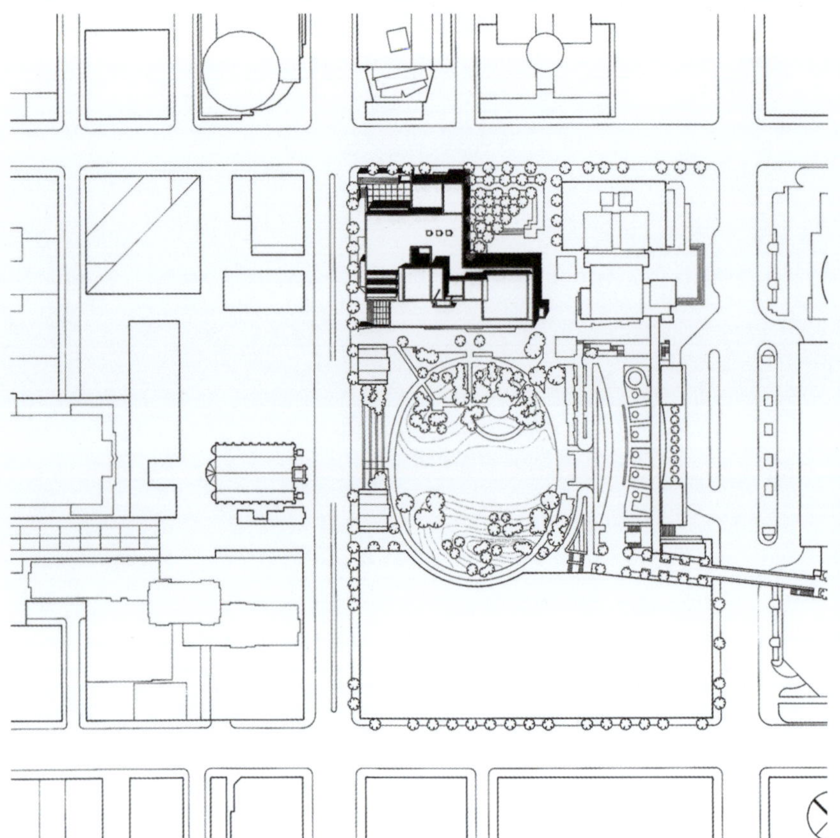
Yerba Buena Center for the Arts site plan.

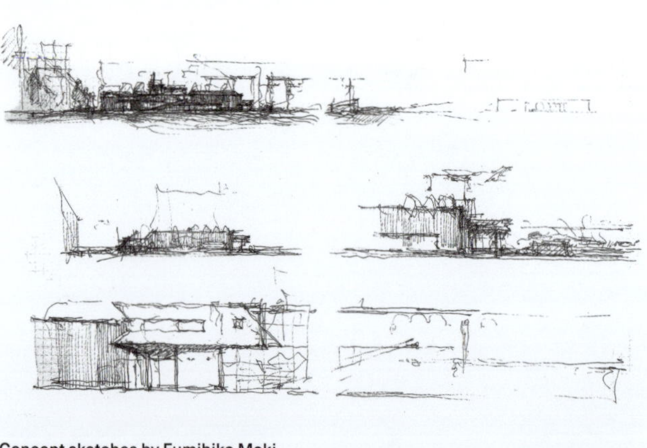
Concept sketches by Fumihiko Maki.

The opening ceremony on 12 October 1993 welcomed 50,000 people.

The passages are sometimes used as show windows that show the interior scenery, and sometimes as displays.

Protruding passage serving as a visual interface between city and the interior.

Aerial view from the north showing the centre within the downtown San Francisco context.

The entrance lobby facing the Yerba Buena Gardens esplanade is used for a variety of civic events.

Anteroom to galleries. A courtyard garden is visible beyond the glass block screen.

Artworks on show appear within the context of the cityscape beyond.

Nature and the Rural Environment

Toyota Kuragaike Commemorative Hall

Location	Toyota, Aichi Prefecture, Japan
Status	Completed
Year(s)	1974
Typology	Museum
Area	4,340 m^2 (46,715 ft^2)

Central aerial view from the nearby mountain.

Toyota Kuragaike Commemorative Hall, completed in 1974, occupies a spacious site on a hillside overlooking Kuragaike lake. Combining a guest house for visitors to the nearby Toyota Corporation and a public exhibition hall devoted to showing the history of the company and its products, the building's strong geometry belies its careful integration with its site and surrounding nature.

Although the two major components of the building have very different programmes and character, in plan they utilize similar footprints – but with vastly different relationships to the surrounding landscape. The private guest house offers travellers a quiet retreat within a triangular block resting on the land. The public museum uses the site's sloping topography to keep the main exhibition space submerged underground, protecting it from natural light and maintaining the visitor's inward focus on the exhibits. Stepped glazed passageways connect the two sections and enable easy service and staff access for both.

While the museum exhibition space occupies almost the entirety of its triangular footprint, the guest house is divided into several distinct spaces. The formal lounge has a unique semicircular plan, extending into the landscape to a semicircular garden. The reception room is elliptical and aligns on an independent axis, offset from the rest of the building. The dining room occupies one apex of the triangle, with fully glazed openings for unobstructed views of the lake below. A twelve *tatami* mat Japanese-style room, enveloped by sliding shoji doors, fits into the remaining vertex of the triangular plan.

Over time, the building has become well-integrated into its topography, melding with the surroundings to create continuous vistas with the deep greenery of nearby hills. Views to the lake and environs are optimized via subtle level changes in both the architecture and landscape. The result is a building uniquely fitting to its site and a harmonious addition to the area for both tourists and Toyota's distinguished guests alike.

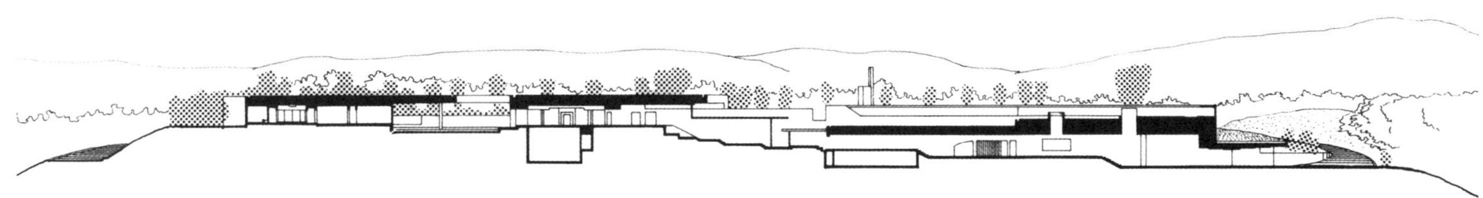

East–west section.

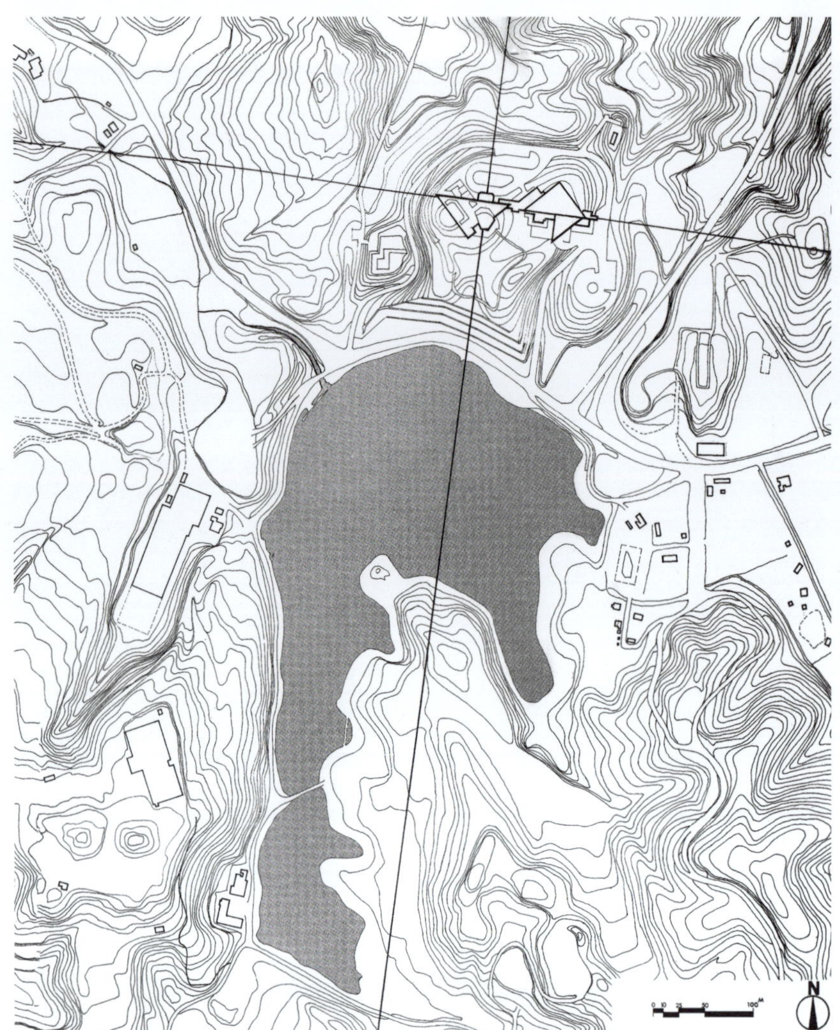

Toyota Kuragaike Commemorative Hall site plan.

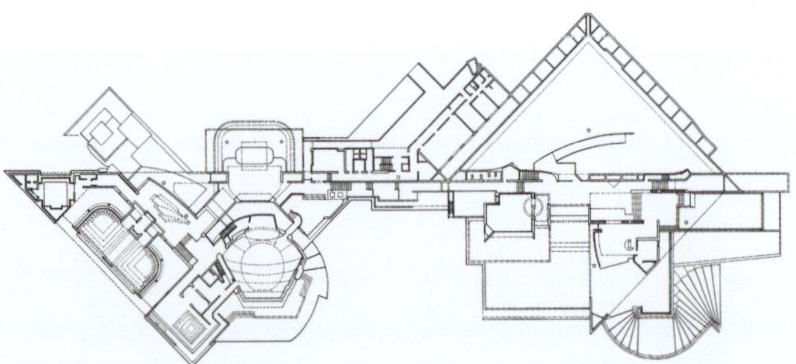

First-floor plan.

Exhibition hall on the right, as seen from the garden in front of the guest house.

View of the guest house from the entrance terrace.

Corridor towards the exhibition space.

Guest house lobby. The steps on the left lead to the lounge; the Japanese-style room is beyond the corridor in the background.

Interior view of dining room, 1974.

YKK Guest House

Location	Kurobe, Toyama Prefecture, Japan
Status	Completed
Year(s)	1982
Typology	Guest House
Area	1,695 m^2 (18,244 ft^2)

The YKK Guest House is a corporate training centre for the YKK Corporation, Japan's leading zipper manufacturer and a major architectural curtain wall/architectural product company. Completed in 1982, the building includes spaces for overseas trainees, lodging for employees and facilities for welcoming distinguished guests. Referencing both traditional private houses and larger Japanese estates, the design combines a sense of monumentality appropriate for larger gatherings with the material and craftsmanship of traditional Japan – creating a unique sense of residential comfort within the context of a modern, institutional facility.

The YKK Guest House is located on a generous hillside site in Toyama Prefecture, near YKK's research, development and production facilities. An elevated approach road and the wide-open surrounding landscape afford views of the facility from all directions. Accordingly, all facades were carefully considered, including references both to local residential roof forms and to the chimneys typical of European country estates. Closer to the building, a more consistent and logical expression of the interior programmes (via glass, glass block and aluminium facade openings) gives the building a modern sensibility and strengthens its connection to the immediate surroundings.

Inside the building, a south-facing entrance lounge forms the heart of the YKK Guest House. Its exposed concrete post and beam structure is reminiscent of traditional Japanese timber-framed *minka* architecture, a residential tradition reinterpreted here via modern building techniques. Bespoke lighting fixtures, wooden furniture and translucent layered interior glazing reinforce both the Japanese sensibility and the residential scale of the space. Meeting, dining and guest rooms surround the entrance lounge and continue similar themes. Overall, the result is a pleasant amalgam of traditional craft with modern comforts, combining a sense of familiarity for visitors with unique local touches.

In 2019 an exterior pergola and landscaped amphitheatre was added to support the YKK Guest House's vibrant year-round programming. Its longevity is a testament both to the success of its design and to the commitment and vision of its owner – and it remains in use today.

(Opposite) The high-ceiling lobby in the YKK Guest House.

YKK Guest House sketch.

Seminar room, located in the library wing.

View from the southern lawn. The two-storey living room is between the gabled guest wing (on right) and the library (left).

The high ceiling and exposed structure in the living room of the YKK Guest House evoke traditional Japanese folk houses. A central staircase leading to the guest room is enclosed by translucent fibreglass panels reminiscent of shoji screens.

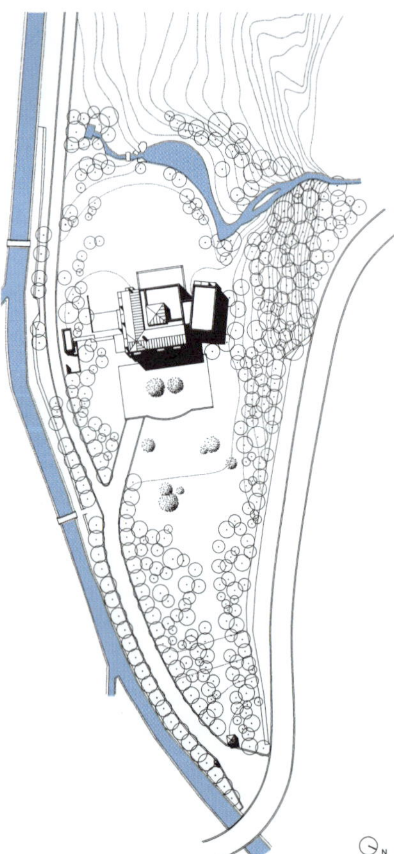

YKK Guest House site plan.

Staircase leading to the library on the first floor.

Floating Pavilion

Location	Groningen, Netherlands
Status	Completed
Year(s)	1996
Typology	Performance Stage
Area	150 m^2 (1,615 ft^2)

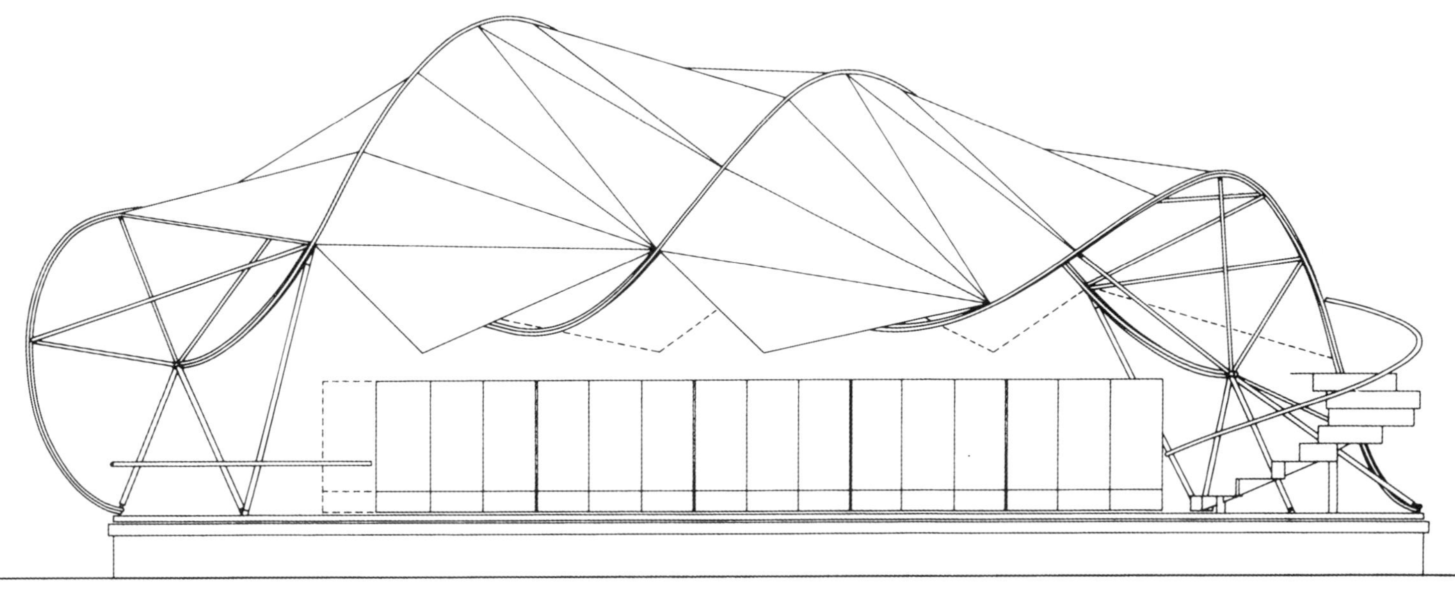

Elevation with the detail of the double-spiral structure.

The Floating Pavilion was commissioned in 1994 by the City of Groningen, part of a larger programme inviting foreign architects to design public facilities for this municipality in the northern Netherlands. The pavilion is characterized by a spiral-shaped white cloth shade, supported on a minimal steel substructure, which shelters a small stage below. Despite its modest size, this non-site-specific architecture has a commanding presence, largely because of the dynamic form and scale of the shade, reflecting the colour and light of its changing surroundings. Completely transfigured depending on its location and the viewer's vantage point, the structure has been described alternately as a snail, a heron, or a cluster of clouds.

The pavilion's concept was developed in collaboration with the avant-garde Antwerp-based theatre director/producer, Dora van der Groen, who proposed multiple key words – *movement*, *memory*, *silence*, *dream*, *freedom* and *surprise* – as the basis for the design. Finalized via a series of workshops, these key words were translated into an open 6 × 25-metre (20 × 82-ft) stage, sheltered by the double-helical shade overhead. The stage rests on a movable barge which is pulled through the canals of Groningen via tugboat. Custom perforated metal side benches lining the edges are intended for passenger use when the stage is not used for performances, but can be folded down and out of sight when necessary. Dressing rooms and storage space are provided below deck, inside the barge structure itself.

The pavilion was first used as a stage for the city's A Star is Born festival in 1996 and subsequently travelled Groningen's canals for almost twenty years as a floating venue for music, vocal and theatrical performances. In 2015, having outlived its use as a portable performance stage, the pavilion was afforded a second life and was donated to a local maritime school to be used for training and educational purposes.

(Opposite) The Floating Pavilion in central Groningen.

Concept model.

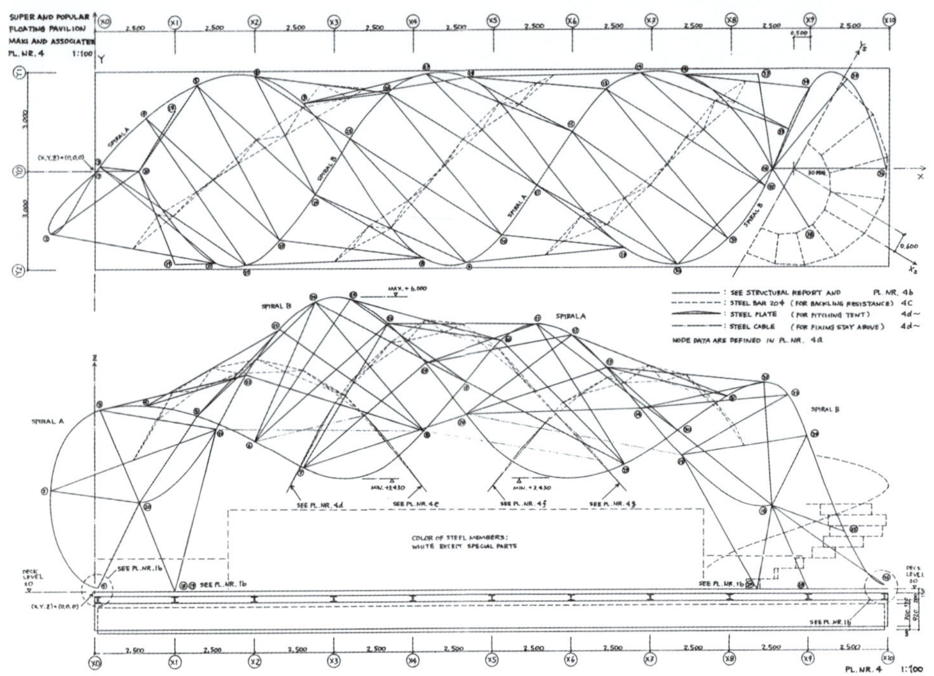

Structural frame of the Floating Pavilion.

The Floating Pavilion travelling through the Dutch countryside.

Side benches made of perforated steel can be folded during performances.

Site plan of central Groningen. The Floating Pavilion's route is shown in red dots.

Cross-section.

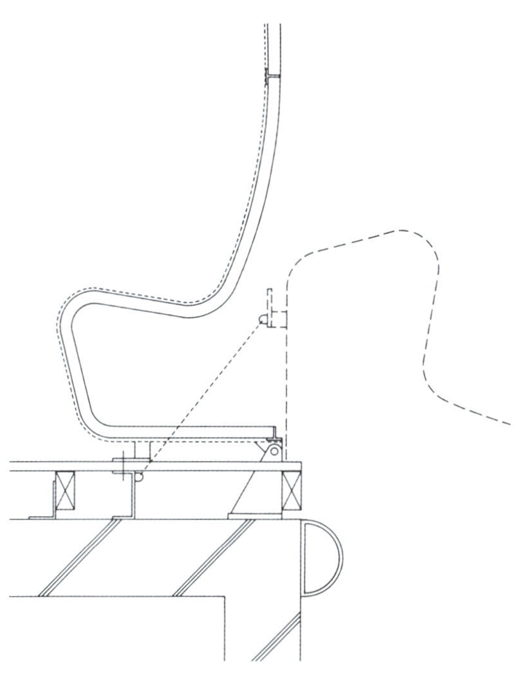

Bench detail.

The roof consists of two spiral elements that coil in opposite directions, with a polyester membrane spanned between them.

Evening view of the pavilion in use as a stage. Both the pavilion itself and the nearby shoreline serve as spectator seating.

TRIAD

Location	Minamiazumi-gun, Nagano Prefecture, Japan
Status	Completed
Year(s)	2002
Typology	Gallery, Laboratory
Area	1,100 m^2 (11,840 ft^2)

Completed in 2002, TRIAD is a complex of independent buildings serving the Harmonic Drive Corporation in Nagano, Japan. Harmonic Drive is the Japanese division of a multi-national corporation manufacturing precision decelerators and other instruments used in satellites, spacecraft and telescopes. Its Japanese director also has a collection of work by the well-known Japanese artist Yoshikuni Iida, which led to TRIAD's unique building programme – combining a Gallery for Iida's work with a new Laboratory for company-based research.

Entrance to the Laboratory with Hotaka mountains seen in the distance.

Model showing the relationship of the three buildings and landscape elements in the interstitial spaces.

The Laboratory is designed to extremely high specifications to maintain constant temperature, humidity and eliminate vibration within the interior. Accordingly, its walls and roof are super insulated, and its concrete floor slab is 1 metre (3.3 ft) deep. The unique complex-curved wall section is optimized (in consultation with mechanical engineers) to ensure extremely stable air-flow velocities and eliminate air pockets. The interior environment remains extremely stable throughout the year, despite the relatively cold winters and hot summers.

In contrast to the Laboratory's curved section, the Gallery uses curved forms only in plan; in section, it is sheltered by a simple pitched roof following a single line. Its three exhibition spaces are fully integrated with the building circulation, the curved plan ensuring a free flow from room to room and allowing views of the art from a variety of distances and perspectives. The largest space displays Iida's most representative sculpture *Screen-Canyon* and can also be used for concerts and events. Two smaller exhibition spaces display smaller Iida works in a more intimate setting.

The Guardhouse for the complex is a simple rectangular form, a concrete box fronted by a frosted glass panel cantilevering over a gentle slope. It has a strong architectural presence that belies its relatively small scale. Combined with the Laboratory and Gallery, it completes a dynamic group of three forms, stitched together via a connecting landscape of elliptical grass mounds and steel plates. Though all different in required volume and function, the combination of these elements produces a lively ensemble against the beautiful rural landscape of the nearby Japanese Alps.

Gallery and the Guardhouse.

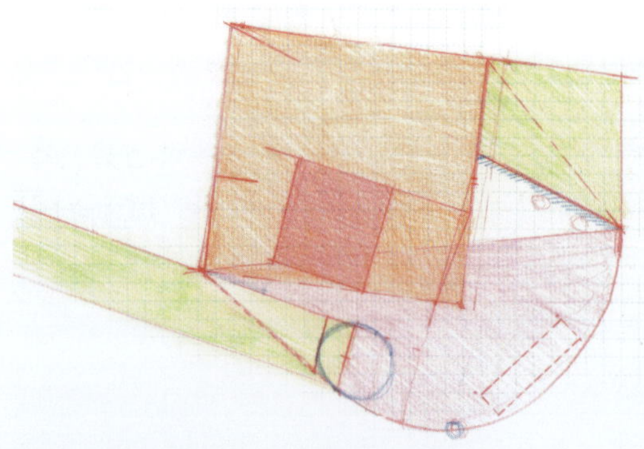

Concept sketch of TRIAD.

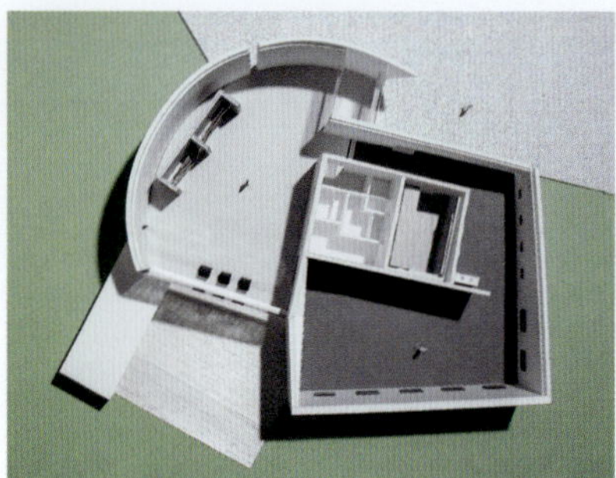

Model of TRIAD.

TRIAD as seen from the Laboratory entrance.

Exhibition hall of the Gallery.

Gallery with Laboratory nestled at the rear, extending towards Mount Hotaka in the distance.

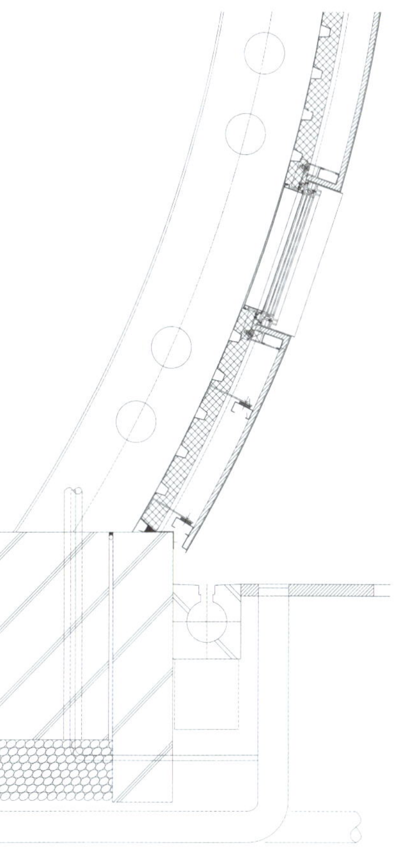

Laboratory section detail.

Inside the Laboratory.

Observation space within the Laboratory.

Drop off entrance between the Gallery and the Laboratory.

Stairs descending from the second-floor observation deck to the first-floor cafe and garden.

Shimane Museum of Ancient Izumo

Location	Izumo, Shimane Prefecture, Japan
Status	Completed
Year(s)	2006
Typology	Museum
Area	11,855 m^2 (127,606 ft^2)

The Shimane Museum of Ancient Izumo, completed in 2006, exhibits cultural artefacts of the Izumo area, one of the cradles of Japanese culture and civilization. Sited adjacent to the Izumo Grand Shrine – itself a source of many important museum artefacts – the building's gentle roof silhouette complements the undulating terrain of the nearby Kitayama mountain range.

The building programme consists primarily of exhibition spaces with adjacent research facilities, a library, hands-on workshop spaces, administrative offices, and miscellaneous support spaces. A glazed three-storey entrance hall, perpendicular to the main building volume, serves as the start and endpoint for each visit, separating the landscaped museum forecourt from a more extensive natural landscape that leads visitors to the Izumo Grand Shrine nearby.

Cladding the main building is a 120-metre-long, 9-metre-high (394 × 30-ft) Cor-ten steel wall. Cor-ten weathering steel is a modern material reminiscent of *tatara* steel, a historically important material in Shimane's economic and trade development. After the glazed entrance hall, visitors pass through this Cor-ten wall and enter the central exhibition lobby space. The lobby serves as a gathering spot from which visitors can move freely between the four main galleries. The lobby also displays remnants of the timber columns from the original Izumo Grand Shrine.

Other artefacts in the collection include national treasures excavated from elsewhere in the Izumo region. Following a tour of the exhibits, visitors pass back through the Cor-ten wall and return to the glazed entrance hall. Here, they can relax in the second-floor cafe or go up to the third-floor observation deck to enjoy panoramic views over the surrounding landscape and the Izumo Grand Shrine. With its prominent siting, memorable architecture and important collections, the Shimane Museum has far exceeded the attendance expectations of the Shimane Prefectural Government.

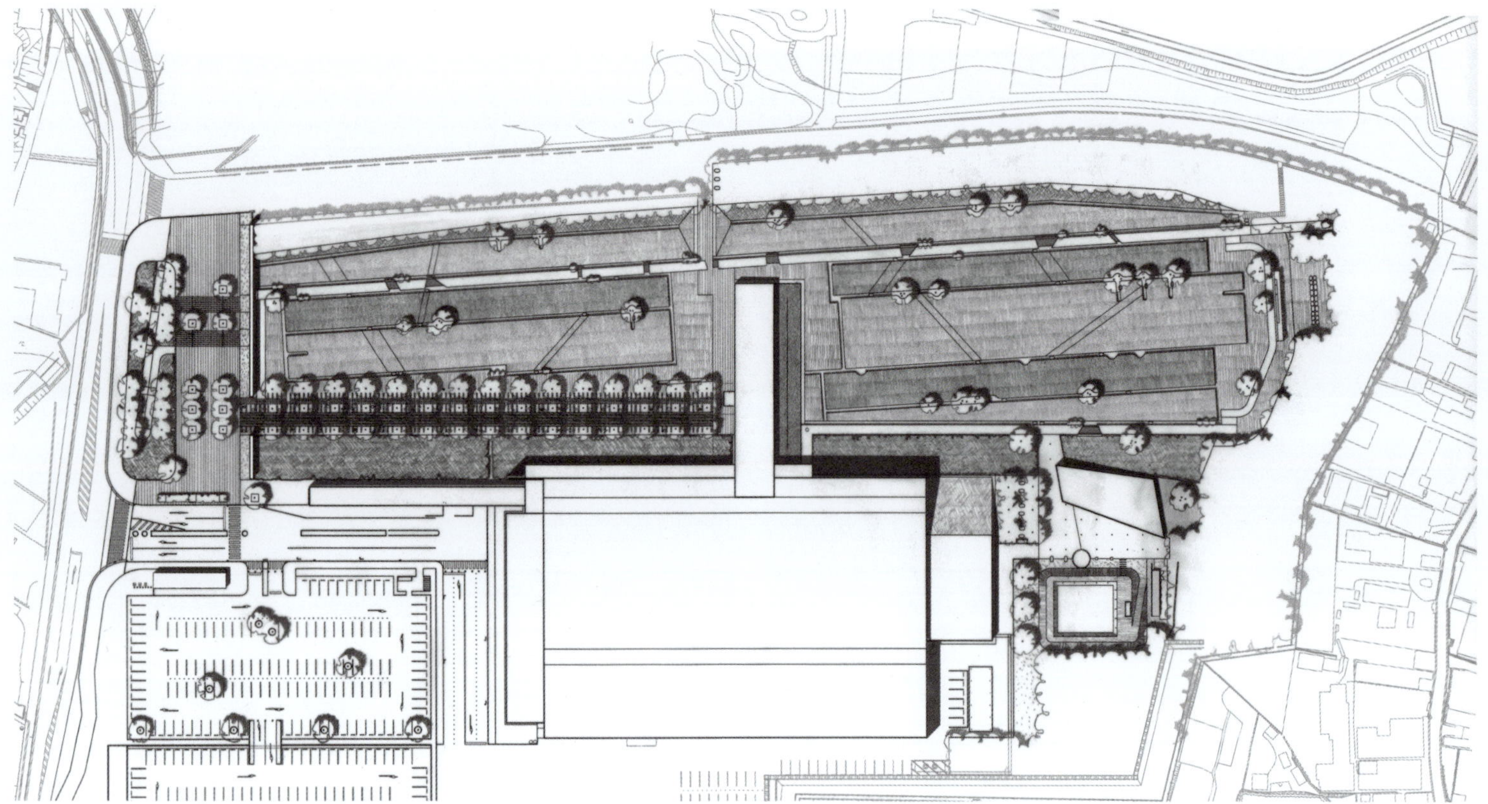

Site plan of the Shimane Museum of Ancient Izumo.

Inside the lobby of the museum.

Lobby exhibition space within the museum.

Aerial view of the site for the museum.

Entrance walkway inside the museum.

Beneath the soft canopy of katsura trees, a pathway unfolds toward the Kitayama mountains, where the Glass Hall draws the landscape through, quietly weaving together the threads of past and present.

Religious Buildings

The porch at the entrance to the Kaze-no-Oka Crematorium. The anteroom of the oratory is visible to the left, in the rear of the room, with the exit on the right.

Kaze-no-Oka Crematorium

Location	Nakatsu, Oita Prefecture, Japan
Status	Completed
Year(s)	1997
Typology	Crematorium
Area	2,260 m^2 (24,326 ft^2)

The Kaze-no-Oka (Hill of the Winds) Crematorium was completed in 1997 in Nakatsu, a small city in southern Japan. Part of the Kaze-no-Oka public park that incorporates an existing cemetery and ancient burial mounds, the new crematorium maintains a modest scale, ensuring it is in balance with its modest surroundings. At the same time, its unique architecture and symbiotic relationship to the landscape combine to ensure a serene and dignified environment for the bereaved.

Aerial view of the crematorium and its pastoral context.

The crematorium is sited within an elliptical grass field, dipping at its centre to form a basin. The surrounding suburban scenery disappears as visitors descend into this basin, providing a sense of separation from the quotidian context and a feeling of embrace within the landscape. From this sheltered vantage point, the new facility appears as a submerged earthwork of three free-standing sculptural forms, avoiding the sense of monumentality that often dominates crematorium design in Japan.

The three embedded forms, while appearing independent, are in fact interconnected – housing a ceremonial area (for funerals), a cremation area (for offering final respects) and a waiting area (for family, friends and relatives of the deceased). These different zones anticipate the distinct states of mind during different rituals but are all carefully integrated for ease of use. Strategic material selection, detailing and natural light all play critical roles in heightening the ritualistic transitions between zones. Outside vistas are limited, focusing awareness on the interior spaces and finishes, where a careful introduction of muted natural light reflects upon primordial materials (wood, concrete, weathering steel, brick and slate) to create an ethereal atmosphere.

Overall, Kaze-no-Oka's highly ceremonial spaces are dramatic but stately, designed for moments of repose and reflection both inside and out. Its unique ensemble of landscape and architecture combine to create a place of lasting memories for all visitors and a tranquil final resting place for generations of residents.

Sketch of south elevation.

Concept sketch.

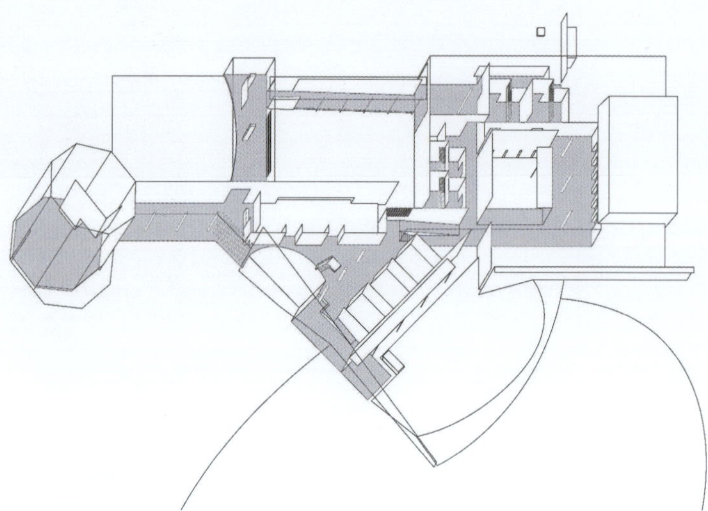
Axonometric plan.

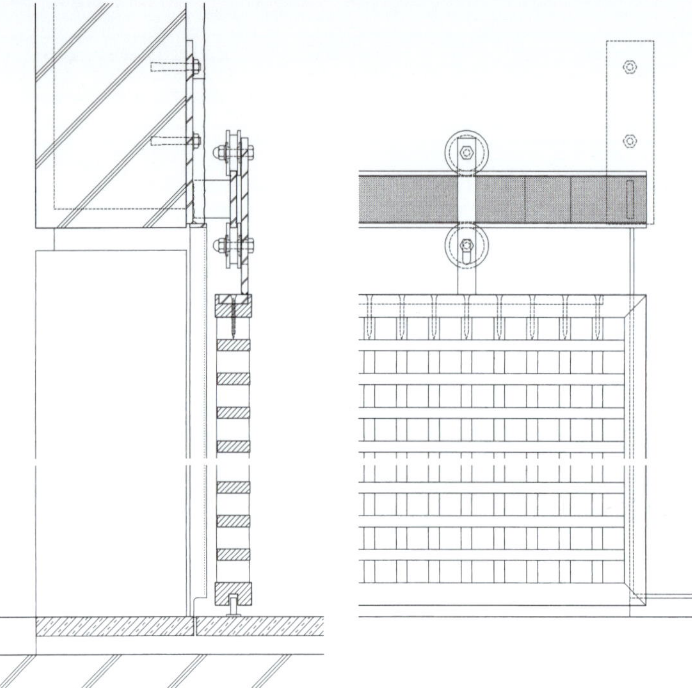
Lattice sliding partition door at the oratory room.

Kaze-no-Oka Park, part of Kaze-no-Oka Crematorium, seen from the nearby ancient burial mounds.

Enshrinement room.

Interior of the oratory.

View of atrium from furnace hall.

Crematory hall with a view of the watercourt.

Waiting room in the lobby.

Evening view of Tokyo Church of Christ. At dusk, the translucent curtain wall glows like a lantern, signalling to passersby that a communal gathering is taking place within.

Tokyo Church of Christ

Location	Shibuya-ku, Tokyo Metropolitan, Japan
Status	Completed
Year(s)	1995
Typology	Religious (Church)
Area	2,243 m^2 (24,143 ft^2)

Tokyo Church of Christ was completed in 1995, replacing a forty-year-old wooden church threatened by road expansion and accommodating a burgeoning congregation. Close to Tokyo's bustling Shibuya district, the new building fulfils the church's changing needs, transforming a tight, challenging site into a uniquely inspiring facility for a growing community.

The church congregation requested a main worship space for 700 people. To ensure the necessary volume for this large population, this main space was raised to the second-floor level to eliminate any constraints on ceiling height and shape. The eventual ceiling design – a shallow curving arch – provides the necessary volume while symbolically expressing the aspirational image of the celestial vault.

The facade of the main hall faces west towards the newly expanded road, its fully glazed curtain wall filling the hall with natural light. A second layer of interior glazing with integrated glass fibres behind the transparent curtain wall helps absorb the visual and auditory chaos of the surrounding city. Recalling the image of a large Japanese shoji screen on the interior, the ventilated double-skin 'light wall' effectively shields the worship space from exterior cacophony and harsh western sun, transforming it with shifting light patterns throughout the day and creating a muted, soft glow in the early evening.

A generous main staircase leads directly from the church entrance lobby to the worship hall, with the remainder of the ground level dedicated to children's play areas, meeting rooms and office space. The hall occupies the bulk of the second level; a mezzanine accessible from the hall interior brings the seating capacity up to the full requirements. Scandinavian birch finishes are used in a variety of configurations throughout, providing a sense of warmth and creating proper acoustic properties for religious services, musical performances and other gatherings. Well-used and well-loved by its members, Tokyo Church of Christ is both a functional and beautiful oasis in a densely packed urban setting.

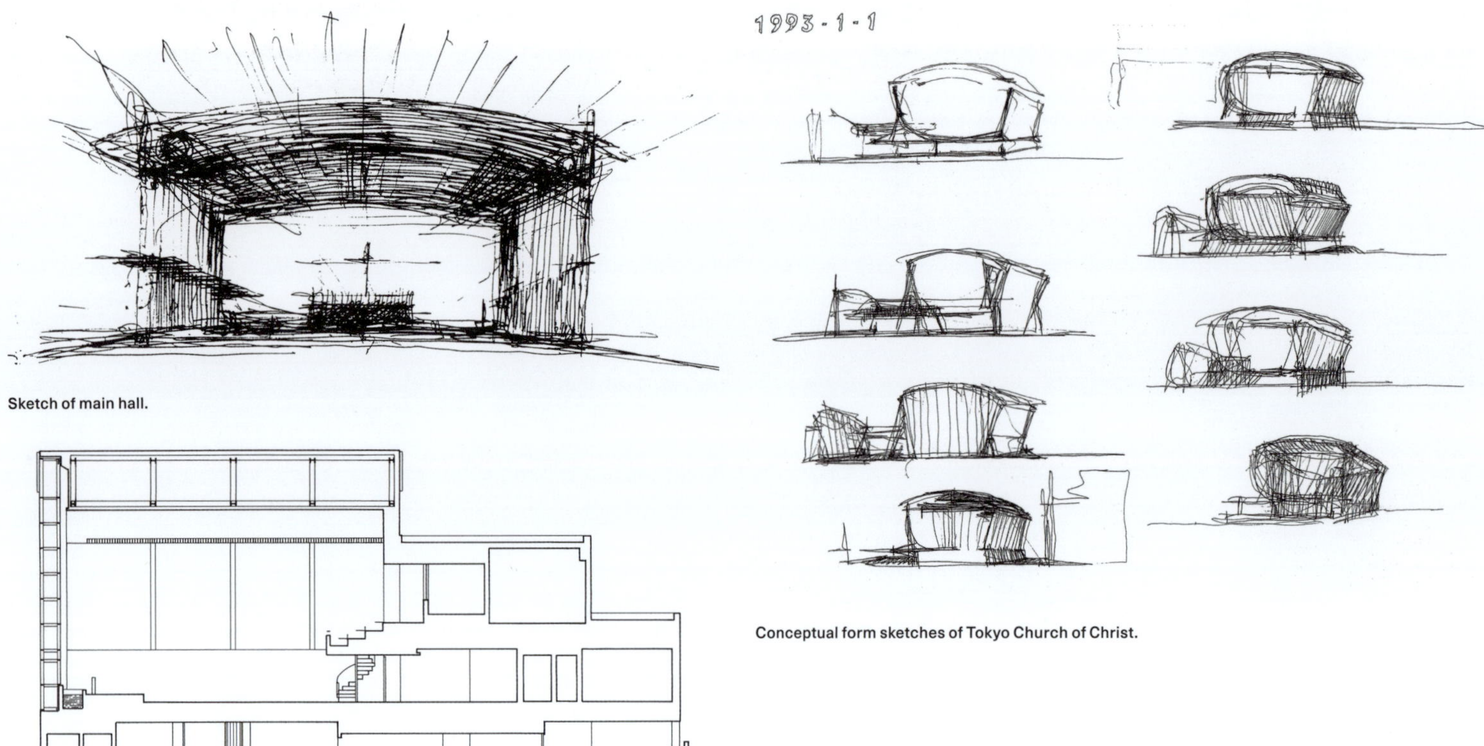

Sketch of main hall.

Conceptual form sketches of Tokyo Church of Christ.

Longitudinal section.

West facade of Tokyo Church of Christ.

Light entering the main hall through the skylight is reflected and softened by the angled, ribbed side walls.

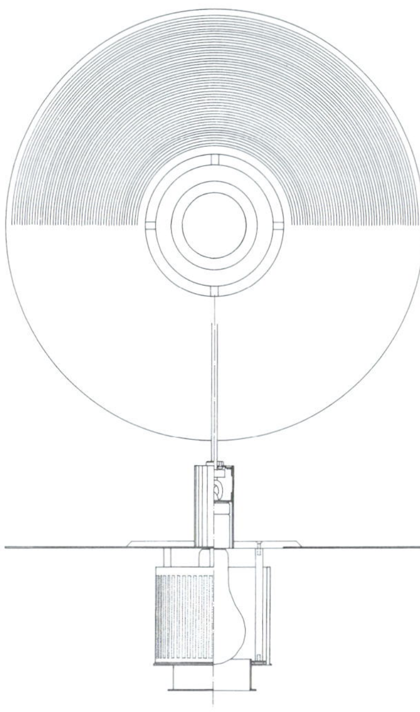

Customized pendant light detail in main hall.

The 'light wall' recalling a shoji screen on the interior.

Customized light fixture.

Jewish Community of Japan Center

Location	Shibuya-ku, Tokyo Metropolitan, Japan
Status	Completed
Year(s)	2009
Typology	Religious (Synagogue), Community Centre
Area	1,915 m^2 (20,612 ft^2)

The Jewish Community of Japan's new building was completed in 2009, replacing an older structure on a tight, centrally located Tokyo site. The new design places renewed emphasis on both religious and communal programmes, while alleviating a variety of problems identified in the previous facility. It answers the community's desire for a building filled with natural light and maximizes flexibility to address their evolving needs long into the future.

The new facility includes many programmes from the earlier building, notably a synagogue, multi-purpose event spaces, a kosher kitchen and rabbi living quarters. However, efficient planning enabled the addition of four dedicated classrooms, larger common spaces and a maximization of both the synagogue and the multi-purpose hall ceiling heights. The new building also houses a library focused on Japanese-language Judaica, as well as expanded office and guest spaces for the rabbi. The lower level includes a ritual *mikveh* bath, extensive storage and parking.

A light-filled entrance lobby and staircase at the centre of the complex serve as the building's heart, where community members linger and meet before and after services. This entrance stitches the entire building and community together – from the synagogue at the second level, to the first-level event rooms and lounges, and the front and rear terraces. It has become an active social space and is often used on its own as the setting for less formal events and parties.

Inside the synagogue, Canadian maple slats line the ceiling, reminiscent of the tree branches that sheltered ceremonies in ancient times. Natural light enters via low south-facing slit windows overlooking the rear terrace and from a skylight directly over the *bimah.* Custom theatre-style seats are finished in Japanese ash, while the front wall and stone accents use Israeli limestone. Complemented by Italian tile flooring and bespoke lighting fixtures manufactured in Japan, the synagogue materials are – like the Jewish community of Japan itself – a diverse composition of different nationalities bound together by their common purpose and shared values.

(Opposite) Hexagonal tile pattern on the north and south facade of the Jewish Community of Japan Center, derived from the geometry of the Star of David.

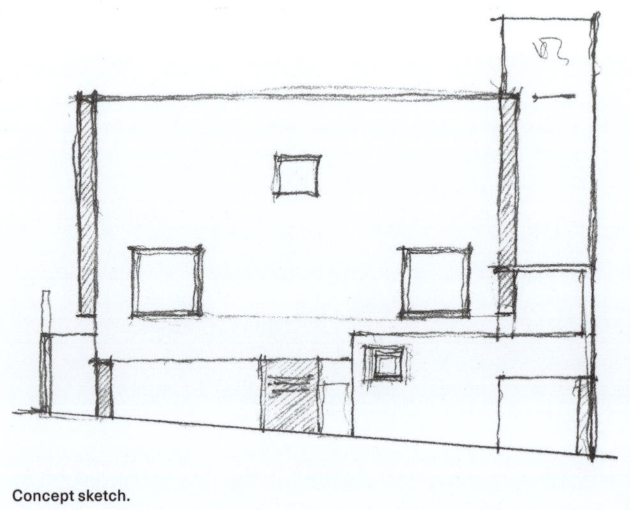

Concept sketch.

North facade with the entrance canopy.

A quiet sanctuary terrace nestled within the bustle of the city.

Second-floor lobby atrium overlooking the urban context beyond.

Inside the synagogue looking towards the bimah.

Lounge space defined by sliding wooden partitions and a stepped ceiling, softly illuminated by a custom light fixture.

Building in Campus

153

Keio University, Mita Campus Library

Location	Minato-ku, Tokyo Metropolitan, Japan
Status	Completed
Year(s)	1981
Typology	Institution (University), Library
Area	15,188 m^2 (163,482 ft^2)

Keio University's Mita Campus is located on a green hilltop near the centre of Tokyo. Completed in 1981, its new central library was the first of three Maki and Associates-designed additions to the campus, which also include the visitor centre (a renovation of the old library) and the Graduate School Building.

The new library stands at a critical hinge point on campus between two exterior courtyards. The north court is the ceremonial campus centre, defined by the original library and administration buildings. The west court, lined with mature gingko trees, serves as the bustling centre of campus life and features as a major pedestrian thoroughfare leading to the university's main gate.

To minimize its size and maintain the delicate balance between these two open plazas, the bulk of the new library's required book storage is kept below grade. Setbacks at its upper levels further mitigate impact on the courtyards and nearby trees. The library's north facade utilizes a structural skeleton mimicking the rhythm of buttresses on the adjacent old library, establishing a clear design kinship to this structure without reverting to overt historicism.

On the interior, a double-height space links the first and second levels to both exterior courtyards, its cladding matching the salmon-pink tiles from the exterior. Further continuity between interior and exterior is strengthened via generous glazed openings, which allow reciprocal views to and from the surrounding campus. The central core planning maximizes window frontage for these reading rooms and other public areas. Chandeliers, lighting fixtures, built-in furnishings, stained glass windows and fabrics were all designed by Maki and Associates, guaranteeing design consistency down to the smallest details.

Following the completion of the new building, Maki and Associates renovated the original library for use as a visitor centre in 1982 (a gallery was added in 2021). In 1985, the Graduate School was opened at the far end of the west court, completing the ensemble of buildings and exterior spaces that still serve the Keio community to this day.

(Opposite) View of catalogues and newspaper reading corner from the entrance hall of Keio University's Mita Campus Library.

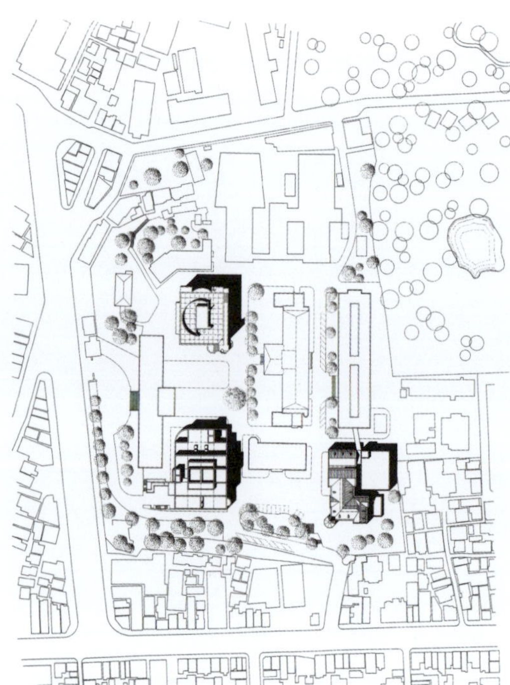

Mita Campus Library site plan.

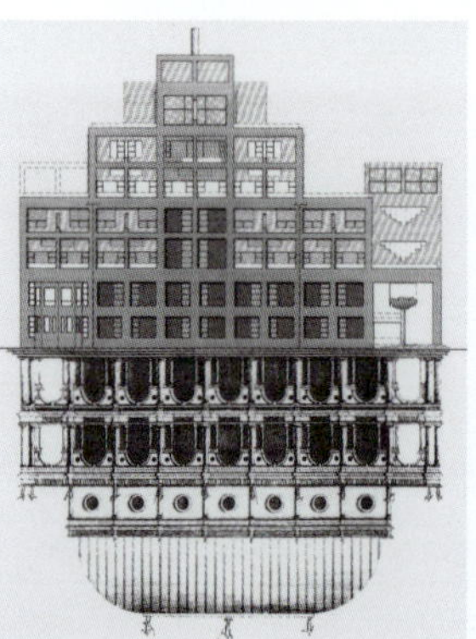

A palimpsest: the library at Mita Campus sits atop an older, classical structure, expressing how different time periods and styles coexist within a single form.

View of new library through the old library arcade.

Stepped silhouette of the building along the west elevation.

The Keio Graduate School building was constructed facing the new library, across an open plaza anchored by a large ginkgo tree.

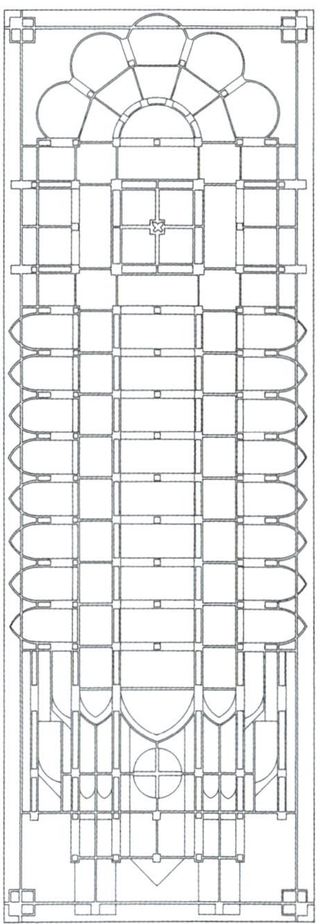

Interior conference carpet pattern.

The remodelling of the old library, built in Tudor Gothic, carries its exterior architectural style into details such as the wall lighting fixtures and carpet design.

View of new library from main entrance.

Reference room with customized light pendant fixture.

Exterior view of Walker Hall.

Sam Fox School of Design & Visual Arts, Washington University in St. Louis

Location	St. Louis, Missouri, USA
Status	Completed
Year(s)	2006
Typology	Institution (University), Museum, Library
Area	9,369 m^2 (100,847 ft^2)

The Sam Fox School of Design & Visual Arts at Washington University in St. Louis consists of two new and three renovated buildings, consolidating five departments: Architecture, Fine Art, Art History and Archaeology, the Gallery of Art and the Art and Architecture Library. The project is sited just below Washington University's main Hilltop Campus (now called the Danforth Campus), in a block known as the 'White Campus' for its consistent use of light beige Indiana limestone. Completed in 2006, the two new buildings by Maki and Associates (Mildred Lane Kemper Art Museum and Walker Hall) combine with their older neighbours (Givens, Steinberg and Bixby Halls) to create an interconnected ensemble of interior and exterior spaces – a mini campus within the larger university.

Kemper Art Museum is centred along the south side of Brookings Drive, the university's ceremonial entrance leading west to the Hilltop Campus and east to St. Louis. The museum combines with Steinberg Hall (designed by Fumihiko Maki in 1960) to create a new north-south axis at the center of the White Campus, connecting Brookings Drive and Steinberg Hall through to the campus southern edge. It includes a sculpture garden prominently located along Brookings Drive, which doubles as a ceremonial outdoor reception space for university functions.

Walker Hall, east of the museum, houses three divisions of the Fine Art School and the Center for Illustrated Books. Walker faces Bixby Hall across a new landscaped courtyard, activated by student art and performances throughout the year. On the interior, its three floors of open studio loft spaces are filled with natural light from clerestory skylights and high side windows.

The exterior envelope of the new buildings utilizes modern reinterpretations of traditional techniques and materials. The cladding is buff limestone cut into 203×762-mm (8×30-in.) linear blocks. This size enabled stoneworkers to lift and install one block at a time, the same craft used in adjacent neoclassical buildings from the 1920s. Additional modern details – crisp aluminium copings, custom embedded light fixtures, extruded ribbed panels and aluminium and glass curtain walls – sharply contrast the traditional stone. Through their deft combination of industrial products and older building techniques, the two new additions warmly integrate with the three existing buildings, creating a harmonic composition of tradition and modernity.

View of the Sam Fox School of Design & Visual Arts from the main campus of Washington University in St. Louis. The skyline of downtown St. Louis is visible beyond the adjacent Forest Park.

View of the Sam Fox School of Design & Visual Arts from the southwest.

View of Brookings Hall from the east: proposed school is on the left.

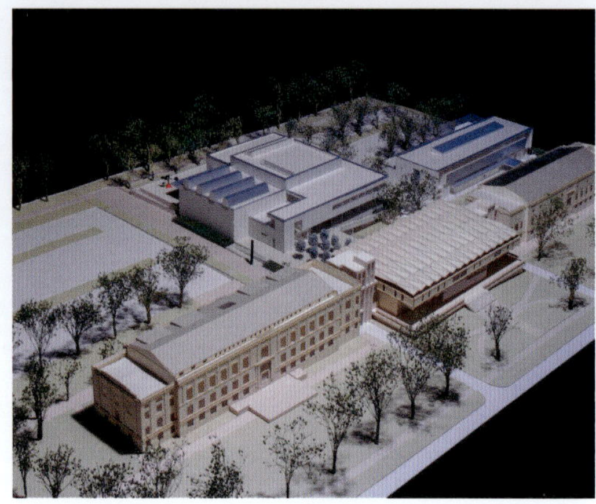

Model showing all five buildings of the school.

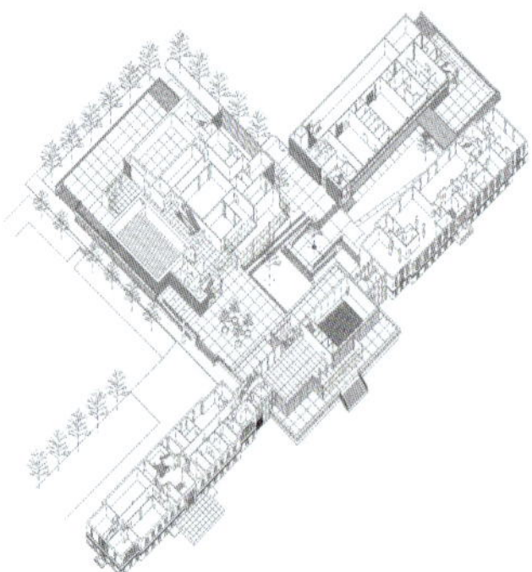

Third-floor axonometric plan.

Second-floor axonometric plan.

Central courtyard formed between the new and old buildings.

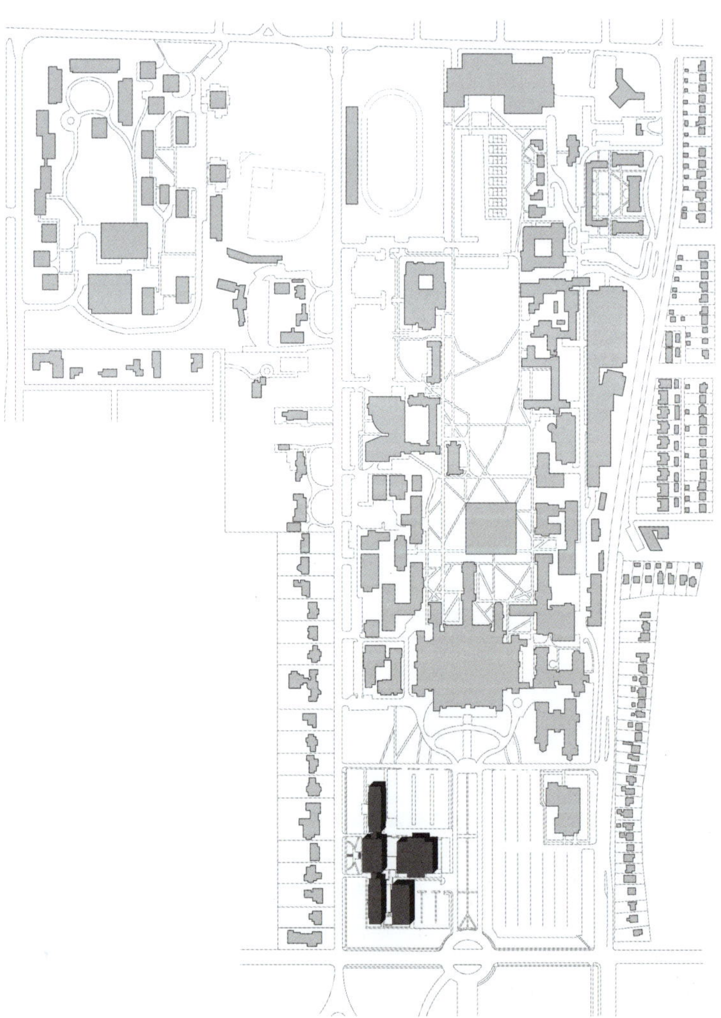

Campus plan.

School of Art Gallery.

The atrium of the Kemper Art Museum.

Permanent gallery on the third floor.

Temporary gallery space within the Kemper Art Museum.

School of Art Gallery.

Annenberg Public Policy Center, University of Pennsylvania

Location	Philadelphia, Pennsylvania, USA
Status	Completed
Year(s)	2009
Typology	Institution (University)
Area	4,562 m^2 (49,104 ft^2)

The Annenberg Public Policy Center (APPC) was established at the University of Pennsylvania in 1994. The centre conducts research and hosts lectures and conferences on media, communication and public policy. Completed in 2009, its new facility contains offices, conference rooms, a broadcast studio and a multi-purpose space for both centre and university events.

The APPC is sited within Penn's historic West Philadelphia campus along 36th Street Walk, a major pedestrian thoroughfare. Immediately to its south is the Arch, a 1928 red brick structure with steeply pitched slate roofs; to its north is Charles Addams Fine Arts Hall, a 1957 red brick building housing the Fine Arts Department; to its west is the Annenberg School complex, built in 1987 and clad in Indiana limestone. The APPC's exterior glass and wood skin complements these nearby buildings, while presenting a modern, open image – a 'warm transparency'. Deference to adjacent building volumes and eave lines further integrates this modern vocabulary with the scale and spirit of its surroundings.

The layered wood and glass facade is the primary aesthetic motif of the project, engineered to enhance comfort and energy performance. Operable exterior windows, sliding wood panels and operable shades allow each user to individually tailor lighting, ventilation, shading and thermal insulation. The result is an ever-changing facade that responds to individual preferences, lighting needs, weather and interior use patterns. In the evening, the APPC glows like a lantern. Wood panels are revealed in silhouette and light spills out to the exterior, creating a bright, secure environment – a beacon for this part of the Penn campus.

Below grade, the building houses a recycling centre that processes all waste from the surrounding facilities. This consolidated material management centre enabled the repurposing of surrounding above-grade open spaces for new walkways and stepped plazas – allowing free passage throughout the block, creating new exterior gathering areas and integrating the APPC seamlessly into its surroundings.

(Opposite) Referred to as the living room, the three-storey atrium is defined by its vertical openness and the soft daylight filtering through the overhead skylight.

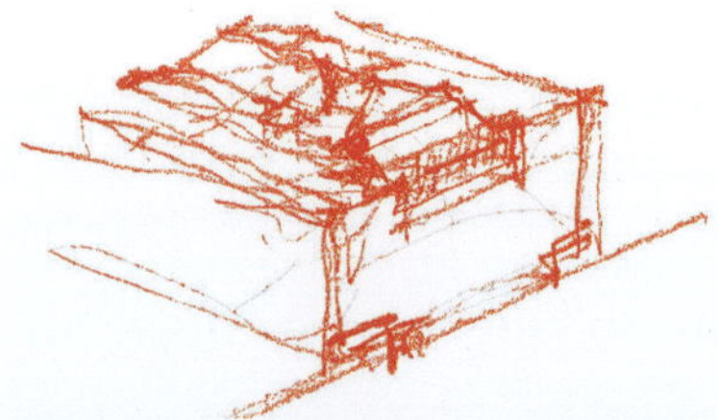

Sketch of the Policy Center.

Site model with Policy Center at the centre.

Evening view from 36th Street.

Agora stairs.

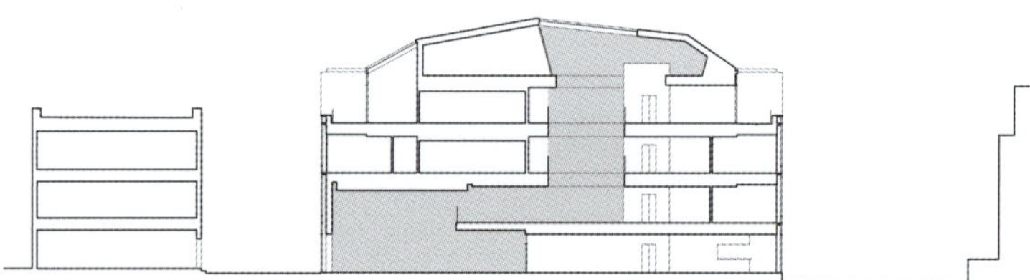

Campus section.

Fourth-floor lounge.

Lobby looking north.

Southeast main entrance.

Anchoring the southwest corner of the Policy Center, the Annenberg Agora is a flexible, multi-use space that supports the organization's programmes.

View of the Annenberg Public Policy Center from across 36th Street Walk, showing the urban context.

Media Lab Complex, Massachusetts Institute of Technology

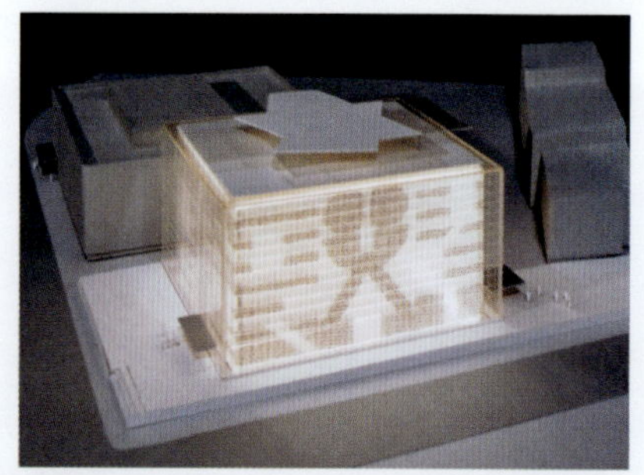

Site model.

Location	Cambridge, Massachusetts, USA
Status	Completed
Year(s)	2009
Typology	Institutional, Research Laboratory
Area	15,159 m² (163,170 ft²)

The original MIT Media Lab building, designed by I. M. Pei & Partners and inaugurated in 1985, was dedicated to research at the forefront of the 'digital revolution'. Unconstrained by traditional disciplines, the lab fosters a unique culture of learning by doing, reinventing how humans experience technology. It is supported by an international consortium of corporate sponsors from a wide range of disciplines.

Maki and Associates' Media Lab expansion, completed in 2009, overlooks the Charles River and Boston skyline. Spatially integrated with the original Pei structure, it adds a variety of flexible spaces supporting the lab's unique interdisciplinary research programmes. The six-storey addition is visible from Boston's Back Bay – its diagonal, curved, cubic glass and aluminium forms distinct against the lower limestone and brick MIT context. But at the ground level, the Media Lab maintains a strong relationship to the larger campus via its integration with the 'infinite corridor' (a series of connected interior spaces stretching across the Institute).

Despite its modern material palette, the expansion exhibits a classical tripartite composition evident in many older campus buildings. A five-foot podium finished in Roman Basaltina stone forms the building's base. A glazed curtain wall assembly with horizontal aluminium shading profiles clads the research labs at the building's *piano nobile*. Finally, a group of celebratory public spaces for the Media Lab and MIT at large (including a winter garden, event spaces and roof terraces) forms the building's crown. Internally, two centrally located atria interconnect the research and public spaces within the old and new buildings, setting the stage for informal social interaction and chance encounters.

Beginning at the entrance lobby, students and researchers experience the Media Lab Complex as a vertical street with a sequence of town squares, all connecting back to MIT's infinite corridor. Meanwhile, the outside community experiences it via the fully glazed labs and atria, putting research on display during the daytime, and creating a muted, lantern-like glow in the evening. This openness has been a welcome addition to the campus, where research is typically hidden behind closed doors – and has made the complex a popular campus destination both for the larger MIT community and its dedicated researchers.

Northeast facade.

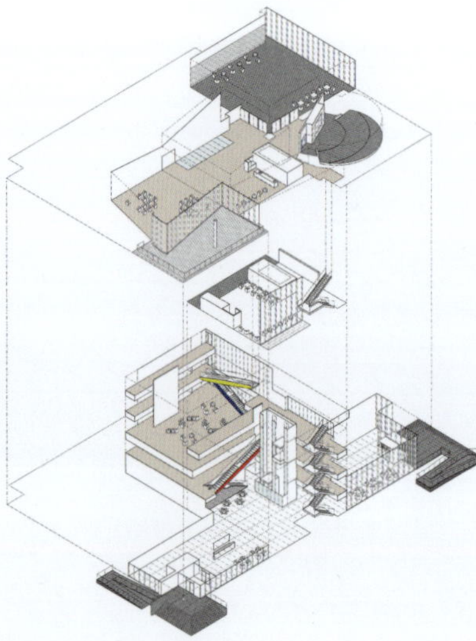

Public space concept.

MIT campus plan.

View from the southeast: a tripartite organization defines the hierarchy of volumes.

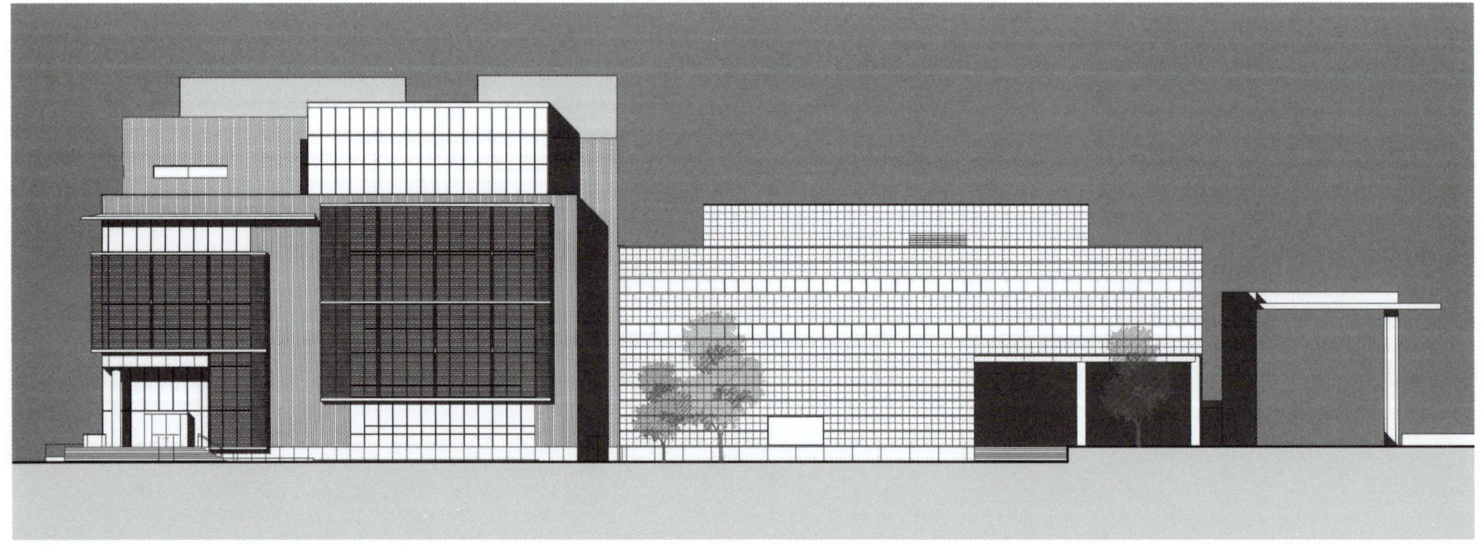

Elevation of the expansion of the Media Lab and the Wiesner Building.

The interior atrium rises as a light-filled core, surrounded by a transparent laboratory that opens onto the shared space – fostering visibility, collaboration and a sense of collective inquiry.

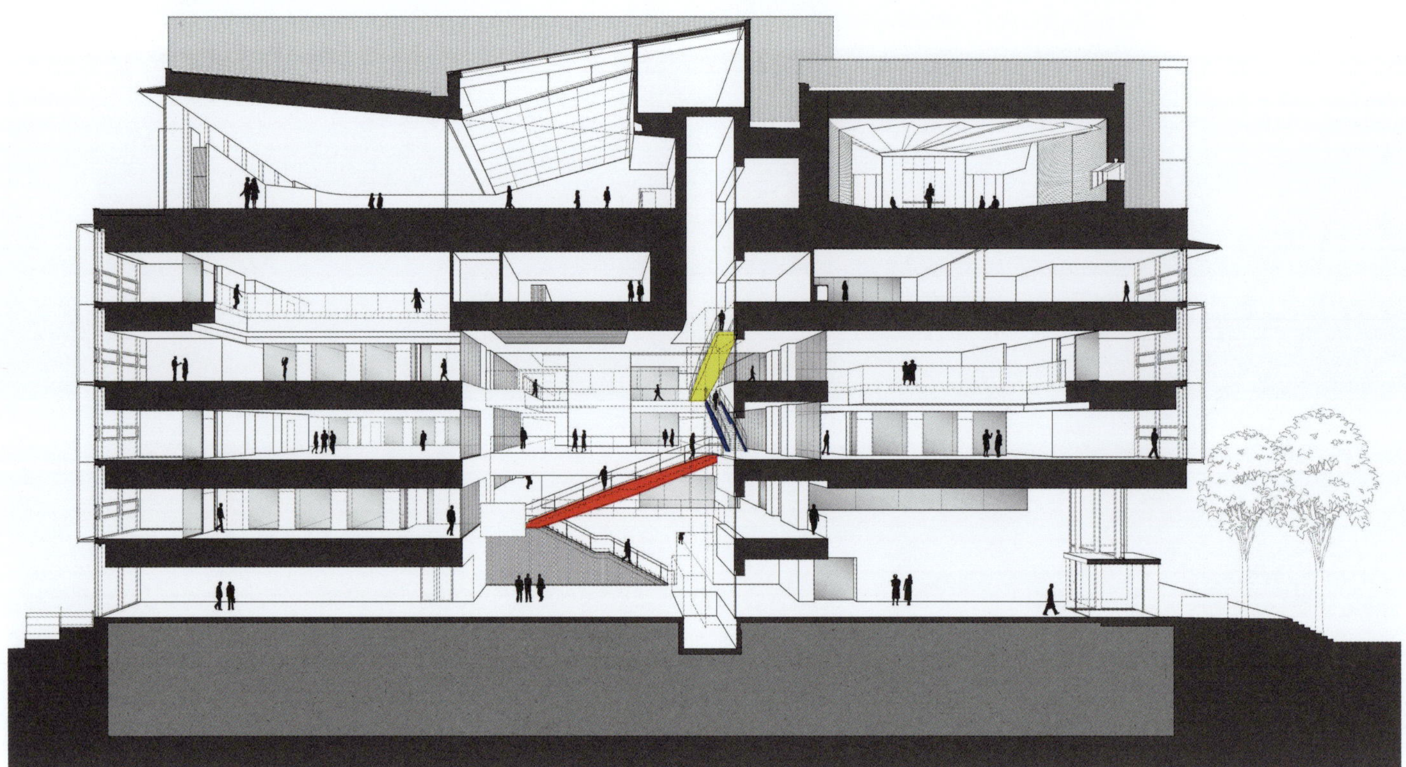

Sectional perspective.

View from across Amherst Street at dusk.

Large conference room; the Boston skyline sets the backdrop.

An elevated perspective above the Charles River; the metallic form contrasts with the surrounding masonry structures, its modern geometry punctuating the urban fabric.

View upon entering the lower atrium; sculptural stairways draw the gaze upward.

The sculptural stair invites interaction and movement.

Lecture Hall.

Social Condenser for MIT

Edward Lifson

The Maki and Associates-designed Massachusetts Institute of Technology Media Lab Complex in Cambridge, Massachusetts, USA, marked its grand opening in March 2010. More than ten years in the making, delayed by a bad economy, the suave $90-million, 163,000-square-feet, six-storey building known as E14 in MIT's nomenclature, adds a most handsome landmark overlooking the Charles River and the Boston skyline.

The MIT Media Lab Complex caps an impressive building campaign that added Frank Gehry's Stata Center, Steven Holl's dormitory, Charles Correa's science complex, and other contemporary works to a campus that already boasts masterpieces by Alvar Aalto and Eero Saarinen. Without calling undue attention to itself, it's the best and the most timeless of the new works. The Media Lab originated in 1980 as the idea of professor Nicholas Negroponte and former MIT president Jerome Wiesner to intermingle researchers from a wide variety of fields. Today, Media Lab research groups include Affective Computing; Biomechatronics; Cognitive Machines; Fluid Interfaces; Lifelong Kindergarten; Mediated Matter; Music, Mind and Machines; New Media Medicine; and even Opera of the Future, which, for example, looks at how 'musical composition, performance, and instrumentation can lead to innovative forms of expression, learning, and health'. Spin-offs over the years include E-ink, Guitar Hero, software for healthcare in the developing world, communications infrastructure for rural communities, and the initiative One Laptop Per Child.

For years the Media Lab was overstuffed into a 1985 I. M. Pei-designed building. Most MIT labs were sealed and secret. Negroponte and William J. Mitchell, dean of MIT's School of Architecture and Planning at that time, approached Fumihiko Maki and asked for a playful and transparent building with floor-to-ceiling glass – and no curtains. They said they wanted unlimited transparency among the various disciplines.

Only an architect very sure of his moves and at the height of his talents could have produced this building. Maki and Associates designed a place whose essence is transparency. Exterior walls of highly transparent glass open the building to the street. From outside you can see all the way through a multi-storey atrium and into and through another. Two fine ground-floor exhibition spaces increase the welcoming spirit and increase the desire to go in. From the lobby, elevators and stairs ascend to the labs.

Strict energy codes in Cambridge limited the amount of glass allowed on the exterior to fifty percent. Maki's elegant solution was to make it virtually all glass, but in front of the labs, the glazing is ¾ inch diameter extruded aluminium pipe louvres horizontally spaced 1½ inches on centre. These horizontals give him the necessary fifty percent shading. Visually, the rods recall a Japanese bamboo screen. The aluminium is exquisitely crafted and connected, and offers the tranquillity of a traditional Japanese screen. It also offers the mystery – you want to peek through. Other window areas achieve the required energy saving performance with a 1⁄16-inch diameter dot screen ceramic frit, which gives the visitor a 'pointillist' transparency to see through.

Silver aluminium could look drab over a long Cambridge winter. I wondered initially whether Maki's aluminium, on a good day, would ennoble New England's transcendent light. H. H. Richardson's use of red brick at Harvard's Sever Hall does that, as does his pink Milford granite at Trinity Church in Copley Square. The grey stone of the Old Cambridge Baptist Church bursts with colour at sunset. The famous all-white New England churches and steeples blend the colours around them to project purity heavenward. But Maki gives us a metallic silver, one he has successfully used elsewhere, and it works here, too. His custom-made silver is not oppressive. The tones are lively and do capture and reflect the serene light of Cambridge. The variety of systems used to cover the glass – from louvres to frits to panels – creates pleasantly varying degrees of shadow, transparency and translucency and dematerializes the mass and the bulk of what could have been a behemoth.

That's one of the beauties of this Media Lab Complex – its seeming contradictions. It is large, yet seems lightweight. Industrial, yet scaled for human needs. Dematerialized, yet it proudly displays materials and joints. It calms, but is exciting. The architecture is thoroughly modern, with classical features, including a five-foot high base finished in Roman Basaltina, a distinct *piano nobile* and (the modernist shudders) a crown! The crown on the corner, under the angled roof, gives the building its memorable profile from afar. We'll see that there had to be a diagonal on the exterior.

Inside, you experience the real magic. From the entrances and the ground-floor exhibition spaces rises a light-filled four-storey atrium. The detailing and the craftsmanship on the interior are as exquisite as they were on the exterior. Every detail is considered, every line is where it should be, and every space, no matter how humble, even a stairwell, is beautifully designed. The detailing and the craftsmanship are on a level almost never seen in America. This adds enormously to the allure.

The walls are white, washed with abundant natural light, and we see two glass elevators illuminated within and underneath, rising and falling like pistons or heartbeats. This atrium acts as a town square, with vertical streets, connected to MIT's campus at every level by the thrilling transparency.

Maki is a master of the modern staircase and he gives us a grand one in this ground-floor atrium. A set of open stairs with a bold diagonal red sidewall that floats above us like Man Ray's image of red lips in the sky, coaxing us to ascend.

Up two flights we go to the second atrium – one of the most exciting spaces in all of modern architecture. Maki has created a composition of planes, lines and points that appear to defy gravity. The ubiquitous white walls and plates of glass dynamically reflect light in all directions and charge the spaces within. Almost anywhere you stand in this atrium, you simultaneously see varying depths and transparencies in two or three or four directions – up and down, diagonally and straight, reflected or across the atrium and even out a glass window. This extraordinary variety of views makes you feel giddy, light on your feet, and inspired.

Maki has staggered seven double-height laboratories around this upper atrium. The double-height labs range from 5,000 to 8,900 square feet and are offset from each other by one floor across the atrium. The floor you stand on is midway up the double-height lab across the way, so you look diagonally down or up into those labs. These double-height spaces are for collective research; you take a white metal spiral stair up to the glazed offices on the mezzanines. Each lab is spatially unique for its location in the building and orientation to the site. Maki has updated the early modernists' *raumplan* with this contemporary masterpiece of transparencies, staggered spaces and perspectives.

This atrium, like the other, acts as a town square. The labs surround the atrium like houses around a piazza, but with the activities inside each lab visible to all. Wide-open floors encourage sociability; to go from one room to another, researchers rarely move in a straight line. This encourages thinking, serendipitous meetings, and a multitude of connections. All the research spaces are open and transparent so anybody can see in; a fellow researcher might get curious, ask a question, and hatch a new, unexpected plan. The projects here change regularly and unpredictably, so Maki has provided highly flexible and adaptable space to accommodate change. But for the exception of a limited number of private offices, the building is shared space!

The double-height labs are a carry-over from Pei's building, where there was a black box theatre-turned research space called the Cube. The much-loved space provided large, double-height areas that the research group shared, with offices in an added mezzanine. So Maki made the Cube the prototype for research spaces in the new building. They work well the way the Media Lab is structured, each project led by a master with several assistants. The master's office is at the top of the lab, reached by the elegant white spiral stair, as if they were a ship's captain.

In the upper atrium, two bold strokes of colour – yellow and blue – spatially link the surrounding labs. These two staircases, with the red one below, evoke the bright primary colours of children's toys, the same colours I. M. Pei put in his Media Lab. What we have, noted by Maki, is an exciting architectural riff on Piet Mondrian's painting *Composition with Yellow, Blue, and Red* – a few bold swatches of colours, against a background of white. The colourful stairs in the subtly changing light make the planes appear to push forward and pull back, breathing more life into the space. And the bright diagonals underscore the diagonal sightlines in the space.

A bulge in the centre of each stair stringer allows for a landing, as required by code. To the eye this bulge increases the tension and compression we feel in the staircases. Do they struggle to hold the building together, or do they demonstrate the cohesion of the masses around them? One's vision and mind is awakened by all the possibilities here. This atrium is so exquisite, satisfying and uplifting that when you leave it and return to your senses it takes a moment to acclimate to being back in daily life. You quickly long to return to Maki's hint of heaven.

MIT furthers the research of Maki's landmark Tepia, designed in the 1980s for the Meiji Memorial Park in Tokyo, which too honours Mondrian and De Stijl with its anti-gravitational composition. At Tepia, Maki deployed finished aluminium, stainless steel and glass in new ways to create sublime transparencies, translucencies and phenomenological effects. The Cambridge building has one more 'town square' to visit. The sixth floor, at the top, crowns the building. There, public spaces for the entire MIT community encourage both formal and informal social interaction, with a cafe, auditorium, meeting and event spaces, conference room, a skylit Winter Garden, and an outdoor rooftop terrace with dazzling panoramic views of the Charles River and the Boston skyline. These and other great views of the city remind us that the work of the labs below is not navel-gazing; it is connected to the lives of ordinary citizens.

And Fumihiko Maki, whose kindness, elegance and thoughtfulness are manifest in his buildings, has a personal reason to enjoy this spectacular view. Besides the goodwill he has for Cambridge, which helped him realize his goals, he also remembers one particular day in 1953, when he was a student at Harvard's Graduate School of Design. He says he went to a rooftop party at a then-new MIT building not far from where the Media Lab Complex is today, and noted the superb river and city views. Only about sixty years later was he able to take advantage of those views with a building of his own design for Cambridge, and give others the chance to enjoy them.

Là, tout n'est qu'ordre et beauté,
Luxe, calme et volupté.

There, all is order and beauty,
Luxury, calm and pleasure.

Charles Baudelaire, 'L'Invitation au Voyage'

Maki recalls, near the beginning of his recent collection of essays *Nurturing Dreams,* that, as a young boy born in 1928, he went with his parents 'to see foreign ships enter the port of Yokohama'. He writes: 'There in front of me would be these layers of decks and vertical masts and stacks, floating like lines and planes in a De Stijl composition.... The polished wood decks, the steel railings... the white painted surfaces – each of these elements projected its own powerful materiality. The ship was a huge machine that constituted a far more powerful statement of modernism than any architecture.'

Look at this Media Lab moored not far from the Charles River, and you see that ship, now, yes, in architecture, ready to explore new ideas and take all aboard to places that, like children, we still dream of. Wherever Maki's ship is sailing, I want to go with it.

Edward Lifson is an American journalist, architecture critic and academic. His diverse and impactful career has included roles as a domestic, foreign and war correspondent for National Public Radio. He was also previously the Director of Communications for the Pritzker Architecture Prize.

Square 3, Novartis Campus

Location	Basel, Switzerland
Status	Completed
Year(s)	2009
Typology	Office
Area	6,150 m^2 (66,198 ft^2)

Square 3 is one of a series of new buildings intended to transform the Novartis headquarters in Basel, Switzerland from an industrial, production-based facility into a modern research and administration campus. Noted urban designer Vittorio Magnago Lampugnani produced the campus plan, which calls for a series of mid and low-rise buildings within a new pedestrian-friendly urban grid enriched by greenery and parks. Completed in 2009, Square 3 is located adjacent to one of these newly planned parks near the River Rhine, which served as a key element in the conceptual development of the building.

Expressive of the cleanliness and hygienic qualities of the medical profession, the Square 3 facade mobilizes a variety of glazing technologies to maximize whiteness and transparency while complying with strict Swiss energy regulations. The unitized curtain wall is broken down into three distinct zones (clear, translucent and white opaque), each using different glass layers and coatings to satisfy performance and aesthetic demands. Surrounded by a patchwork of industrial facilities, the gleaming white facade is a radiant presence against the adjacent open green.

On the interior, the entire building is designed to function as a single, continuous open space, an interpretation of the Novartis working environment guidelines promoting mobility, adaptability and interaction across disciplines. At the ground floor, teakwood stone flooring and the maple slatted ceiling combine with floor-to-ceiling clear glass partitions to extend the warm, natural qualities of the adjacent park into the building. Individual floors are offset in an alternating pattern and connected at each end via a double-height lounge space and a spiral staircase, creating a continuous flow of space that allows staff to move freely from level to level.

The lounges serve as social nodes where employees congregate during breaks and for group meetings, both formal and informal, while the upper level of each lounge includes an integrated exterior terrace, enhancing natural cross-ventilation and serving as additional break and meeting space. These terraces connect the employees back to the exterior campus, effectively integrating the Square 3 community to its neighbouring buildings, parks and the campus as a whole.

(Opposite) View of terrace, which also functions as a private meeting area.

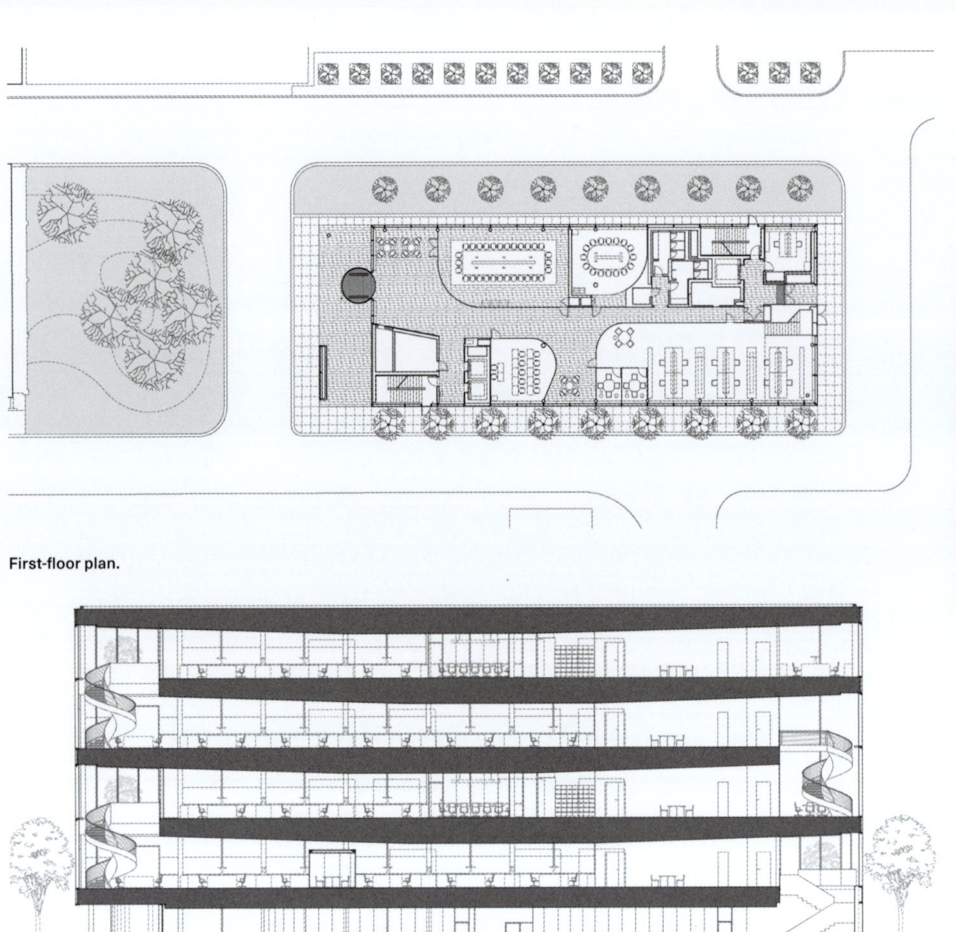

First-floor plan.

Building section.

Circular staircase from above; made of maple wood and bent steel plates, the stairs are supported by the inner guardrail.

Double-height break area: the curves of the stairs highlight the ends of the building.

Site plan of Novartis Campus, highlighting the WSJ-174 office building.

View of exterior terrace from inside.

Southeast facade view with integral roll blinds drawn down within insulated glazing.

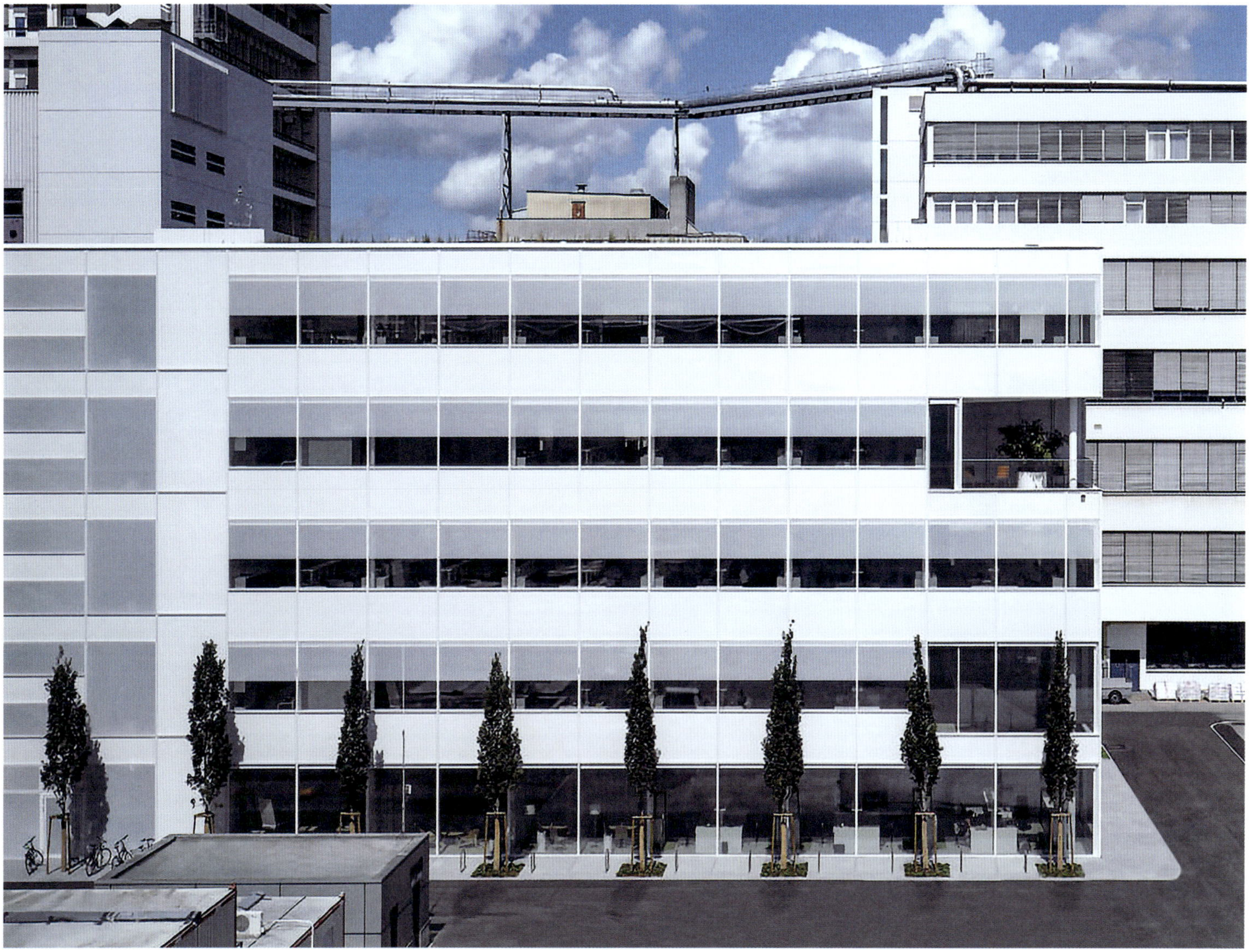

View of south elevation of Square 3, Novartis Campus.

The east facade and the Heian Shrine's grand *torii* gate.

National Museum of Modern Art, Kyoto

Location	Kyoto, Kyoto Prefecture, Japan
Status	Completed
Year(s)	1986
Typology	Museum
Area	9,980 m^2 (107,424 ft^2)

The National Museum of Modern Art is located in Okazaki Park at the northeastern corner of Kyoto, the historic capital of Japan. Symbolized by the enormous red *torii* gate of the rebuilt Heian Shrine, the park concentrates many of the city's major cultural facilities in a single campus. Each reflects the individual design spirit of its time while recognizing Kyoto's history, the strong axis of the ancient city structure and a district-wide 20-metre (66-ft) height limit.

Completed in 1986, the museum follows the patterns of its surroundings, while contributing exceptional new architectural qualities. The facade is primarily composed of massive grey granite resonant with the weight of Kyoto as an ancient capital city. It is divided into three layers, at the lower level integrating larger stones reminiscent of masonry techniques used in traditional castles. At the same time, the museum's glass and metal corner towers introduce a lighter, modern touch, combining transparent glass with fibre inlays similar to traditional Japanese shoji screens. Overall, a dialogue between past, present, Japan and the West informs the exterior design, creating a unique architecture that is unquestionably modern but highly respectful of its historic setting.

The main entrance to the museum faces east, connecting directly to the shrine's main approach. It opens onto a generous first-floor lobby/atrium filled with natural light from above, enabling a wide variety of activities including informal exhibitions and openings to functioning as a space for visitors to gather. A grand stairway leads from the atrium directly to upper-level exhibition spaces, while secondary stairways at the building corners offer more subdued, private routes through the building.

The strategic corner location of these vertical circulation towers enhances the flexibility of the exhibition spaces on the upper floors and serves a vital urban function, creating a clear separation between the museum and the buildings surrounding it. The clear identity established by these open, light-filled corners combines with other modern touches to make the museum an easily approachable yet dignified addition to this campus of historic structures.

Perspective with the museum's abstracted volume shown in relation to the Heian Shrine.

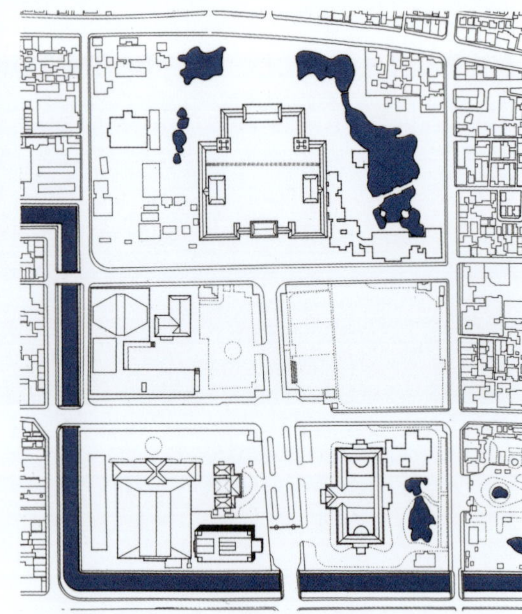

National Museum of Modern Art Kyoto site plan.

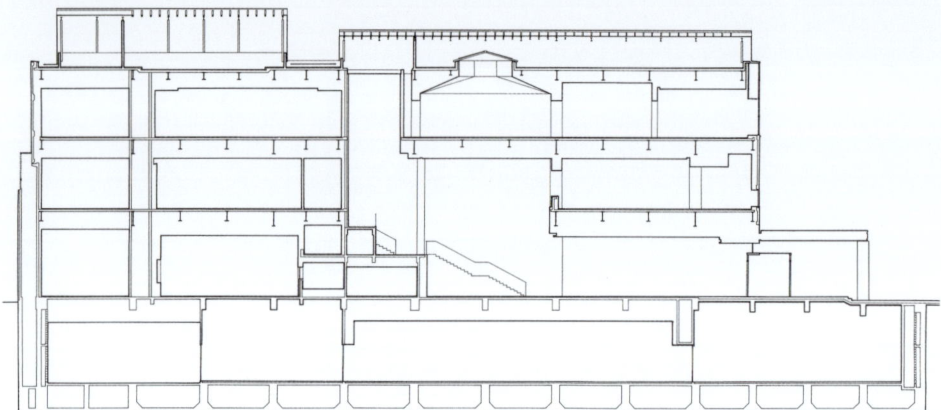

Section.

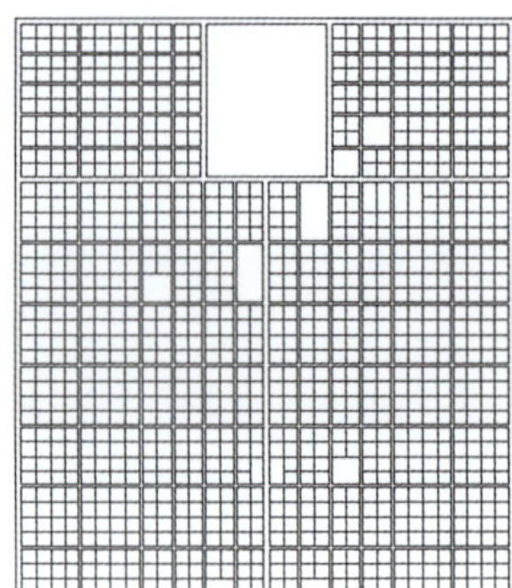

Early city plan of Kyoto during the Heian period.

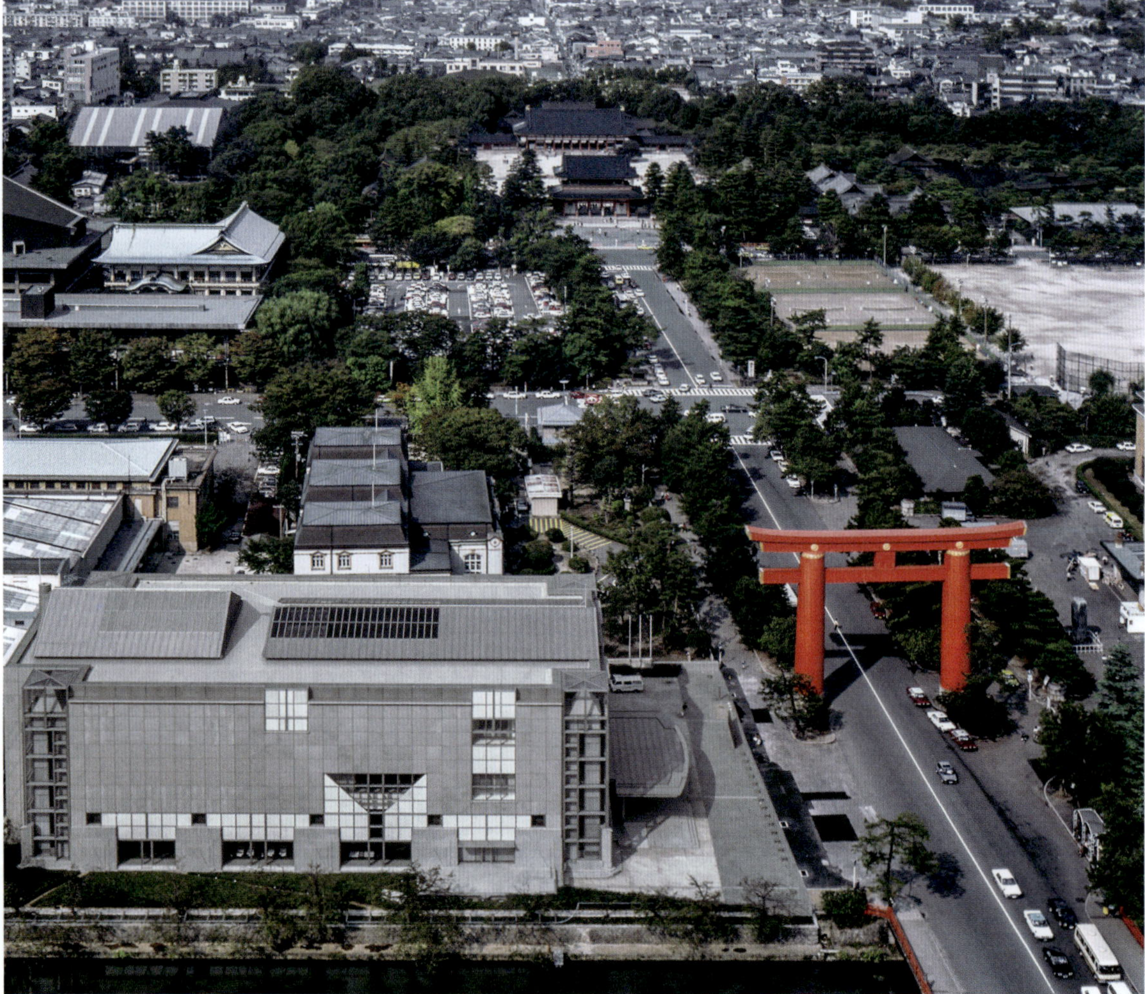

Aerial view of the museum and its urban context, aligned along a direct axis to the Heian Shrine.

The elevation of the National Museum of Modern Art Kyoto, seen from beyond the canal.

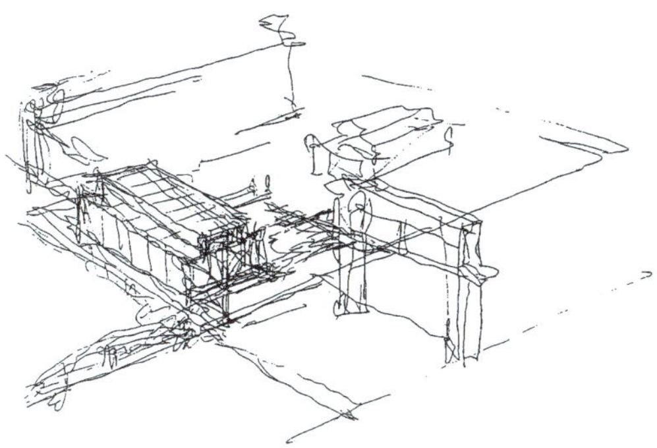

Conceptual sketch.

The first-floor gallery is an extension of the entrance hall.

Main stairs in the entrance hall.

Modernism and Islamic Culture

The Delegation of the Ismaili Imamat

Location	Ottawa, Ontario, Canada
Status	Completed
Year(s)	2008
Typology	Offices, Assembly Hall, Residence
Area	8,916 m^2 (95,971 ft^2)

The Delegation of the Ismaili Imamat, completed in 2008, is located on a prominent site facing Confederation Boulevard in Ottawa, Canada, establishing a formal and symbolic presence for His Highness the Aga Khan, the 49th Imam of the Shia Imami Ismaili Muslims. Its programmes foster intellectual exchange and partnerships with the Canadian government and the private sector, while simultaneously sharing Islamic culture and its spiritual dimensions to all visitors.

The Aga Khan's vision for the project was inspired by the characteristics of rock crystals. With its inherent mystique, faceted geometry, and its unique interactivity with light, the crystal is a distinct symbol of the interwoven beauty, mystery and intellect in Islamic thought. Its image and intrinsic characteristics served as the foundation for the Delegation building design.

The building has an elongated rectangular footprint, with programmes concentrated at its perimeter. This allowed for the creation of an inner sanctuary at the centre of the site, removed from the everyday world. Within this central zone, two symbolic spaces (an interior glass atrium and an exterior landscaped courtyard) integrate the perimeter programmes, while simultaneously enhancing their independence and privacy. The 16-metre-high (53-ft) glass atrium, formally reminiscent of a crystal, is supplemented by an asymmetrical inner membrane of triangulated glass fibre and fabric panels. This hovering membrane shades the interior, while narrow slots between its panels emit direct light shafts, creating a kaleidoscope of light and shadow on the floor.

The exterior utilizes a variety of glass materials with varying degrees of transparency and coatings. Even the solid exterior walls are clad in Neopariés, white crystallized opaque glass panels that subtly reflect their surroundings. The result is an ephemeral interplay of transparency and opacity, overlaid with a variety of translucent layers – all combining to create gentle light patterns that change throughout the day and season. Like the natural beauty of the crystals that inspired it, the Delegation building is a source of optimism, fascination and enlightenment, and a vibrant cultural ambassador in the heart of Canada's capital city.

East entrance featuring a custom crystallized white glass wall.

Early conceptual sketch.

Atrium detail; aluminium lattice screens are hung along the periphery.

Exterior view of the translucent atrium drawing inspiration from a rock crystal.

Gallery view of main entrance; aluminium cast screens and fabric shades create rich qualities of light.

Evening view from the east.

Evening view of the west facade on Sussex Drive.

Gallery 2 with view to the courtyard.

The spatial layering of intricately detailed die-cast aluminium screens is inspired by Islamic geometric motifs.

Approach via the drop-off area.

Aga Khan Museum

Location	Toronto, Ontario, Canada
Status	Completed
Year(s)	2014
Typology	Museum, Auditorium, Restaurant
Area	10,511 m^2 (113,139 ft^2)

The Aga Khan Museum was completed in 2014 and is part of a larger master plan by Maki and Associates for a 6.8-hectare site north of downtown Toronto. As the first museum in North America devoted to Islamic art and culture, the museum seeks to foster knowledge and understanding within diverse Muslim societies, and between these societies and other cultures. To this end, it exhibits a permanent collection of over 1,000 objects across a broad range of styles, materials and time – supplemented by classrooms, a reference library, a 300-seat auditorium and a restaurant.

In a vision statement entitled 'Light', His Highness the Aga Khan expressed hope that the building would become a celebration of light and its mysteries, a founding concept present throughout Islamic texts. Inspired by this vision, the museum is strategically oriented forty-five degrees off solar north (exposing all sides to direct sunlight throughout the year), while its mass (clad in sandblasted white Brazilian granite) is chiselled into a concave angular form. These angled stone surfaces are set into motion with the sun's movement throughout each day.

The museum interior is characterized by free-flowing public spaces surrounding a fully glazed courtyard. The public spaces are non-prescriptive – enabling performances, installations, public gatherings and receptions – while the courtyard remains a peaceful sanctuary. Its layered glass walls are imprinted with offset geometric patterns recalling traditional Islamic jali screens, and create moving patterned shadows that animate the walls and floor of the public spaces on sunny days. From the second level, large openings with cast zinc screens – a reinterpretation of Mashrabiya Islamic bay windows – overlook the busy public area below. Surrounding galleries are illuminated via aluminium panelled skylights with tight hexagonal openings, emitting soft natural light and again recalling traditional jali patterns.

In this way both the exhibits and the architecture itself educate visitors about the living traditions of Muslim societies and the artistic and cultural practices across Islam, past and present. The museum further reflects the Aga Khan's long-standing relationship with Canada and his appreciation for the country's commitment to pluralism and cultural diversity.

Domed aluminium auditorium roof.

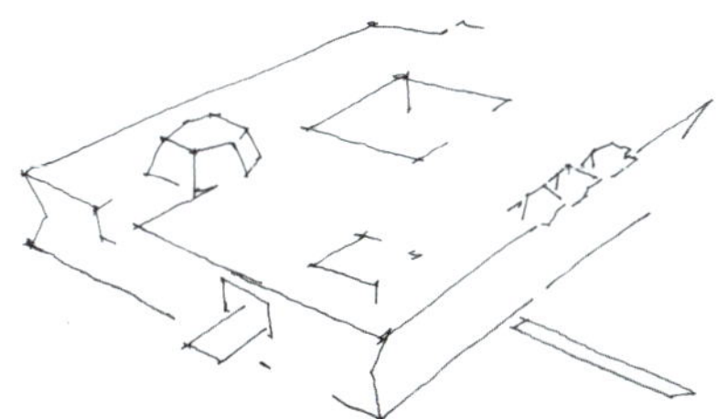

Conceptual sketch.

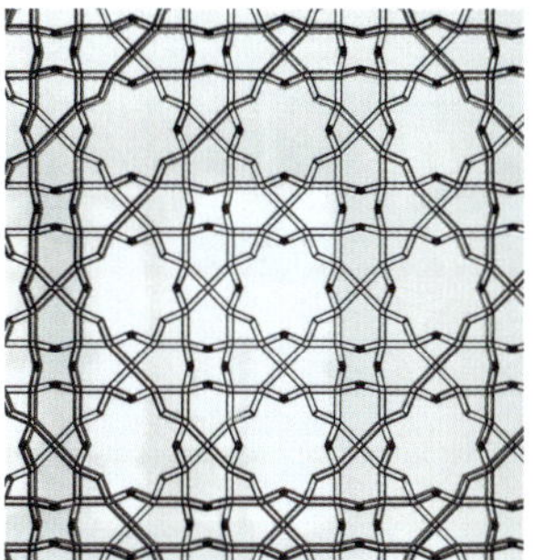

Zinc screen with sandblasted finish.

The Aga Khan Museum facing the formal garden.

Mashrabiya screen case in zinc.

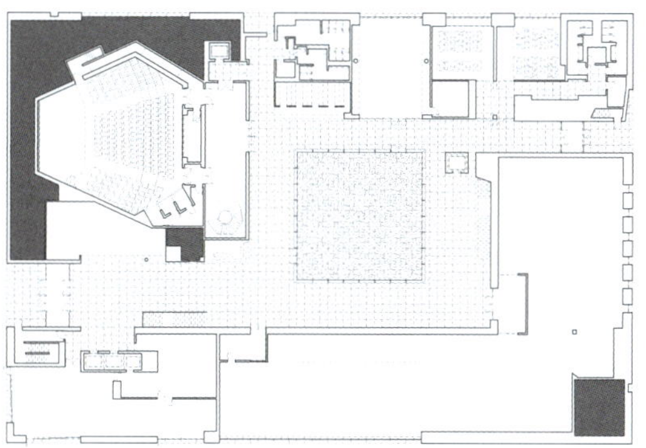

Ground-floor plan.

Patron's lounge with panoramic views of gardens and Toronto skyline.

Double-height permanent exhibition space and honeycomb skylights.

The Aga Khan Park: Ismaili Centre, formal gardens and Aga Khan Museum.

A performance in the courtyard.

View of courtyard from exhibition and reception.

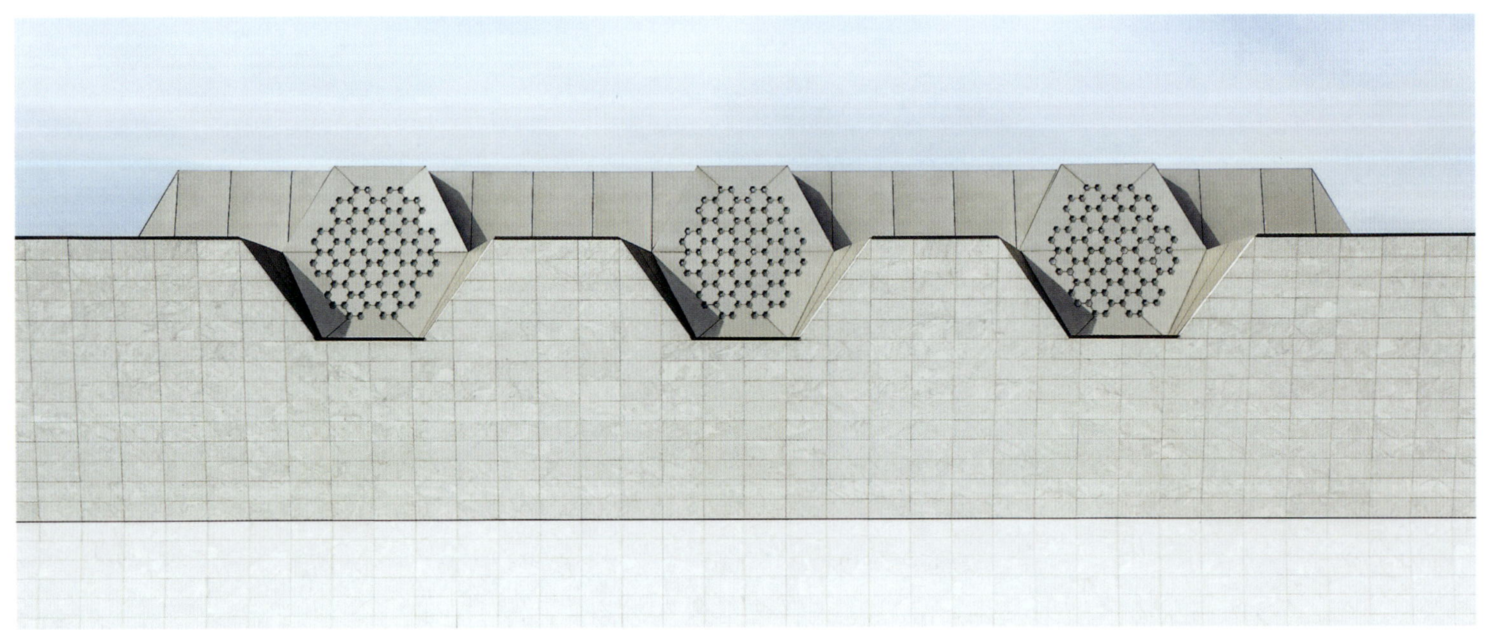

Exterior view of honeycomb skylight.

The 350-seat, multi-purpose auditorium features a prismatic dome inspired by mosque interiors.

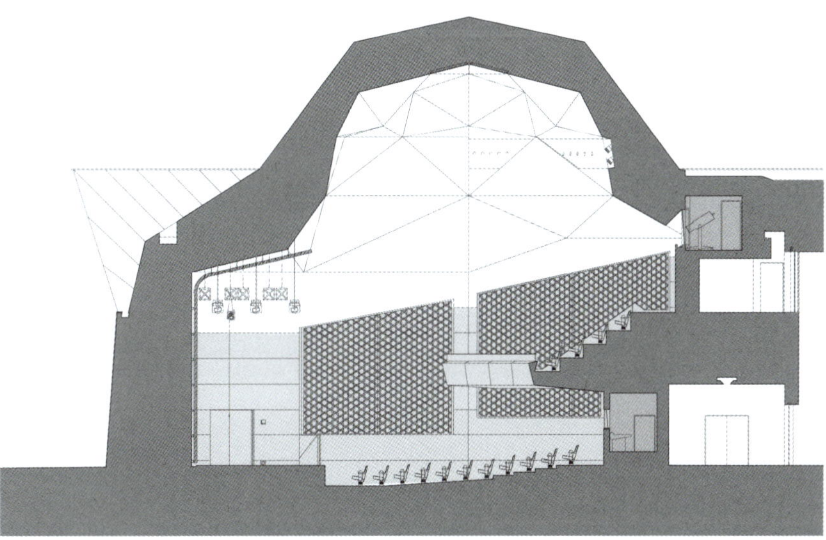

Auditorium section.

Auditorium ceiling.

Architecture of Pluralism

Toshiko Mori

His Highness Aga Khan has always promoted Pluralism as a concept that truly represents Islamic culture. The idea calls for a more precise understanding of Islam as inclusive of diverse ethnic and social groups, that has developed in multiple regions in coexistence with other cultures. It explains the dynamic and diverse aspects of Islam that have resulted from its unique history of continuous integration into different societies.

The Aga Khan Museum, which opened in Toronto, Canada in September 2014, has a modern and contemporary design that seamlessly integrates the building into the progressive milieu of the city. His Highness wished for visitors to spatially experience the essence of traditional Islamic culture, in paradox with the modern architectural language. There was also no attachment to historic nostalgia neither on the part of the client nor the architect. Instead, their mission was to make this museum relevant to its time and place.

The Aga Khan Museum is located in the North York district of Toronto due to the city's values and diversity. Toronto has a rich and tolerant multicultural community that makes it the number one multi-ethnic city in the world. There are more than 100 languages spoken and over 200 ethnicities represented who live together peacefully. In addition to its social agenda that fosters a vibrant and mosaic city, Toronto sees diversity as an asset that promotes economic growth and competitiveness. It was necessary to place the museum in an environment with shared goals and the potential to represent a precise message of inclusiveness. The museum presents Islamic tradition through historical and contemporary representations of cultural and artistic activities. An important mission of the museum is to promote humanism in Islamic art and culture and to educate the public of its multiple complex expressions and rich historical backgrounds.

As the first Islamic art museum in North America, the Aga Khan Museum carries with it the enormous challenge of presenting a balanced and positive face of Islam by confronting and rejecting stereotypes and misunderstandings. Therefore, the building's iconic presence had to be something ahistorical, new and fresh, while carrying with it an undeniable characteristic of Islamic architecture.

This project is the result of a long arduous conversation and extensive collaboration. The result is an architecture of clarity and simplicity, unfolding experiences of nuance and complexity. An important dialogue bridges the gap between the cultural backgrounds of the client and the architect. A superb hybrid was produced, two minds merging seamlessly into one building that exudes positive energy and forward outlook shared by the personalities of both His Highness and Fumihiko Maki.

Included in this collaboration is the contribution by the French exhibition designer, Adrian Gardère. His imaginative design offers an interpretive potential for the visitors. In an intimate conversation with displayed artefacts, each visitor can find a rich narrative that gradually unfolds to reveal mystery and wonder.

The exterior of the museum is simple, strong and restrained. As in traditional Islamic architecture in regions where defence from harsh natural elements and various enemies is requisite, it has a familiar monumental and fortress-like quality. The building's exterior envelope opens to the sky as a vessel to receive light. The spatial theme of the museum is light, the most fundamental metaphor in Islamic scriptures. This special quality, which one can only describe as 'benevolent', envelopes us immediately. The facade has a fold in the middle where light reflects to reveal the contrasting subtle shade on the surface and bright white of the stone. After two years of searching, the architect was able to find the whitest granite in Brazil. The soft daylight can therefore be amplified, giving the illusion of finding an iconic place. Approaching the building, one cannot help but notice the impeccable craftsmanship of the exterior wall. Our mind is trained to enter the building with a sense of calm and reverence. His Highness requested an emphasis on Islamic architecture's extreme sensitivity to light, wishing to have it expressed in a modern and contemporary language while avoiding the insertion of traditional motifs.

The building introduces many 'episodes' of daylight filtering techniques that have precedents in Islamic architecture. The screen, for example, is an important element traditionally used to designate spatial boundaries to assure privacy while letting light filter through spaces. In the Aga Khan Museum, the results are abstracted, refined, and folded into a contemporary museum experience. The courtyard curtain wall reflects and refracts layered geometric patterns, leaving the atmosphere sensitive to the time of day and season. The area around the courtyard is used as a public space where people are meeting, chatting and enjoying the cafe. Indoor spaces filled with natural light are appreciated by the public, as Toronto is a city with long winters.

The architectural plan consists of four blocks, reminiscent of the bazaar typology and scale, making it a more relaxed urban space with quiet music playing and a cafe displaying an abundance of sweets from different parts of the world. The highly popular restaurant also curates global and local Islamic cuisine. These personal touches help ease visitors into the mood and enjoyment of the culture beyond the museum experience. The architecture facilitates the successful blending of a foreign tradition with the everyday lives of the local community.

As we face crisis and problems of staggering global scale, we often question the role of architecture as a tool to confront these growing issues and propose solutions. The Aga Khan Museum gives a clear, precise and positive answer through its careful analysis of the programme, thoughtful architectural and cultural interpretations, informed methodology and discursive dialogue. Here, architecture works as a new bridge for culture, society and history, transcending multiple boundaries. Different values can coexist when a refined philosophy, thoughtfulness and empathy allow for open dialogue and conversation.

For civilization to move forward, the role of architecture as its steward engages in a continuous dialogue to achieve balance. The architecture of Pluralism quietly, with dignity, demonstrates the potential of architecture as a productive mediator in our complex society.

Toshiko Mori is the Robert P. Hubbard Professor in the Practice of Architecture at Harvard University Graduate School of Design and was chair of the Department of Architecture from 2002 to 2008. She is principal of Toshiko Mori Architect, which she established in 1981 in New York. Previously, Mori taught at the Cooper Union School of Architecture from 1983 before joining the Harvard GSD faculty with tenure in 1995.

View from Lewis Cubitt Square.

Aga Khan Centre

Location	London, United Kingdom
Status	Completed
Year(s)	2018
Typology	Institutional, Library, Classrooms, Offices
Area	10,930 m^2 (117,650 ft^2)

The Aga Khan Centre is part of the newly revitalized King's Cross area in London which is characterized by repurposed historic buildings and a network of pedestrian-friendly urban squares and parks. Completed in 2018 as part of this emerging creative district and tech hub, the centre integrates teaching, research, archival and development activities for three primary institutions of the Ismaili Imamat and the Aga Khan Development Network: the Aga Khan University, the Institute of Islamic Studies and the Aga Khan Foundation United Kingdom. It also promotes public engagement with Islamic culture through its active programme of exhibitions, lectures and conferences.

King's Cross is characterized by dark brick reflecting its industrial past. In contrast, the centre utilizes a light beige limestone sourced in Spain (visually similar to the Portland limestone used for British public and institutional buildings but with better durability). Overall, the building follows a familiar tripartite composition also common to older structures. At the same time, flush detailing and white ceramic fritting at the windows transform it into a more singular, sculpted block, carved out by a series of terraces and gardens. Overall, the effect is respectful to its context and British traditions, while distinguishing itself with calm dignity and modern detailing.

A thematic series of six ascending roof gardens, courtyards and terraces – tightly integrated with interior programmes – showcase the diversity of Muslim societies and cultures over a variety of geographic regions. Varying in scale, proportion and orientation, they also reflect the abiding British interest in horticulture and garden design. The vertical journey unfolds in a sequence of interwoven internal and external spaces around the ten-storey skylit atrium – a vessel of light and the centre's community living room.

The lines and forms of the Aga Khan Centre are deceptively simple, belying the great care taken with its details and finishes. It is an ensemble of British and European artisanship, which adds – via its carefully curated exterior spaces – a respectful integration of essential Islamic themes.

Fifth-floor sky court.

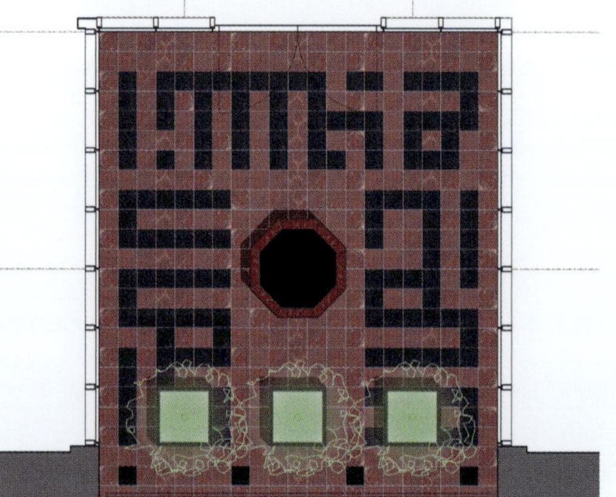

Fifth-floor sky court plan.

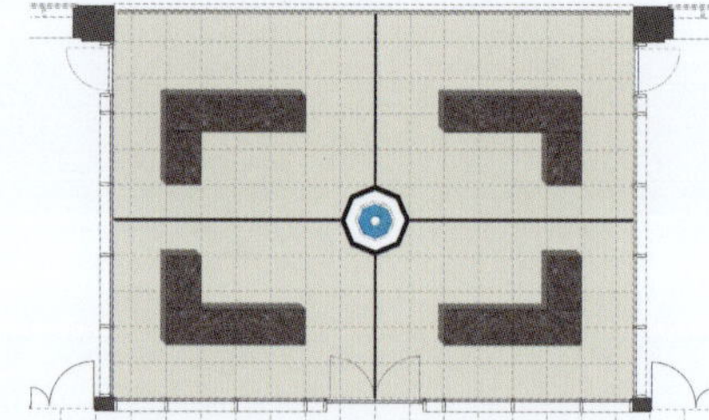

Terrace balcony guardrail design.

First-floor atrium terrace plan.

Ninth-floor meeting room terrace – Talar.

First-floor atrium terrace with vista of nearby urban fabric.

Ninth-floor anteroom garden – Chahar Bagh.

Entrance foyer.

Landscape stacking diagram.

View of entrance foyer from first-floor atrium.

Ninth-floor meeting room.

Making a Living Environment

205

PREVI Low-Cost Housing

Location	Lima, Peru
Status	Completed
Year(s)	1972
Typology	Residential
Area	80–150 m^2 (861–1,615 ft^2) per household

In 1965, the Peruvian Government and the United Nations invited British architect Peter Land to develop new housing strategies, in response to the massive informal settlements overtaking Lima during that period. Land proposed an international competition for the design of 1,500 housing units on forty acres north of the capital, based on six design goals:

1 A high-density, low-rise model for future urban expansion.
2 A 'growing house concept' including courtyards.
3 Ensuring identifiable housing clusters within the larger master plan.
4 Ensuring human-scaled pedestrian environments.
5 Utilizing improved building methods with earthquake resistance.
6 Inclusion within an overall landscape plan including the surroundings.

Among the thirteen international architects participating, Herbert Ohl, Atelier 5 and a team from Japan (including Kiyonori Kikutake, Kisho Kurokawa and Fumihiko Maki) were selected and joined three local architects to develop designs for six neighbourhoods in the master plan. The Maki team utilized pre-cast concrete to save costs and enable tight construction timelines, grouping mechanical and plumbing services in anticipation of kitchen and toilet zones likely to come but not yet planned. Vehicles were removed from pedestrian zones, enabling freer use of adjacent exterior spaces by residents and visitors. The Maki team proposal also included unit entry points from both the front and rear of the buildings.

Although by 1972 only one-third of the originally planned 1,500 dwellings were realized, the Maki team design has been lauded for its success – not as a finished product, but as a platform for expansion and adaptation, in the spirit of the original brief. Evolution was effectively anticipated by the Maki team design and, according to one recent survey, only one house out of the forty constructed remains as originally built. All others exhibit a variety of infills, updates and extensions that have radically transformed them, programmatically and formally, through their long years of active use.

(Opposite) Model of PREVI Low-Cost Housing, Lima

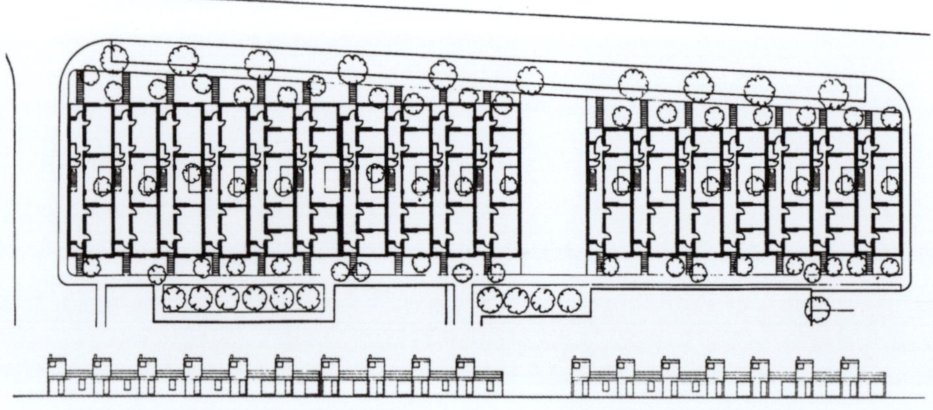

Site plan illustrating spatial layout and pedestrian street.

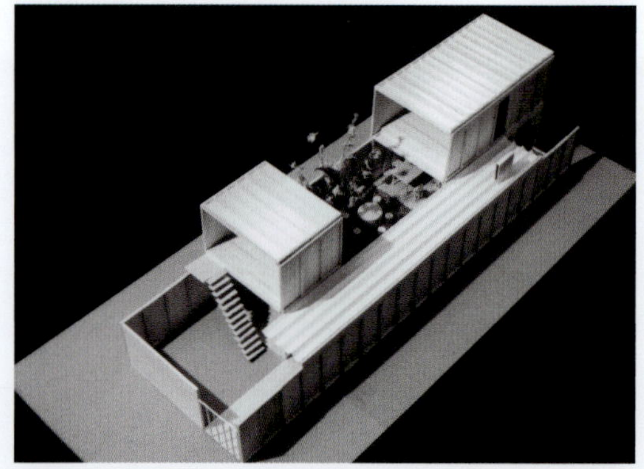

Concept model of typical unit.

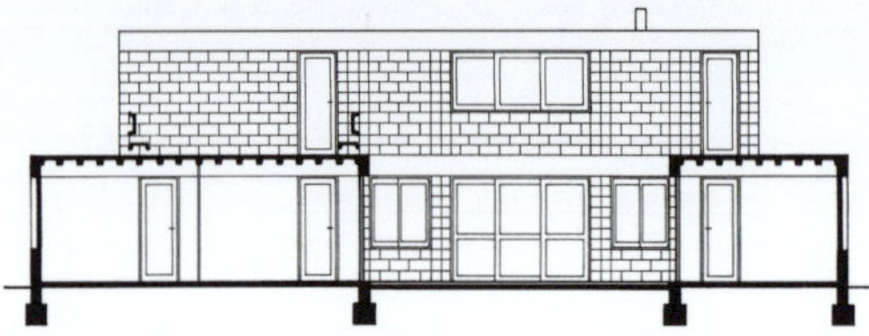

Section.

Aerial view of site-plan model.

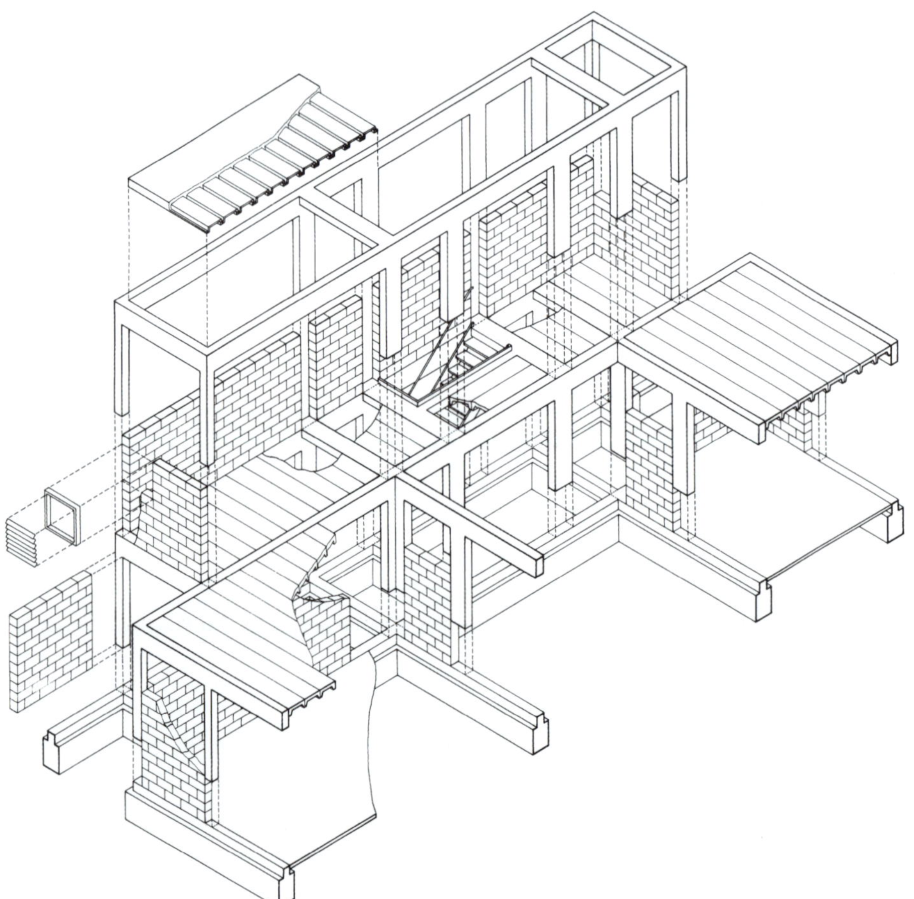

Axonometric section of structure.

View depicting the 'Omnibelt' – a continuous spatial band where public functions and circulation seamlessly intersect.

A typical barriada near Lima.

Facade after adaptation by residents.

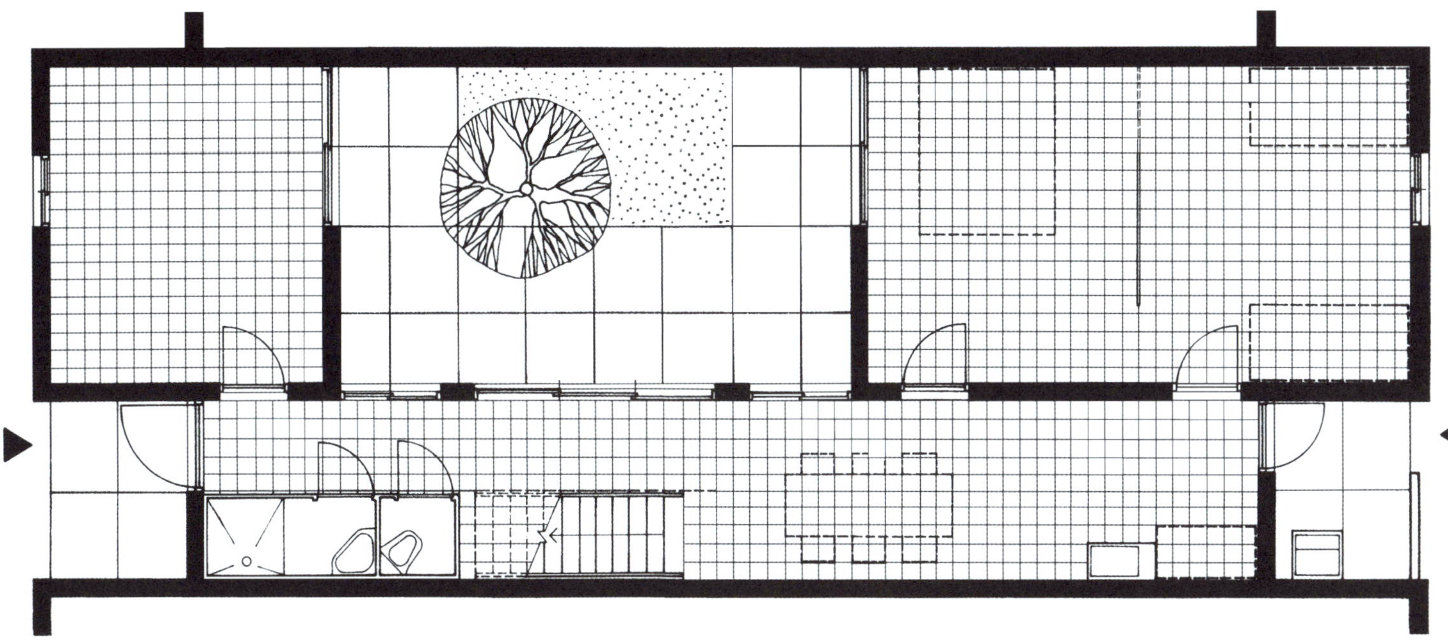

First-floor plan.

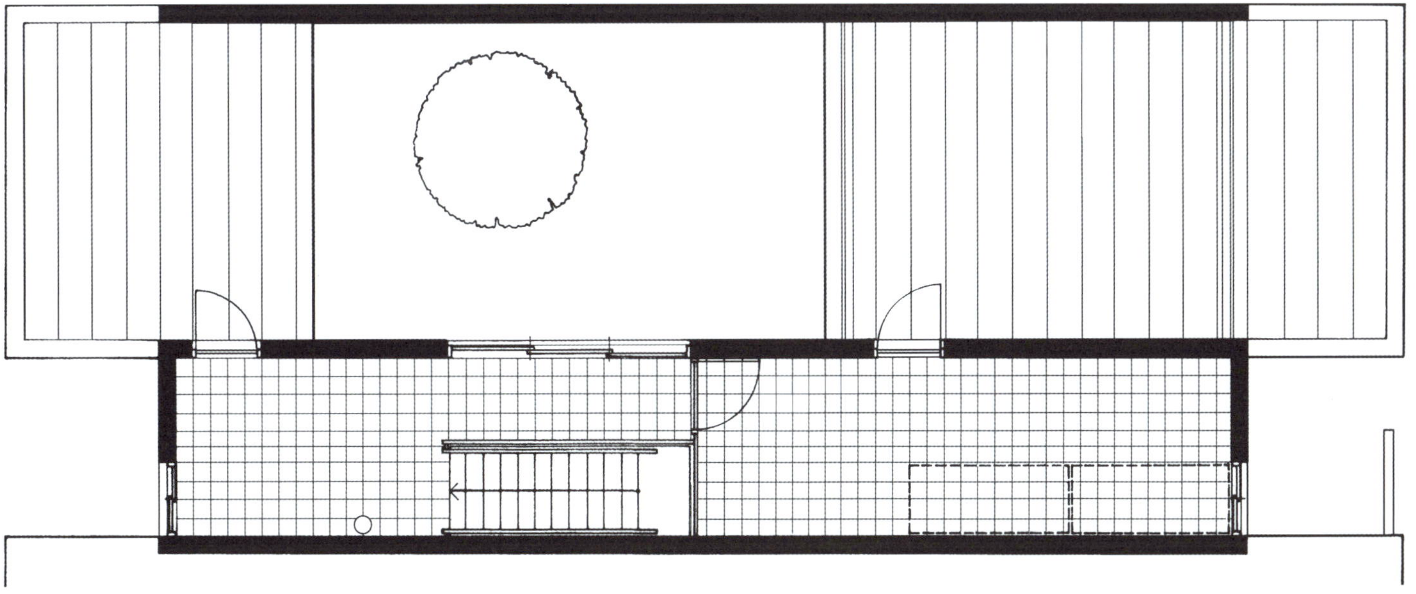

Second-floor plan.

Skyline @ Orchard Boulevard

Location	Orchard Road, Singapore
Status	Completed
Year(s)	2015
Typology	Residential
Area	21,666 m^2 (233,211 ft^2)

Completed in 2015, Skyline @ Orchard Boulevard was commissioned by Far East Organization, a private developer in Singapore offering bespoke luxury residences at coveted addresses. This project, perched on a small hill only one block from Orchard Boulevard, is a thirty-three-storey residential tower rising 147 metres (482 ft) above ground. The building makes full use of the site's height allowance and ensures better views for all residences by raising the lowest units 20 metres (66 ft) above grade, simultaneously allowing for the enrichment of its lower-level garden and amenity spaces.

On the exterior, the entire tower is clad in custom coloured aluminium panels, providing a shimmering sense of luxury and elegance in the tropical sunlight. Protruding bay windows and carved corner balconies cast deep shadows on the silver panels, enlivening the building's silhouette and shading the cladding from the harsh sun. These corner balconies function as outdoor extensions for living, dining and bedroom areas, creating an open environment that takes full advantage of Singapore's warm climate.

Skyline's first and second floors are layered in an unfolding sequence of indoor and outdoor spaces that reach into the inner depths of the site, utilizing a wide variety of plants, stone, timber and water. With the layering of numerous green spaces at the ground level, and the greenery lining the building's corner balconies, the residential units appear to seamlessly grow out of a lush landscape, blending the architecture with Singapore's abundant flora.

On the interior, a variety of unit types – including two-storey maisonette units – are serviced by an array of private elevators. Rich finishes and furnishings with a Japanese sensibility create a sophisticated and elegant atmosphere for residents on the inside, while remaining connected to the exterior via the generously finished corner balcony spaces. This unique combination of privacy and openness has made Skyline a flagship property and a destination address in its prestigious central location.

(Opposite) View of protruding living rooms with open view from Orchard Boulevard.

Model of Skyline @ Orchard Boulevard.

The residential tower as seen in its entirety from Orchard Boulevard on the eastern approach to the site.

Clad in aluminium panels, the building's facade responds to shifting daylight with a subtle play of reflections and tonal variation, while corner balconies on each floor extend the interior spaces outward as private terraces.

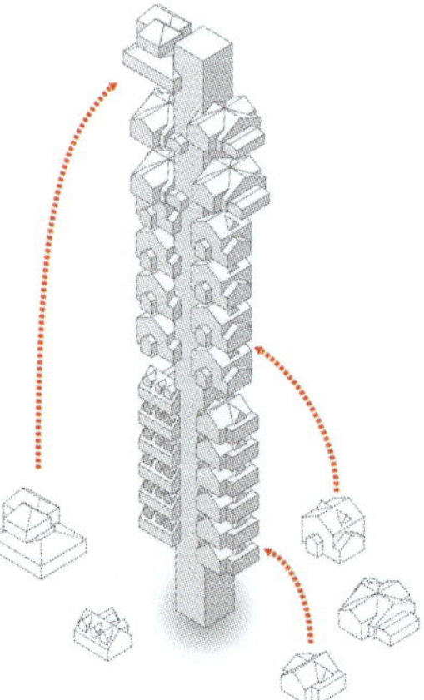

The 'bungalows in the sky' concept.

Drop-off lobby.

Residential interior unit; a blend of light wood and white marble creates a serene atmosphere.

Corner terrace; the greenery along the parapet rises with the tower.

From the roof terrace, an expansive view unfolds – Singapore's skyline in the foreground, with vistas stretching into the distance.

From the dining pavilion, the view unfolds across a water basin anchored by an Isamu Noguchi sculpture.

Site model view from the west.

YKK Passive Town

Location	Kurobe, Toyama Prefecture, Japan
Status	Completed
Year(s)	2016
Typology	Residential
Area	6,792 m^2 (73,108 ft^2)

YKK is Japan's leading zipper manufacturer and a major architectural curtain wall/architectural product company. The YKK Passive Town development is an initiative to realize a sustainable residential community in Kurobe, near the company's main research, development and manufacturing centre along the Japan Sea coast. Highlighting many of YKK's own sustainable architectural products, Maki and Associates' contribution to Passive Town employs a variety of high and low-tech technologies to create comfortable living spaces with a relatively small environmental footprint.

The 3.7-hectare master plan for Passive Town includes 250 apartment units in six sectors, all surrounding a central zone with shared open spaces and communal facilities. Three sectors have been realized to date. The Maki site, completed in 2016, is located along the eastern edge of the development and consists of two 'Street Buildings' (including both housing and commercial space, facing a roadway) and four 'Residence Buildings' (with housing only, on the inner side of the block).

Energy consumption at Passive Town is minimized via strategic deployment of thermal insulation, high specification window glazing and well-sealed doors/windows that reduce air infiltration. Rigorous three-dimensional air-flow modelling at both the site and unit planning level was studied to optimize both block-to-block site plan relationships and the locations and sizes of exterior openings within each unit. Living room terraces, bedroom balconies, sunrooms and verandas take advantage of sunlight and prevailing winds to create natural ventilation and shade in the summer while maximizing solar gain in the winter. Elimination of heat-bridges at openings and balconies and thorough insulation coverage add to the energy savings and comfort for the residents.

As a result of these initiatives, Passive Town residents enjoy daily comfort and remain better connected to their environment and the different seasons throughout the year. Only nine years since completion, the new buildings have begun to blend in with the trees and surrounding landscape, and this model of co-habitation with nature and sustainable living practices is thriving and growing.

The malls on the east side of Buildings D and G have shops and a water basin facing the street.

Early concept sketch.

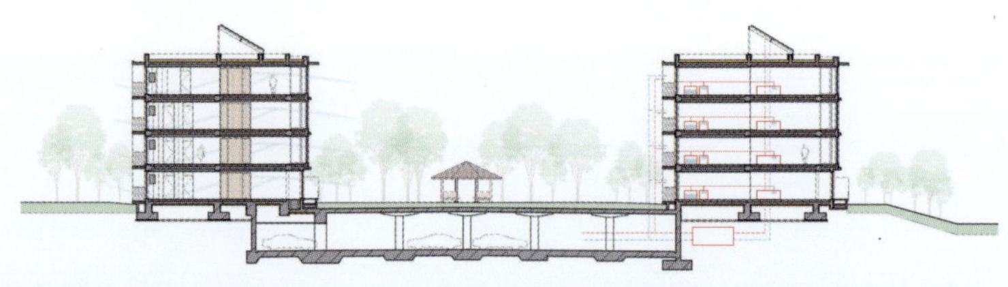

Section.

A continuous street mall was proposed across the first, second and third blocks, creating a human-scale streetscape.

A water basin, parallel to the street mall along the roadside, uses well water for regular irrigation.

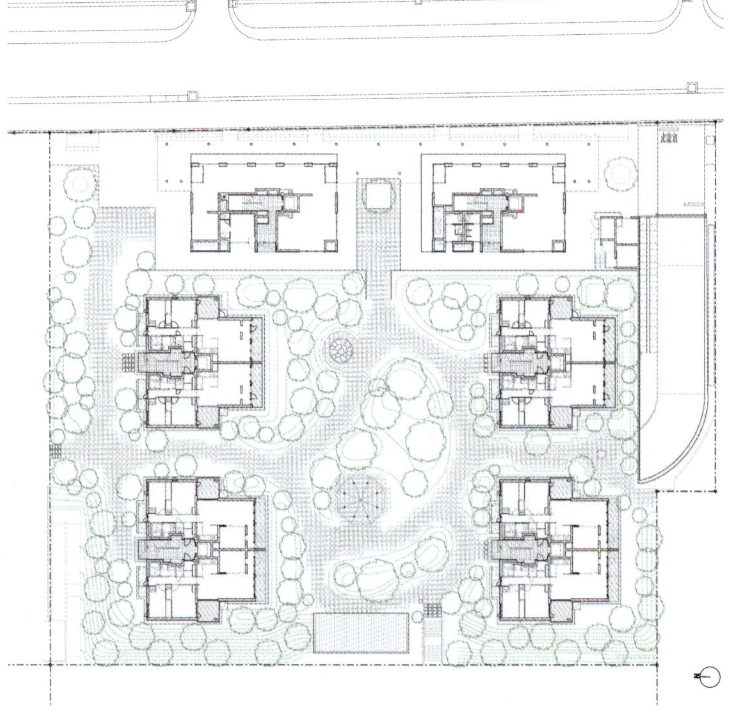

First-floor site plan.

Aerial view of roof.

Typical three-bedroom unit with a living room, dining area and kitchen in Building F or I.

A green shared space surrounding the azumaya.

The common space – defined by six residential buildings centred around a gazebo – unfolds against the backdrop of the Tateyama mountains.

The terrace, connected to the living room, uses louvres to maintain privacy from adjacent units, while controlling direct sunlight and allowing natural light and breeze to enter.

Hiroo Residential Renewal Project

Location	Minato-Ku, Tokyo Metropolitan, Japan
Status	Completed
Year(s)	2023
Typology	Residential
Area	9,914 m² / 106,713 ft² Studio unit 67 m² / 721 ft²

Garden Plaza and Hiroo Towers.

Located in one of the most upscale residential neighbourhoods in Tokyo, the Hiroo Apartments were an embodiment of affluent modern life at their completion in 1973. Two towers, Hiroo Homes and Hiroo Towers, demonstrate how both urban design and architectural design are employed to create a total environment. The facilities and the buildings, housing 158 dwelling units, have been carefully planned with a clear intention that has taken a period of fifteen years to execute.

Commercial activities were located at the periphery of the site to activate the streetscape. The buildings here were kept low so as to not disturb the views from the residential towers. The residential activities were concentrated at the centre of the site, away from the noise and traffic of the busy boulevard. The elevated residential units take advantage of natural light, air and most importantly bring in the lush greens of the surrounding garden, a scarcity in most of Tokyo today. An effort was made to preserve as much of the original greenery that the site possessed, which has matured over the years along with the architecture.

Continuing earlier efforts of total environment and responding to the context of present-day sustainable living, the recently renovated residential unit – completed in February 2023 – realized this ambition, creating an open living space suited for the modern lifestyle. The existing compact core and the continuous run of a 7.3-metre-long (24-ft) ribbon window were fully utilized and their functions augmented, with the strategic removal of walls and efficient planning of living elements. Without compromising on function or privacy, this renewal creates a sense of spaciousness where spaces merge seamlessly, allowing a stream of natural light to pour into all living spaces, as well as an unobstructed view of the pre-existing greenery of the outdoors.

View of residential tower.

View from living space.

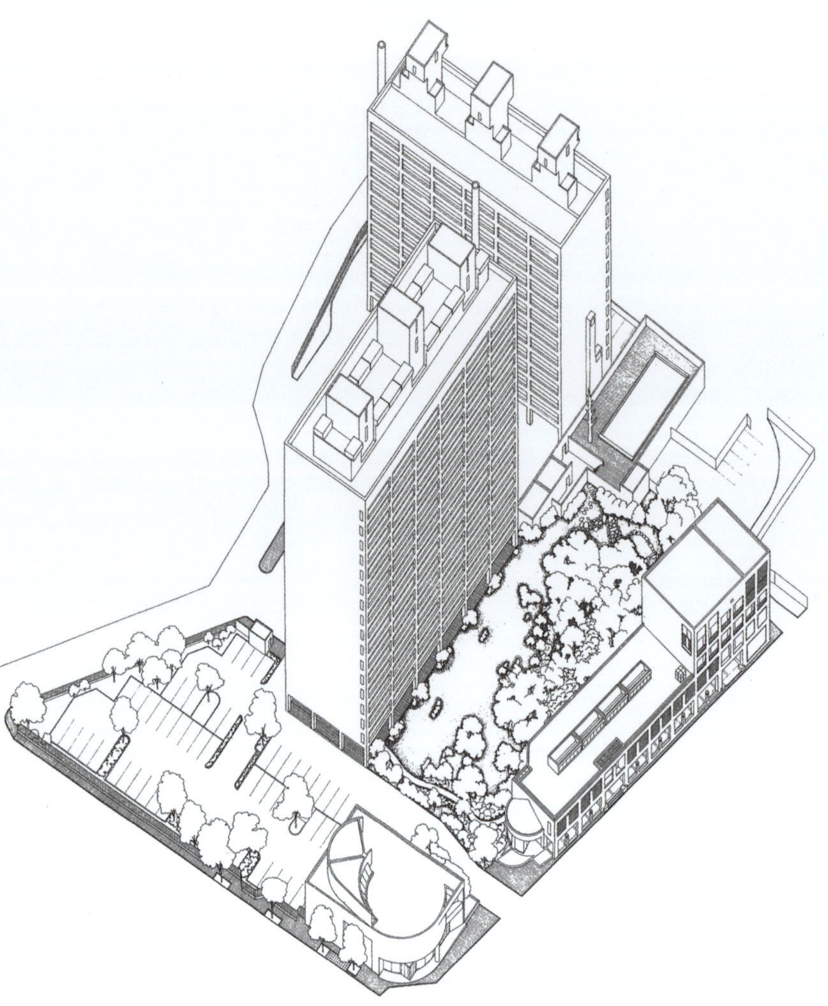

Axonometric drawing.

Overall view of Hiroo Project and its urban context leading to Arisugawa Park.

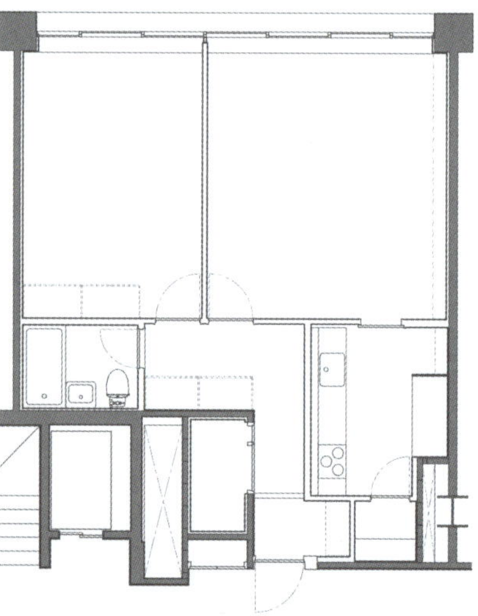

Existing plan of unit.

The open-plan living space is framed by broad, unobstructed views of the city.

Open-plan design encourages spatial permeability and unimpeded visual connections.

The revitalized integrated living space is designed to address modern spatial needs.

Children's World

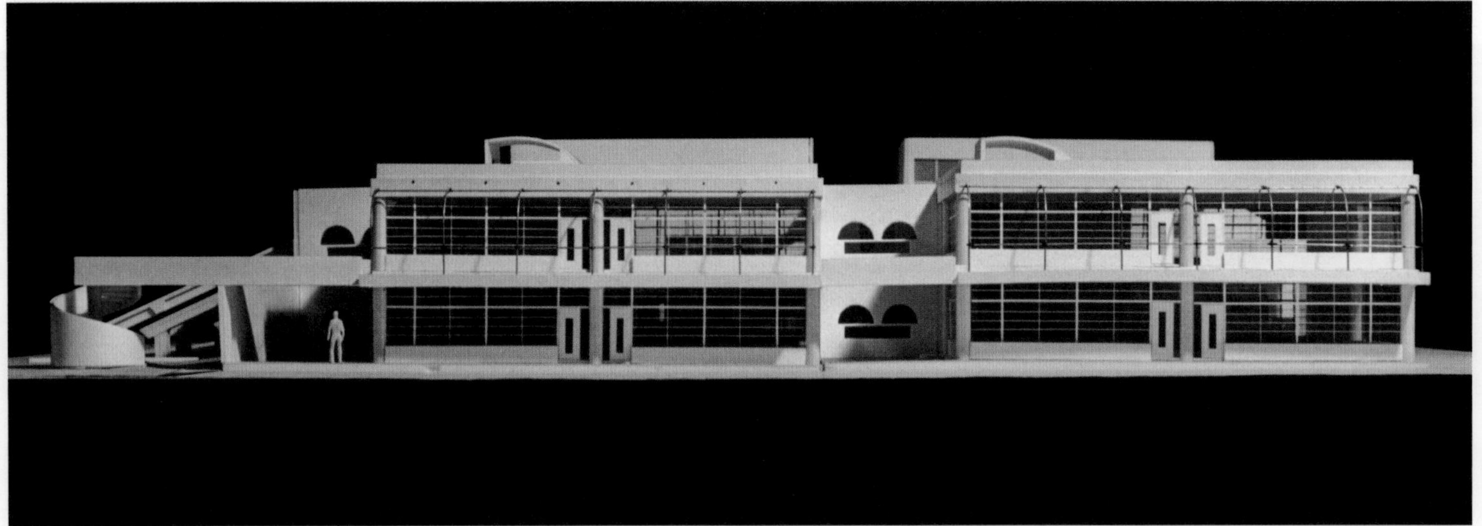

East elevation view of model.

Katoh Gakuen Elementary School

Location	Numazu, Shizuoka Prefecture, Japan
Status	Completed
Year(s)	1972
Typology	Institution (School) Library, Classrooms
Area	3,148 m^2 (33,885 ft^2)

Katoh Gakuen elementary school opened in April 1972 in Numazu and supports a curriculum that follows educational philosophies imported from the United States. Prioritizing educational flexibility, classes are conducted by teaching groups and students are subdivided according to proficiency regardless of age. The education is therefore structured to students' individual abilities and efforts, rather than their birthdates.

Building on this unique educational vision, the design for Katoh Gakuen was inspired by Aldo van Eyck's dictum that a city is a large house and a house a small city. Designed to feel like a 'house' for the students and the teachers, its closed exterior facade maintains privacy against its chaotic surroundings, while a series of small internal courtyards bring ample light and ventilation throughout the interior. Students are afforded a bright and open learning environment while maintaining sufficient auditory privacy between classrooms. Extensive use of carpeting encourages children to sit on the floor (similar to their home environments) and helps absorb sound. Door heights limited to 1.85 metres (6.1 ft) and low window ledges and benches at the peripheries of the rooms reinforce the informal, residential scale within the school.

A large library/multi-purpose room forms the centre of all school activities and study. Here, students gather for both learning and playing, formally and informally. Four 8.1 × 8.1-metre (26.6 × 26.6-ft) classrooms (two per floor) are located adjacent to this central space, each equipped with movable partitions to allow for further subdivision into four smaller spaces. When subdivided, the area adjacent to the bathroom is used as a locker room, with the remaining three spaces serving as breakout classrooms: a generous matrix of differently scaled gatherings is possible to address changing student needs.

This unique combination of flexible multivalent spaces with residential-scaled planning touches has kept Katoh Gakuen in use to this day. It is a well-loved neighbourhood landmark and has become a foundational educational experience for generations of Japanese students.

Aerial view of Katoh Gakuen elementary school. Cast-in-place concrete walls bear the imprint of plywood formwork and a sloping roof over the stair and entrance is clad in glazed tile.

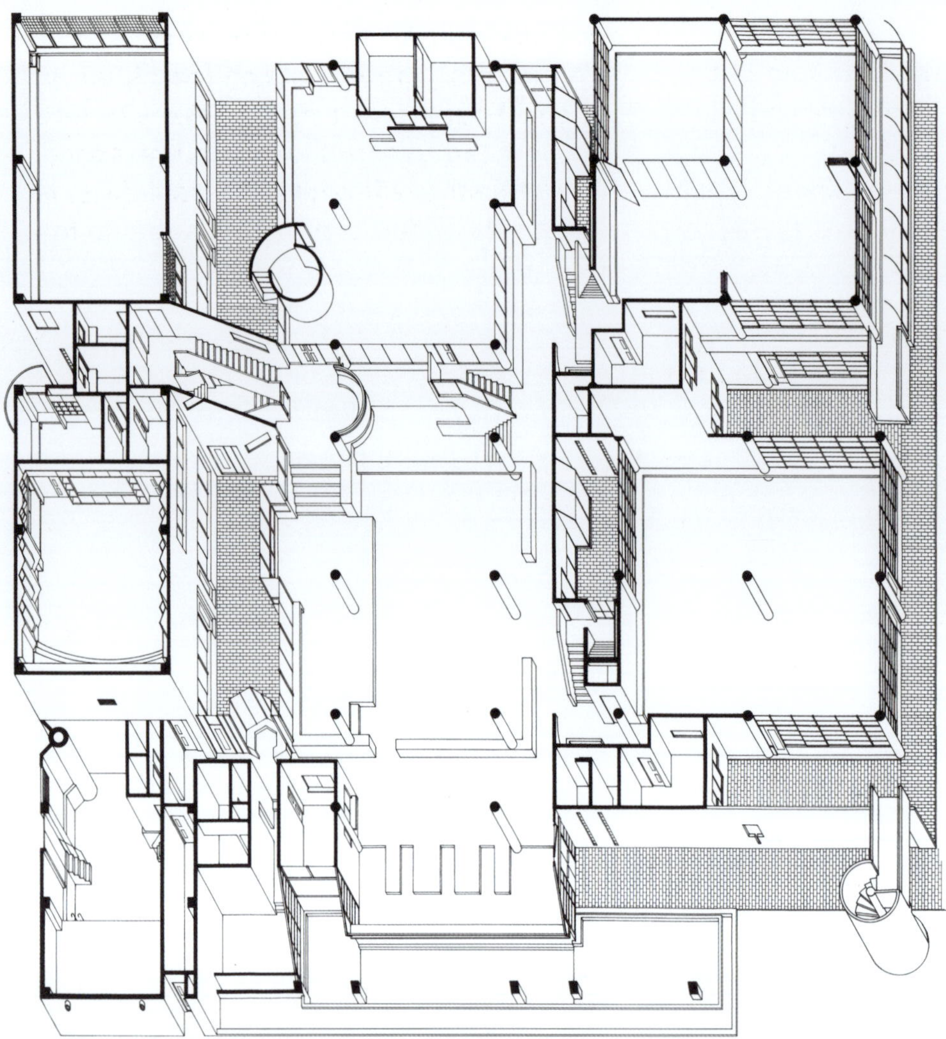

Axonometric drawing of the school.

Custom-designed furniture installed and used in a classroom.

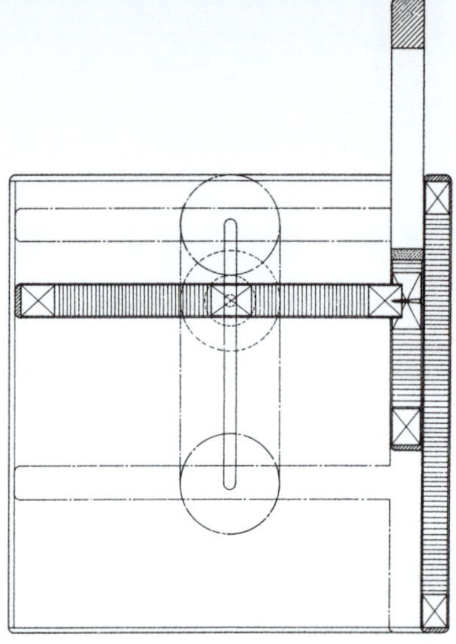

Section of a chair with adjustable height.

Model.

Open-plan classroom with movable partitions that divide the large space into four smaller rooms as needed.

Atrium space between multi-purpose rooms.

Arts and crafts room.

Children playing on the rooftop terrace.

Music classroom.

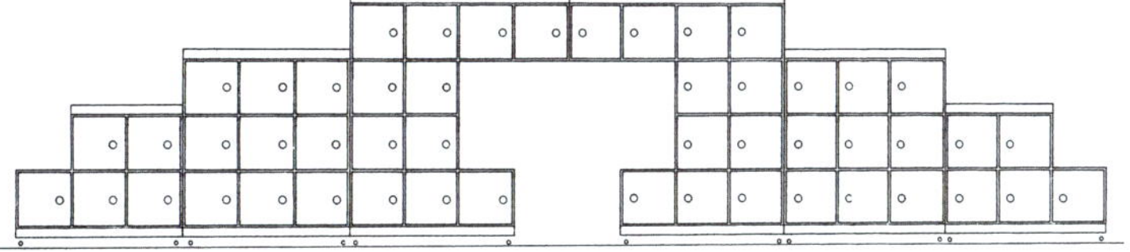

Elevation of custom-designed lockers.

Children playing on custom-designed lockers, which serve as a buffer zone between the staircase, corridors and classrooms.

Cantilevered seating area overlooking to the atrium.

Semi-enclosed sloping roof over entrance and staircase.

Haus der Hoffnung

Plan of Haus der Hoffnung.

Location	Natori, Miyagi Prefecture, Japan
Status	Completed
Year(s)	2012
Typology	Community Centre
Area	234 m^2 (2,518 ft^2)

The Great East Japan Earthquake of 11 March 2011 resulted in a tsunami that completely engulfed Yuriage Port in the northeast of the country. Although the tsunami almost reached the Natori Performing Arts Center, completed by Maki and Associates in 1997, the building was fortunately left undamaged and able to serve as a temporary shelter for displaced residents in the immediate weeks following the disaster.

After learning of the tragic earthquake news, the Reinhard and Sonja Ernst Foundation in Germany proposed to work with Maki and Associates to donate a community centre to Natori in the Performing Arts Center's garden. The community centre – named the 'Haus der Hoffnung' (House of Hope) – opened in November of 2012 and was widely celebrated by the local community. It has since become a valuable asset and a symbol of the recovery efforts in Natori and beyond.

Haus der Hoffnung is organized as a single-storey wooden structure, a series of small interior volumes arranged under two nested circular roofs. The small volumes contain counselling rooms, play spaces, a *tatami* room and a kitchenette, while also supporting the roof structure. The larger roof, above the individual rooms, shelters a dynamic common space which rises to a central height of over 6 metres (20 ft) and can support larger gatherings. A smaller crescent-shaped roof encloses the entry spaces and an outdoor terrace that can be used in combination with the Arts Center garden for special events.

A wide variety of spaces and functions are housed under the single, symbolic roofs at Haus der Hoffnung. These intimate, inviting spaces also inspire unique events and new uses, extending a warm welcome to all age groups. The building continues to serve the community long after its recovery from the tragic events of 2011 and has become a well-loved part of daily life in the local area.

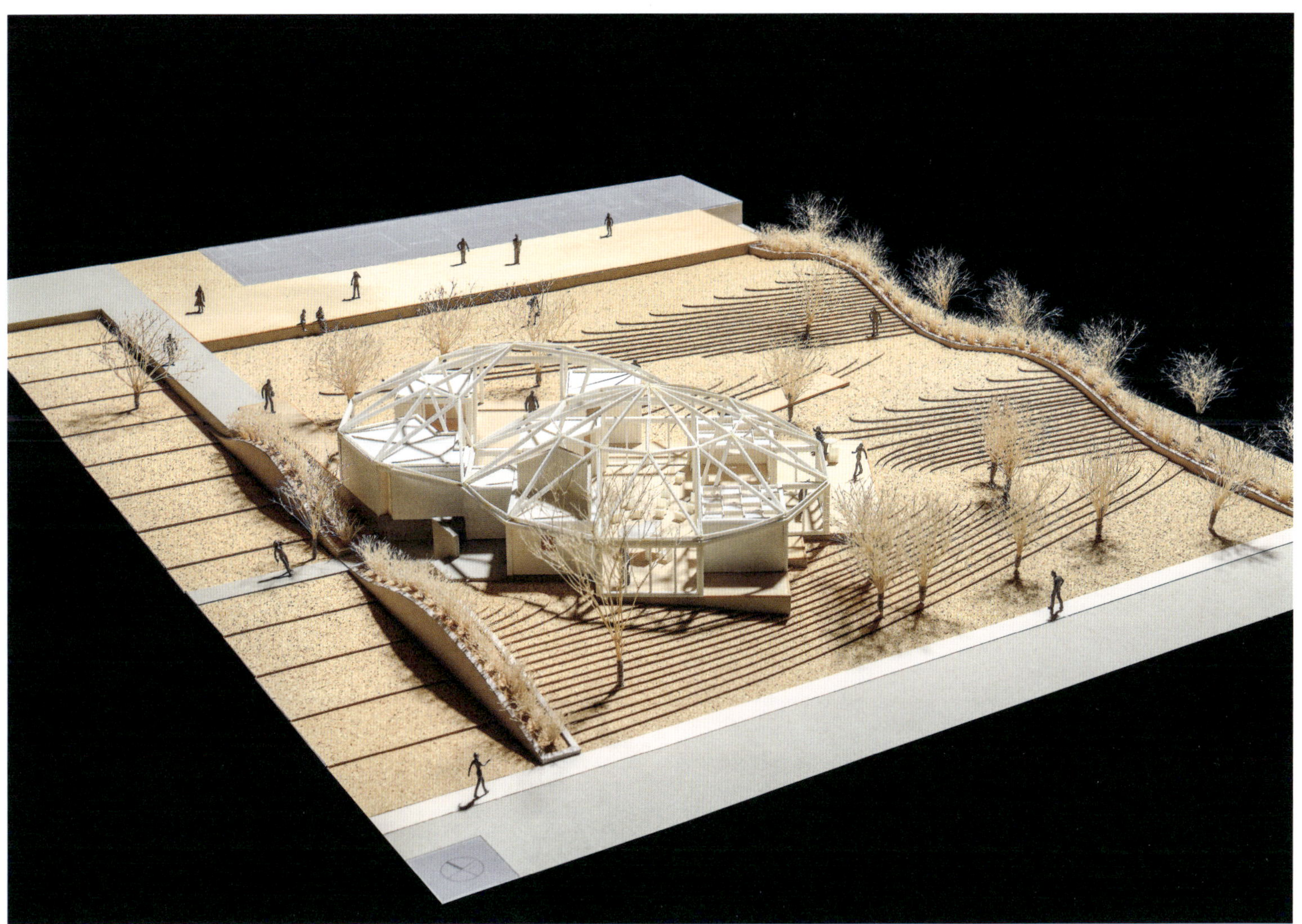

Site model with structural frame.

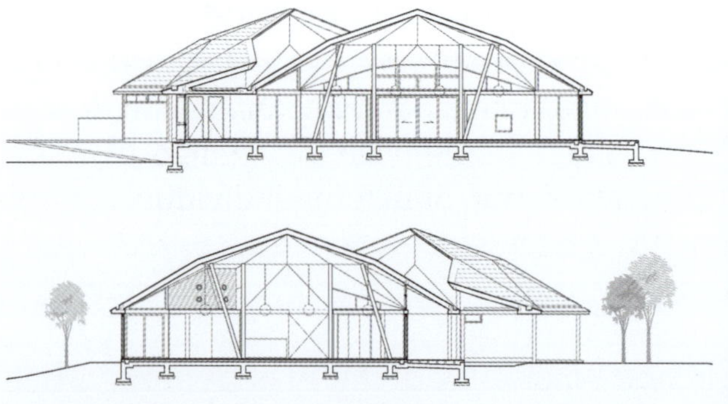

Sectional drawings showing the structural frame.

View of the Haus der Hoffnung from the south garden, with children's drawings on the mural along the terrace.

Haus der Hoffnung and Natori Performing Arts Center.

A semi-exterior space at the main entrance, located beneath the apex of the crescent-shaped roof. The mural along the terrace symbolizes hope for the recovery effort and friendship between Germany and Japan.

Full-height openings on the periphery yield exterior views from various points of the multi-purpose room.

Multi-purpose room during a community event.

The staircase hall functions as an active space and a seamless extension of the nursery room.

Location	Yokohama City, Kanagawa Prefecture, Japan
Status	Completed
Year(s)	1974
Typology	Institution (School)
Area	768 m² (8,267 ft²)

Noba Kindergarten

Completed in 1974, Noba Kindergarten is designed to serve the educational needs of a large-scale housing complex 6 kilometres (3.7 mi) southwest of central Yokohama. Contrasting the densely developed and small apartments surrounding it, the school interior is organized around a single, large, flexible space and strives to achieve a playground-like atmosphere via its welcoming exterior massing, spacious double-height interior rooms, flexible use patterns and inventive and colourful interior finishes. The goal was to have Noba's students feel both comfortable and inspired with each visit.

The building's exterior is characterized by exposed concrete surfaces, with its main volume divided into three zones via two generous striped skylights which bring filtered light into the main school space. Stairs and slides for emergency egress are enlarged and formally expressive, to create interest for children and to strengthen the school's connection to its surroundings. Overall, the exterior is inviting and friendly, with generous glazed openings overlooking outdoor play spaces.

On the interior, the oversized main stair landing doubles as a stage as it enters the central open space. This is an ideal area for students to play and perform, or from which school administrators can make announcements. Skip floors add spatial interest to the circulation zones while also ensuring efficient space use within office and support areas. While the main interior walls have primarily neutral white finishes, wooden furniture, wood wall accents and brightly coloured carpeted floors animate the space, reflecting the sun entering from the skylights above.

Added colour accents on walls further brighten the atmosphere and tented furniture/space dividers can be freely arranged by the children – guided by their imagination to create and re-create different separations of the main space. Allowing the children to help shape their own environment has engendered a sense of connection and ownership, making Noba a popular and well-loved part of the local community.

(Opposite) View of the staircase hall from the nursery room, where natural light floods the stage-like space painted with graphics of forests and clouds.

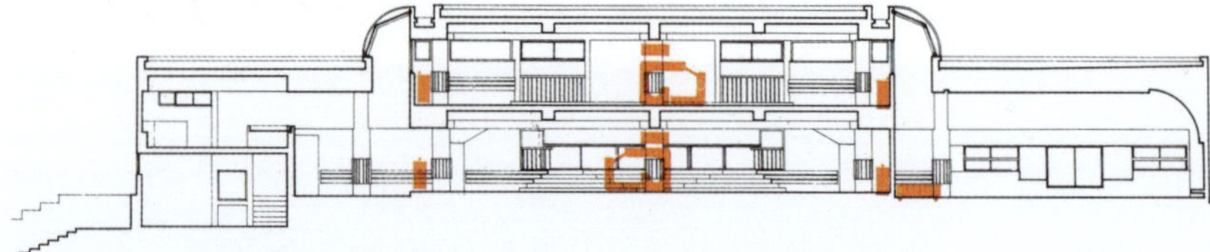

Section.

Children playing on the stairs that also function as a slide.

Opened on 1 April 1974, alongside the Noba housing complex, Noba Kindergarten was the first kindergarten in the area. Its modern open-plan design helps children ease into the school environment while fostering independence.

External view of Noba Kindergarten. The stairs between the office zone and nursery room, visible beneath the skylight, also function as a slide, with the building itself designed as a playground.

View of nursery and staircase hall.

Tent playground equipment where children can freely play.

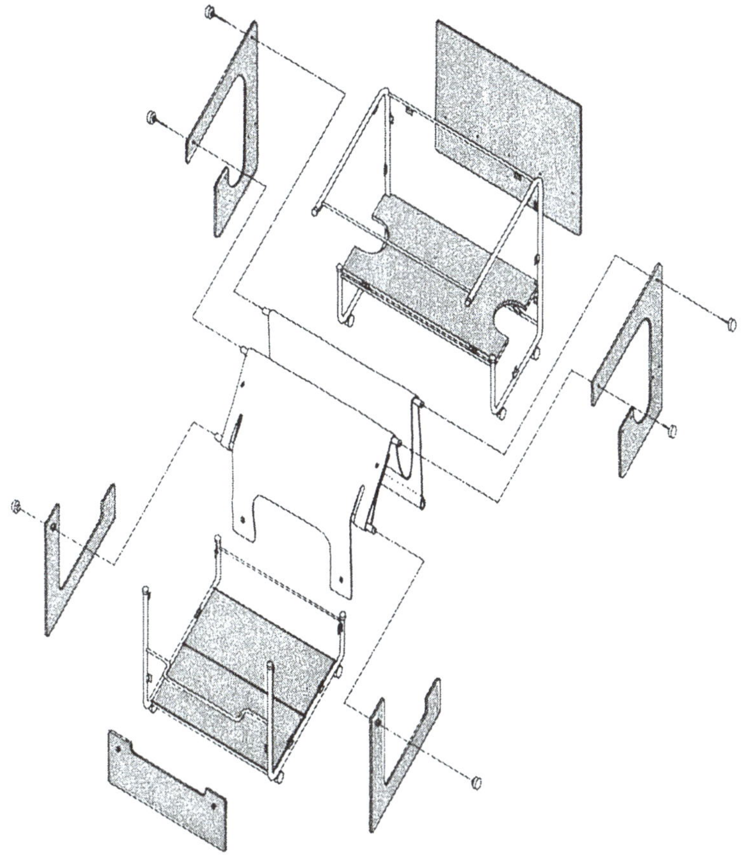

Play equipment assembly diagram.

Model of the Children's House.

Children's House

Location	Oświęcim, Poland
Status	Not realized
Year(s)	1991 initiated
Typology	Community Centre
Area	200 m^2 (2,153 ft^2)

Maki and Associates designed the Children's House as part of a Children's Village which is currently being developed for orphans in Oświęcim, Poland. The village is dedicated to the memory of Dr Janusz Korczak, a philanthropist who organized homes for orphans in pre-war Poland. Twelve architects from several countries, including Poland, are working together to create an environment that will embody Dr Korczak's ideas concerning children belonging to both a family and to a larger community.

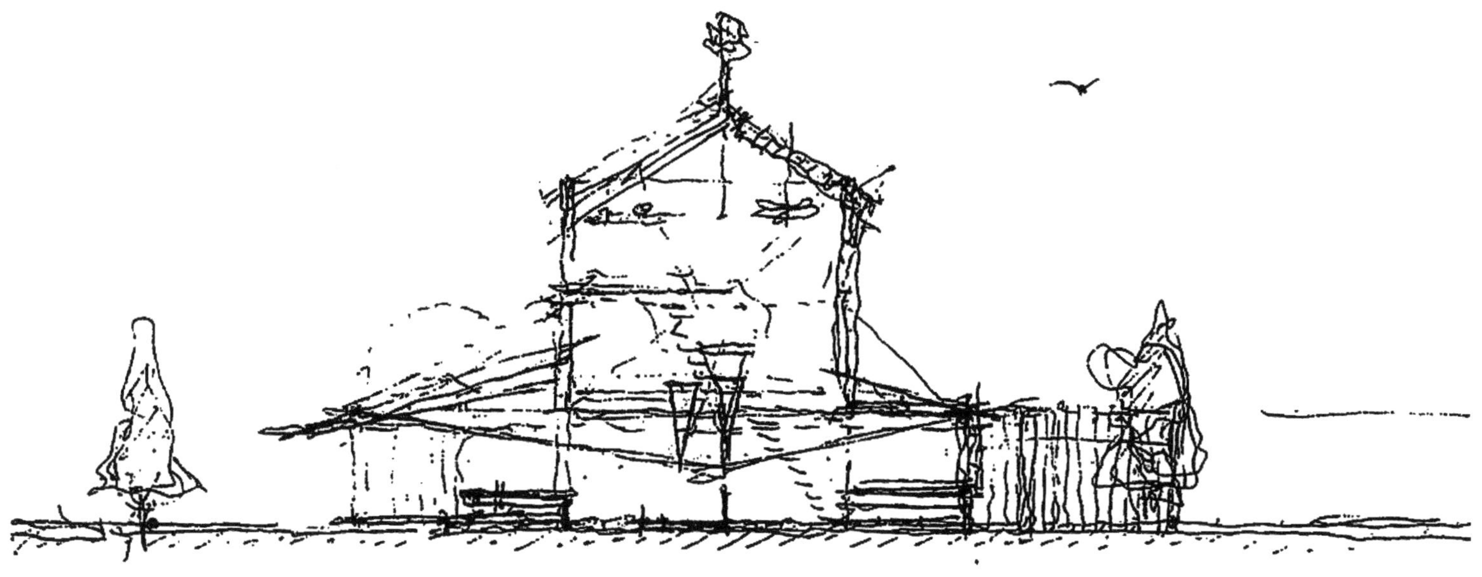

Section sketch.

Professor Tomasz Mańkowski of Krakow Technical University developed the master plan, which consists of twelve individual houses grouped around a common recreation space, a community centre and administration buildings at the village entrance. The programme for each of the houses is quite modest, consisting of living quarters for eight children (between three-months and eighteen years of age) and a single foster mother. The Maki site in the southeast corner of the village is a 25 × 25-metre (82 × 82-ft) square and the total floor area is 200 m^2 (2,153 ft^2). To keep costs moderate, Maki and Associates has considered working with local materials for the house, primarily using brick and wood.

The Children's House presents the unmistakable figurative image of a house, yet its central tower expresses something extraordinary about the structure of the family within. As the imbalance between the upper and lower volumes is slight, the house adheres to expectations of a 'house' and questions the conventional definition of a 'family'. A small tower containing two loft floors (one for girls, one for boys) rises above the lower mass of the communal spaces, giving the older children smaller residential zones within the larger house. Rooms for the mother and two infants are on the ground floor, more convenient to the house's central functions. Spatially, the house is structured as a series of interlocking L-shaped zones: cooking-eating-gathering spaces, mother and infants' rooms, boys' and girls' loft quarters, and so on. The inherent flexibility of the L shape (left open or subdivided) allows the house to adapt and accommodate unforeseen developments in the family. On the ground floor, places of communal importance – dining table, reading alcove, fireplace, entryway facing the common green – provide space for family interaction.

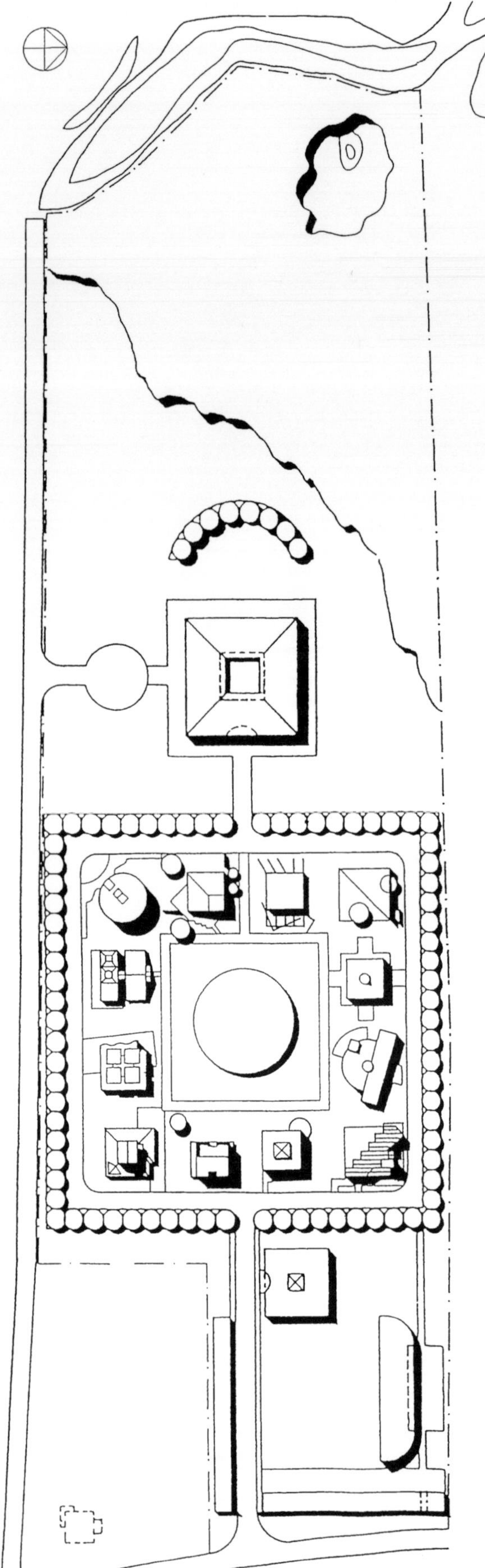

Schematic site plan with twelve houses arranged around a central playground.

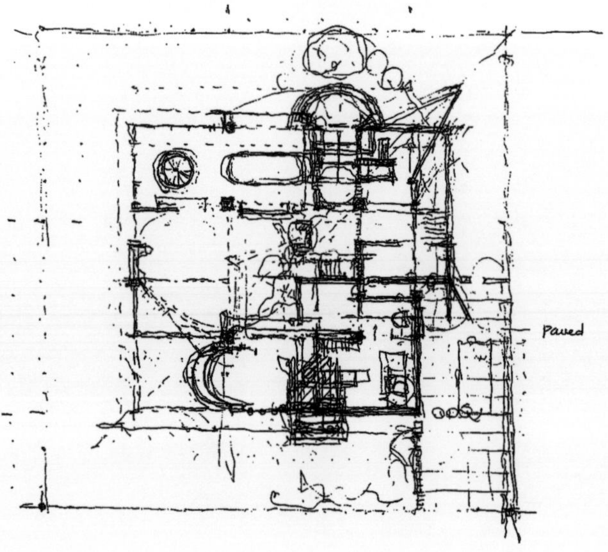

Plan sketch.

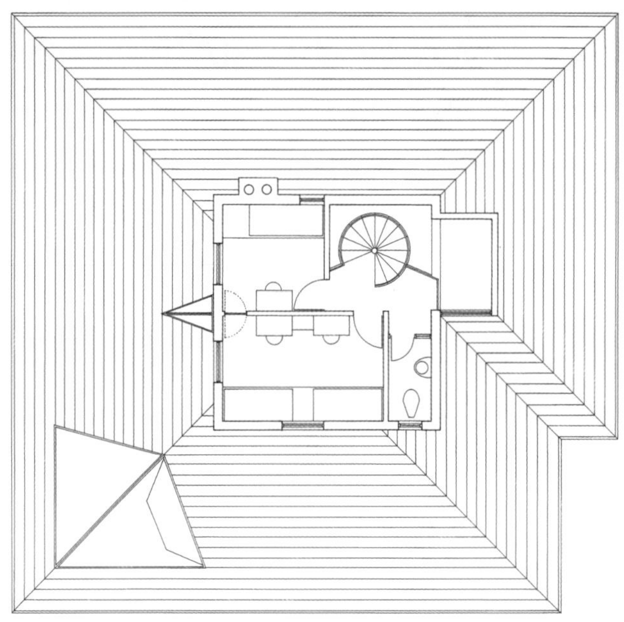

Second-floor plan.

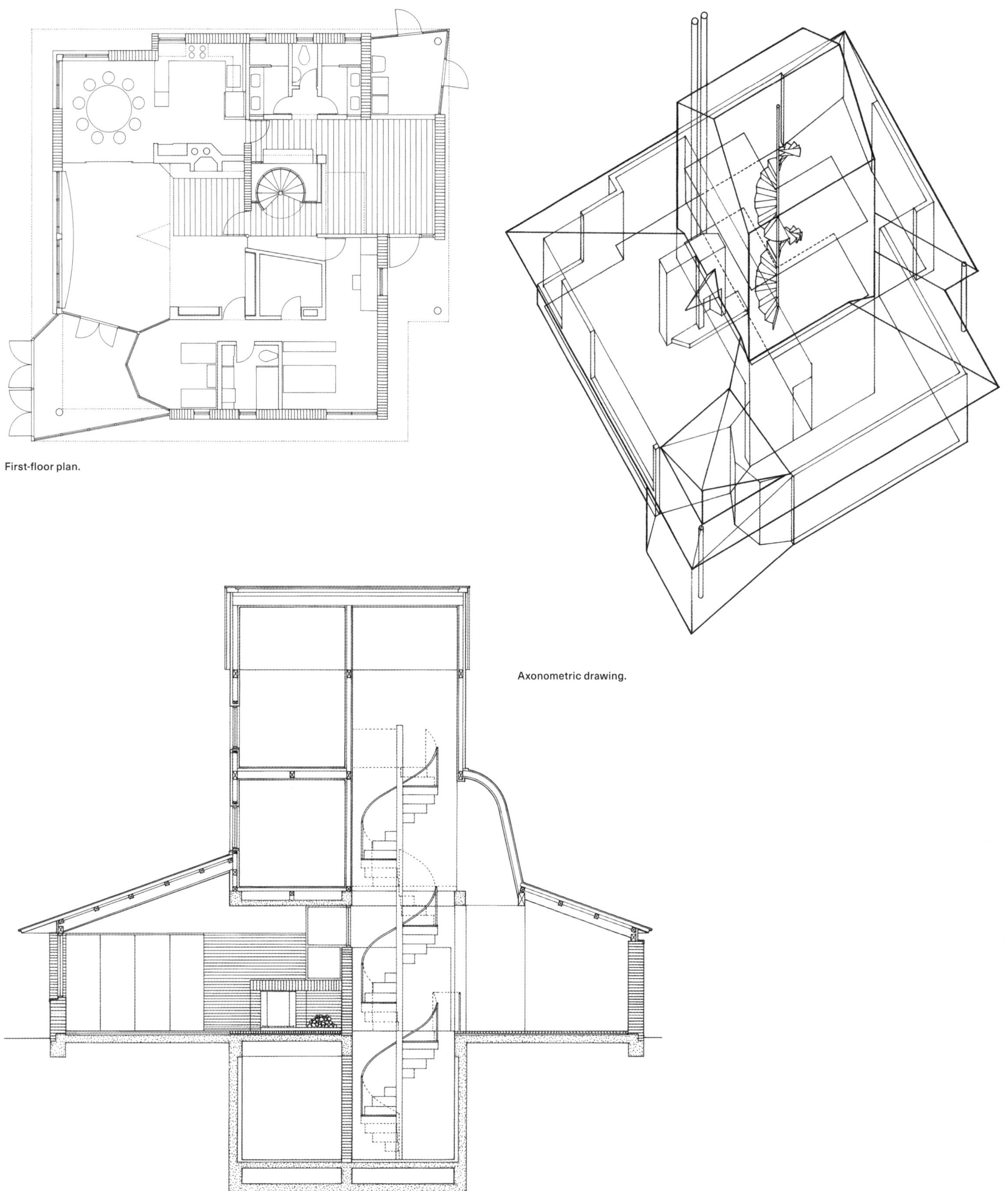

First-floor plan.

Axonometric drawing.

Section.

7

Technology and Construction

243

Steinberg Hall, Washington University in St. Louis

Location	St. Louis, Missouri, USA
Status	Completed
Year(s)	1960
Typology	Institution (University)
Area	3,400 m^2 (36,597 ft^2)

Steinberg Hall is the first project designed by Fumihiko Maki in the United States. Completed in 1960 during Maki's tenure as an instructor of urban design at Washington University's School of Architecture, the building was funded by Etta Steinberg (in memory of her husband, Mark Steinberg, a native St. Louisan and noted philanthropist) on the condition that Maki would be its architect. The project was later revisited by Maki and Associates, re-programmed and re-integrated into the campus as part of the Sam Fox School of Design & Visual Arts in 2006 (p158).

South entrance to Steinberg Hall, 1960.

Structural model of the roof of Steinberg Hall.

Sited between two neoclassical limestone structures (Bixby and Givens Halls), Steinberg is notable for its dramatically cantilevered folded plate roof. Utilizing post-tensioned cast-in-place technology, the roof shelters a generous terrace space that extends across the front and rear facades. As Bixby and Givens house the Schools of Art and Architecture, Steinberg was programmed with shared functions for these two schools, including an auditorium on the ground floor and the art and architecture library on the upper level. Steinberg Hall was also the first home of the Mildred Lane Kemper Art Museum (formerly the Washington University Gallery of Art), on its lower level.

As part of Washington University's 'White Campus' (named for its consistent use of light beige Indiana limestone), Steinberg Hall makes use of pre-cast concrete, cast-in-place concrete and white travertine stone to create a sympathetic yet modern addition – different in detail from its neighbours but still connected in scale and spirit. With the addition of two new buildings by Maki and Associates (Kemper Art Museum and Walker Hall) in 2006, Steinberg Hall was integrated into a new ensemble of interior and exterior spaces, a mini campus within the larger university. Its library and museum functions were shifted to the Kemper Art Museum, the auditorium renewed, and its generous open interior spaces repurposed to serve the architecture school.

Sketch.

Hoisting of the pre-cast structural folded roof plate.

Construction in progress for the folded plate, emphasizing the design intent of a more ethereal, informal character.

View of the structural cantilevered folded roof plate.

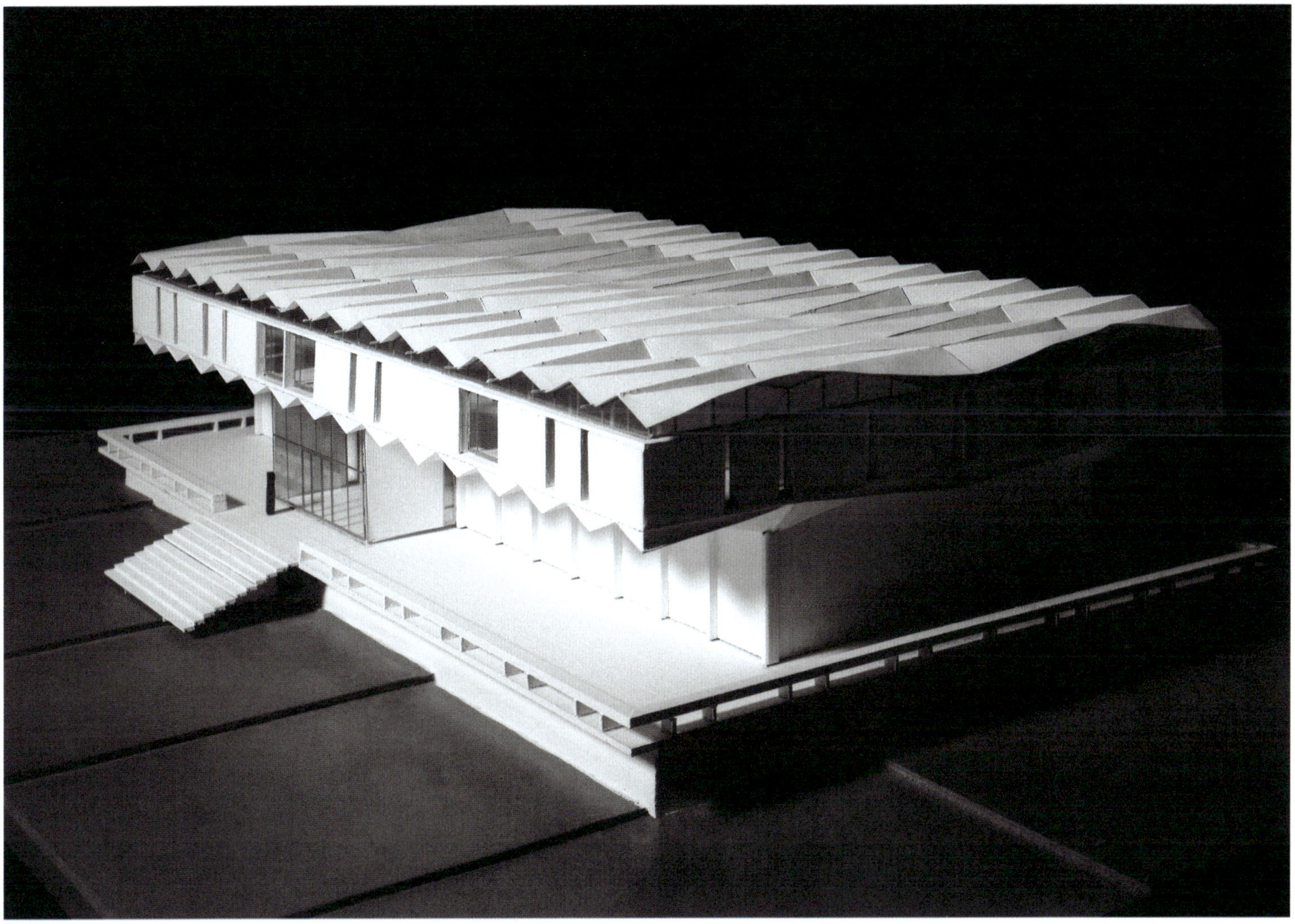

Model of Steinberg Hall.

Front entrance with plaza of the Osaka Prefectural Rinkai Sports Center.

Osaka Prefectural Rinkai Sports Center

Location	Takaishi City, Osaka Prefecture, Japan
Status	Completed
Year(s)	1972
Typology	Sports Centre
Area	11,930 m^2 (128,413 ft^2)

Osaka Prefectural Rinkai Sports Center was completed in 1972 on a narrow industrial parcel of reclaimed land in Takaishi, south of Osaka's downtown district. Intended to inspire athletic participation across a broad population, the project includes a wide range of public amenities and is designed to project an intimate, approachable image. The centre includes main and sub gymnasia, an indoor swimming pool that doubles as a skating rink in winter, communal and support facilities, and restaurants.

To promote continuity between different programmes, the design incorporates a variety of both visual and physical interconnections between different facilities. A single shared circulation spine connects all elements at the ground level and serves as informal breakout and social space. Courtyards and terraces surrounding the facilities improve natural lighting and provide further open spaces for relaxation and cross-programming. These open spaces also imbue the interior with natural light and views of surrounding water and greenery from the canal and its embankments.

The long-span roofing units consist of spindle and rectangular-section trusses bound together to form large, unified panels. These standard units are deployed in different combinations to shelter the main gym, the small gym, the entrance hall and the swimming pool. Clad in curved steel plate, the hollow units are structured similar to bamboo stalks, with added ribbing at fixed intervals for localized strength. Their open shape allows for easy integration of axial-flow exhaust fans, helping to keep the spaces below well-ventilated and comfortable throughout the year.

As this site is in a congested industrial zone, prefabricated parts (with sizes maximized according to transport limits) were used wherever possible and elements staged together on site prior to erection. Installation of reinforcing steel plates, interior insulation, exhaust ducts, light-fixture stabilizers, steel ceiling mesh and other mechanical equipment – even finish painting – was completed on grade before the units were hoisted into position. This system allowed the total structural framework to be erected in only twelve days.

Model of the Sports Center.

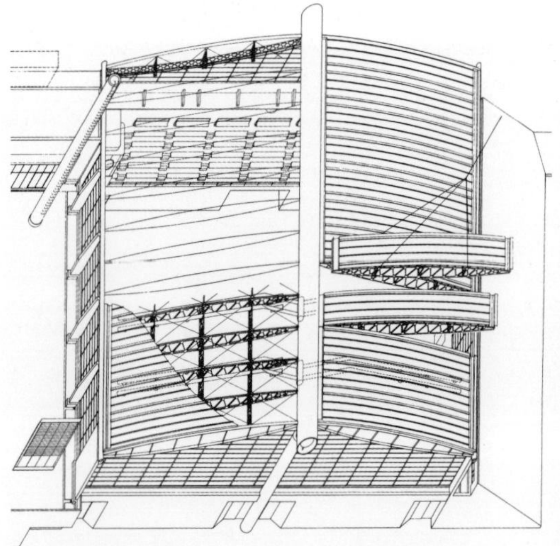

Axonometric showing the assembly of the prefabricated structural units. The roof over each of the major blocks of the building is composed of connected units resting on independent peripheral posts.

Each truss unit was pre-fitted with ductwork and ceiling panels while on the ground, before being hoisted into position.

View of the axial-flow exhaust fans, which provide ventilation to the spaces below while also serving as part of the roof beam structure.

The indoor swimming pool can be used as a skating rink in winter. A translucent glass curtain wall provides diffused natural light.

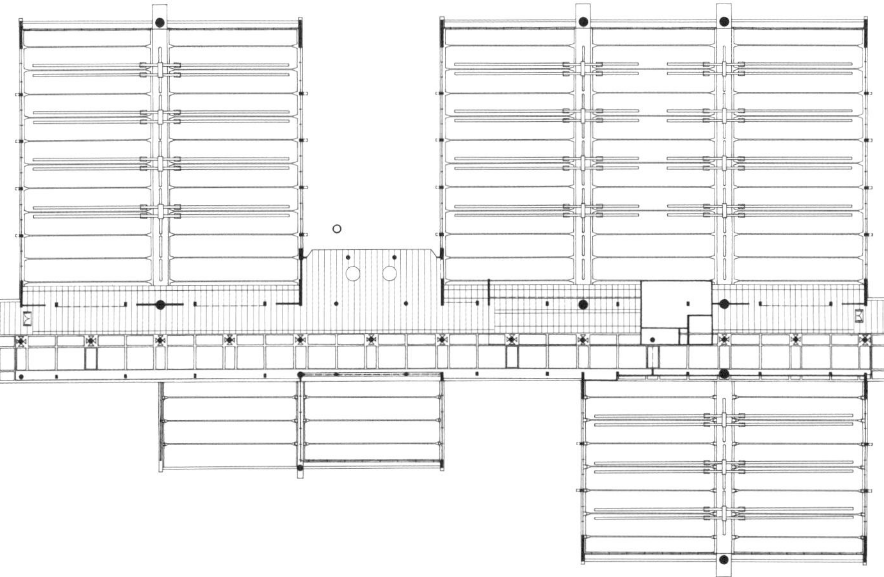

Reflected ceiling plan, showing aggregation of structural units and air ducting.

Okinawa Ocean Expo Aquarium

Location	Motobu, Okinawa Prefecture, Japan
Status	Completed
Year(s)	1975
Typology	Aquarium
Area	7,700 m^2 (82,882 ft^2)

Located in Motobu, Okinawa, the National Aquarium (officially known as the Okinawa Ocean Expo Aquarium and now the Okinawa Churaumi Aquarium) was the centrepiece of the 1975 International Ocean Exposition 'The Sea We Would Like to See', and remained as a permanent facility following the Expo's conclusion. Overlooking a 10-metre (33-ft) bluff along the oceanfront, the complex consists of the aquarium proper, a fronting plaza, a dolphin island to the south and extensive surrounding landscaping.

A majority of similar facilities from this era rely on highly functional but limited arrays of smaller display tanks. In contrast, the National Aquarium incorporates two immense tanks that recreate virtual slices of the sea and its group biology at their natural scale. This larger (and therefore more biologically realistic) type of tank was unprecedented and required new technology to successfully realize, but eventually became a model for subsequent aquarium projects across Japan.

To provide for uninterrupted viewing, the tanks themselves are composed of five layers of 50 mm-thick (2 in.) acrylic (total 250 mm / 9⅞ in.) cantilevered from the ground. This approach eliminates the need for bulky vertical or horizontal support mullions. These large tanks and other visitor amenities, such as built-in alcove seating and advanced audio-visual systems, established new standards for public aquarium design.

The necessary protection from the hot sun also inspired a unique architectural vocabulary for the National Aquarium – but one rooted in local traditions and the subtropical climate of Okinawa. A low-scaled prefabricated concrete arcade around the periphery of the aquarium combines with planted trees to shade the exterior spaces between the entrance plaza and the aquarium for visitors. The arcade's pre-cast elements are formed from circle quadrants and assembled via simple bolt connections, reducing construction time while ensuring structural stability. Pergolas and tents offer further shade for spectators.

This simple but effective design vocabulary responds to the climactic demands of this region, while recognizing the limitations of skilled construction labour available on the island at that time. It is an early example of sustainable building practice, exercised long before such interests became commonplace.

(Opposite) The simple arch elements of the aquarium are configured to produce a rhythmical arcade along the seaside.

Oceanside elevation.

Elevation.

Section.

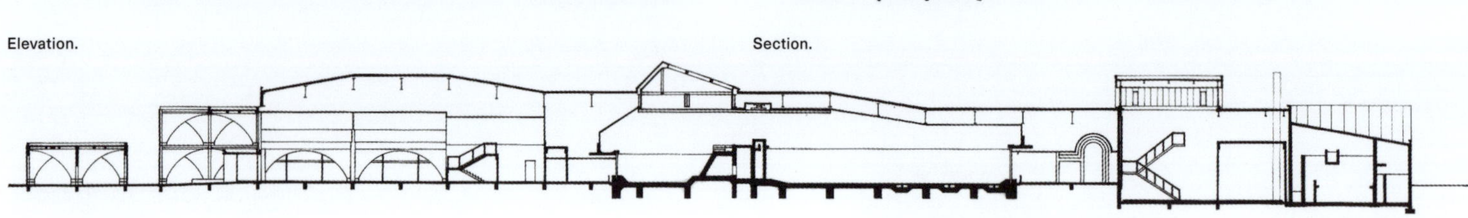

Longitudinal section.

Concrete arch sections were pre-cast off site, transported individually, and hoisted in place.

Curved seating elements follow the geometry of the arch supports, reinforcing the structural rhythm.

Night-time view.

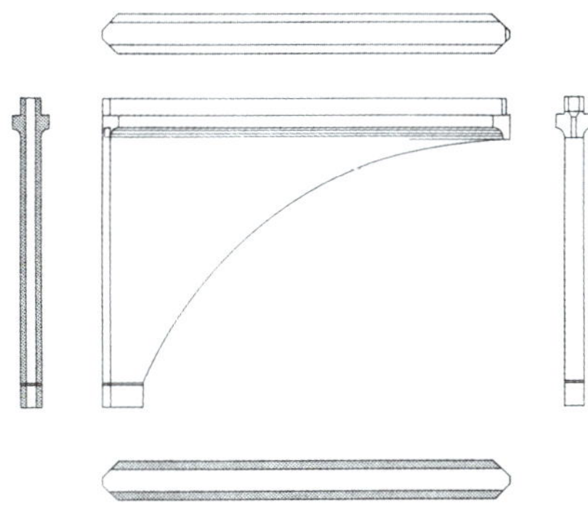
Assembly of the pre-cast elements for the arcade.

Aerial view of the aquarium complex.

View to the sea from the arcade at sunset.

Interior of the aquarium with alcove seating offering views into the two main tanks – the Coral Sea and the Deep Sea.

Fujisawa Municipal Gymnasium

Location	Fujisawa, Kanagawa Prefecture, Japan
Status	Completed
Year(s)	1984
Typology	Gymnasium
Area	11,100 m² (119,479 ft²)

In 1980, in response to its increasing population and popularity as a Tokyo commuter suburb, Fujisawa announced a plan to create a new sports complex close to its downtown area. The first stage of the project, including the gymnasium, a soccer field, an outdoor pool and an archery field, was completed in 1984. The gymnasium, designed by Maki and Associates, consists of a 2,000-seat main arena, a sub-arena, a martial-arts practice hall and support facilities.

Within its low-scaled surroundings, the dynamic roof forms of the arenas immediately create a memorable impact. The main arena roof is supported by two spanning arches with a 3.5 × 3.5-metre (12 × 12-ft) triangular section, 80 metres (262 ft) long. Large crescent-shaped concrete podia are cantilevered on both sides under these arches, each supporting 1,000 spectator seats. Located in a separate volume, the 20 × 12-metre (66 × 39-ft) sub-arena on the upper level is crowned with a pointed arch roof. Practice halls for judo and kendo, a restaurant and administrative spaces are arrayed on the two levels below. A third rectangular volume connects the main and sub-arena, serving as the entrance for users, spectators and restaurant patrons. Its grand exterior staircase leads visitors up to a central lobby, with direct connections to the restaurant and arena spectator areas, stairs down to the arena support spaces and stairs up to the sub-arena floor.

Both arena roofs are clad in 0.4 mm-thick (1⁄64 in.) stainless steel, creating a sense of lightness and ethereality despite their large volume. They also share continuous linear window openings and, via careful detailing at the transition between the light steel roof and the solid concrete base, emphasize the roof's floating quality. Even exterior lightning rods were designed and located with care, adding vertical punctuation points to the composition.

Overall, the project's advanced detailing in stainless steel and formal exuberance evoke a futuristic landscape while paying homage to the recent industrial past. The metallic roofs – suggestive at times of medieval helmets or futuristic spaceships – remain to this day a remarkable, forward-looking landscape for visitors and residents alike.

(Opposite) Skylights along the main structural frame allow natural light into the main arena.

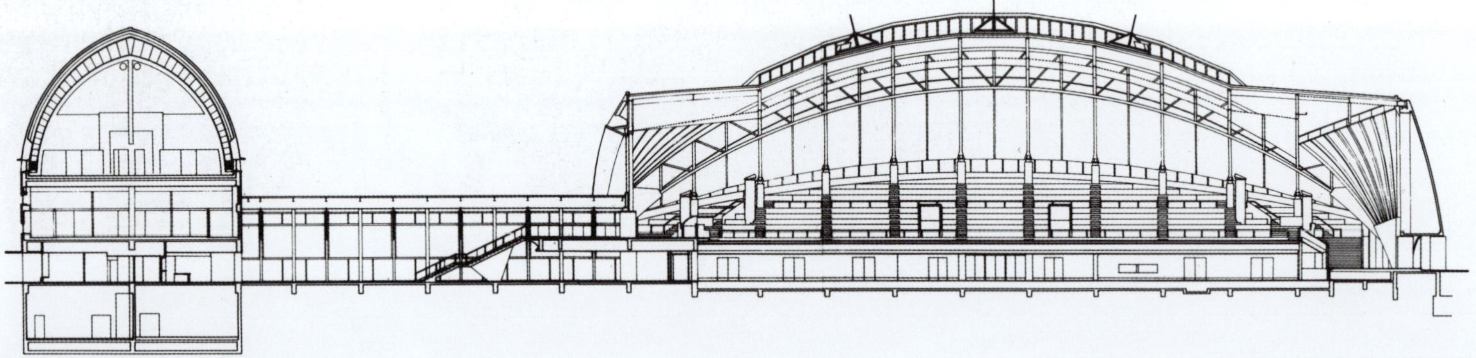

Longitudinal section.

Aerial view of the Fujisawa Municipal Gymnasium with the main arena and sub-arena.

View of steel roof under construction.

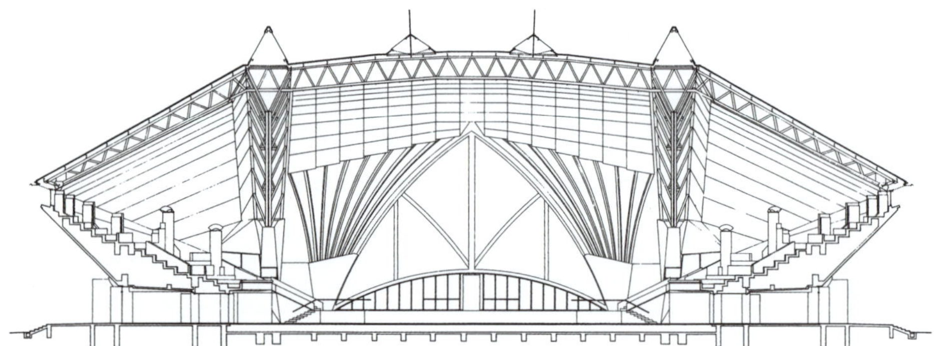

Main arena section of Fujisawa Municipal Gymnasium.

Exterior view: a Japanese warrior's helmet was one of the design inspirations for Fujisawa's distended form.

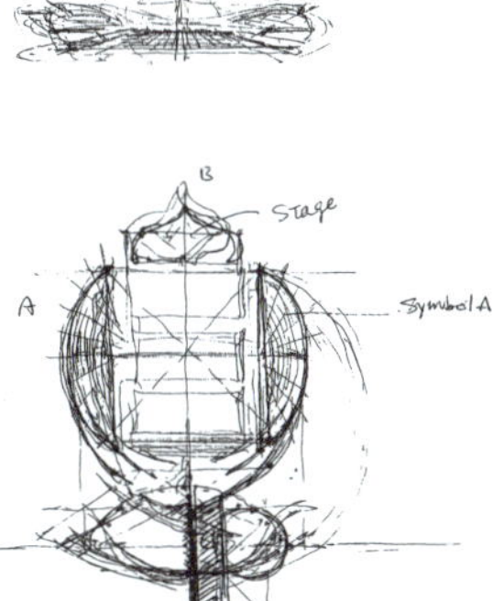

Sketch.

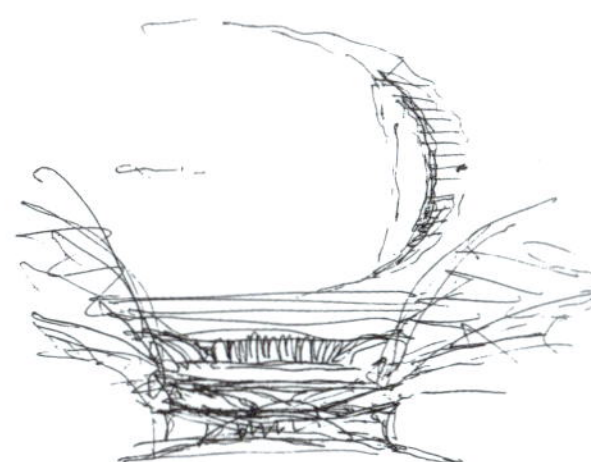

Sketch of the interior.

View of the main arena. The perforated metal edge accentuates the thinness of the stainless-steel roof panels.

Practice gymnasium on the third floor of the sub-arena.

Collage image of the sub-arena under construction.

Close-up of the roof of the main arena of Fujisawa Municipal Gymnasium.

Roof view of the main arena at the Tokyo Metropolitan Gymnasium, featuring a sculpture by Hidetoshi Ohno.

Tokyo Metropolitan Gymnasium

Location	Shibuya-ku, Tokyo Metropolitan, Japan
Status	Completed
Year(s)	1990
Typology	Gymnasium
Area	43,971 m^2 (473,300 ft^2)

Tokyo Metropolitan Gymnasium is located on a four-hectare site in central Tokyo and includes a 10,000-seat main arena, a swimming centre with 25- and 50-metre (82- and 164-ft) pools, a sub-arena and related support facilities. Open to all Tokyo residents, since its rebuild in 1990 it has served as the stage for a wide variety of national and international sporting events, including the 2020 Summer Olympics.

The site for the project is part of Meiji Park, bound by Sendagaya Station to the north, residential and commercial complexes to the south and west, and the Japan National Stadium to the east. In deference to its scale and location, Maki and Associates treated the entire site as an urban park. Sendagaya Station, the gateway for most visitors, is the centre point from which paths disperse radially toward the main arena, the swimming centre and the sub-arena.

A height restriction of 30 metres (98 ft) necessitated lowering most facilities below ground level. The complex therefore avoids an overly massive appearance and harmonizes well with nearby residential and commercial buildings. At the same time, the roof shapes are architecturally expressive – the main arena is a gently curving shell, the sub-arena a ziggurat, the swimming centre an undulating roof with hovering eaves, while the entrance is a glass pyramid. Together with exterior sculptures and bespoke lighting fixtures, visitors to the complex enjoy views juxtaposing the various buildings with the surrounding park and city, an experience reminiscent of traditional Japanese *kaiyushiki* (promenade) gardens.

On the interior, the main arena is a dynamic, double-curved space with a circular plan; its main structural girders rest on four massive piers, with additional stabilization from a perimeter tension ring. The swimming centre interior is characterized by its ethereal floating quality, with soft natural light filtering through its Teflon roof. The sub-arena has a rectilinear interior structure, directly lit via side windows. Though all three structures are independent in size, shape and form, they are knitted together by similar materials – metal, glass and concrete – and their consistent attention to detail.

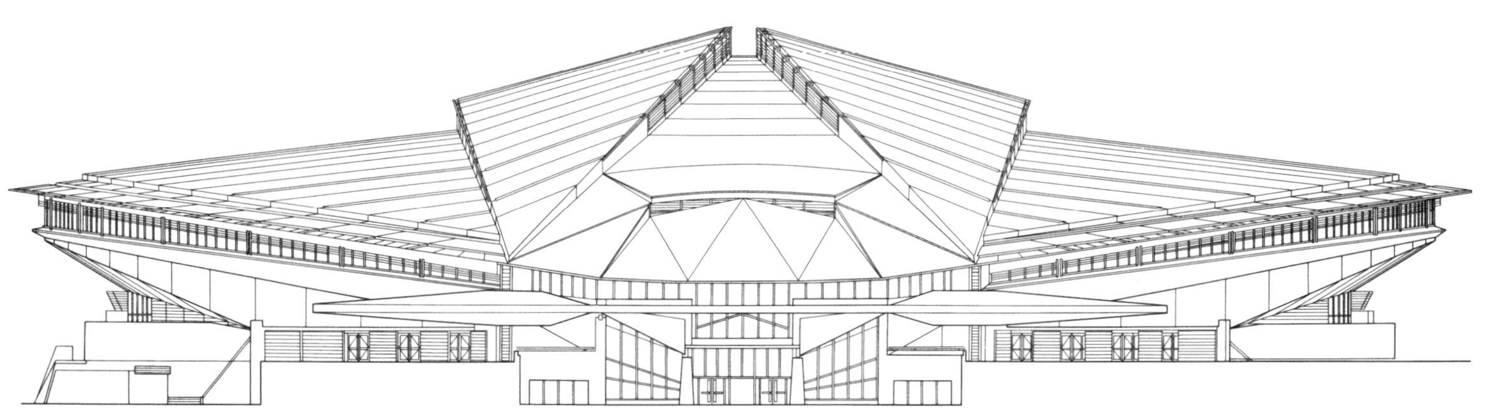

Detailed east elevation of the main arena.

Sketch of the interior of the main arena.

The shell-like roof of the main arena and the membrane over the swimming pavilion make for a varied skyline.

Aerial view of the sports complex with Shinjuku's skyscrapers in the background.

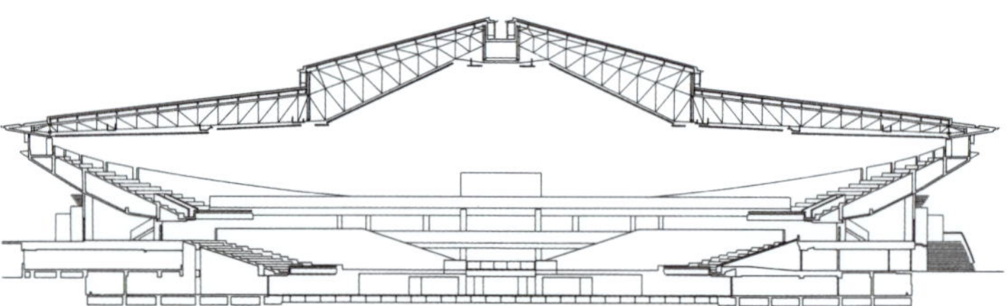

Section of main arena with the spectator seating.

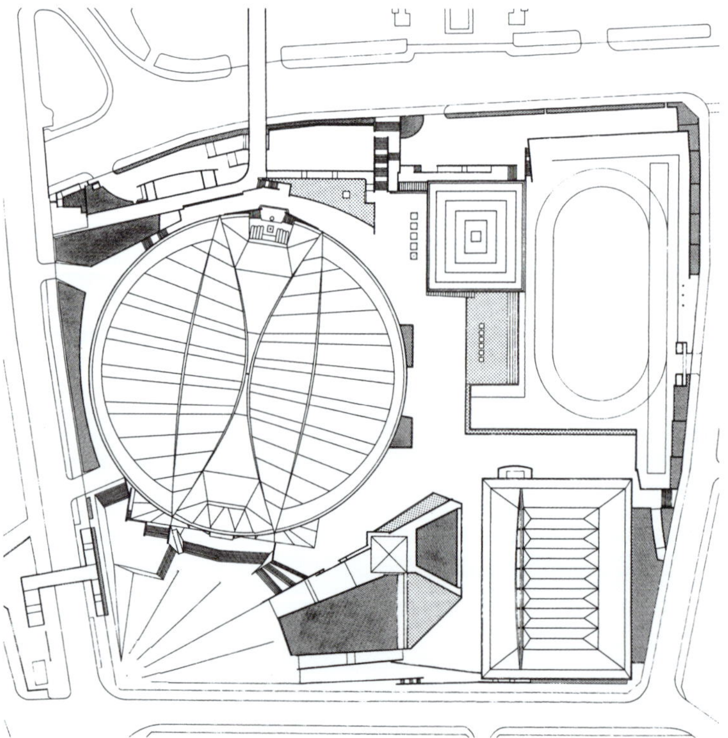

Tokyo Metropolitan Gymnasium site plan.

Interior view of the 50-metre (164-ft) swimming pool with adjacent spectator seating, illuminated by soft, ethereal light filtering through the Teflon roof and fibre-grating ceiling. A clerestory, separating the curving wall and hovering roof, allows light of a stronger intensity to find its way into the space to offer a mood of lightness.

Natural light entering the main arena, through the continuous windows along the edge of the spectator lobby, gives the roof a floating appearance.

Interior of the sub-arena, used primarily as a practice gym, with training courts, meeting rooms for sports seminars, exhibition space, generous administrative areas, and a restaurant.

The curvilinear main arena roof contrasts with the glazed pyramid.

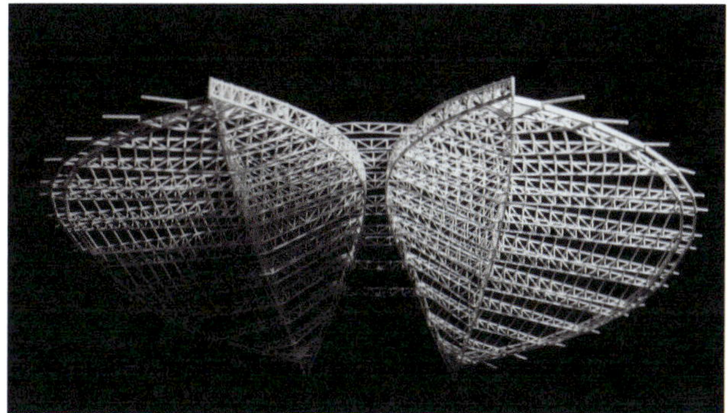

Model of the roof structure of the main arena.

Stairs and ramps leading to the entrance of the North Hall.

Makuhari Messe Convention Center

Location	Mihama-ku, Chiba Prefecture, Japan
Status	Completed
Year(s)	1989, 1997, 2009 Phase I 1989 Phase II 1997 Phase III 2009
Typology	Exhibition Hall
Area	131,043 m^2 (1.4m ft^2) 37,176 m^2 (400,159 ft^2) 593 m^2 (6,383 ft^2)

The Nippon Convention Center 'Makuhari Messe' was Maki and Associates' winning scheme in an invited national competition held in 1986. Designed for a flat parcel of reclaimed land facing Tokyo Bay halfway between Narita Airport and Central Tokyo, Makuhari Messe was the first comprehensive convention complex in Japan.

Phase I has three main components: a Main Exhibition Hall, a secondary Event Hall and a Conference Center. The Main Exhibition Hall roofline is an abstraction of a mountainous landscape – a poetic juxtaposition of natural and geometric elements in this otherwise indistinct location. The roof extends over eight identical 120 × 60-metre (394 × 197-ft) bays, sweeping a total span of 540 metres (1,772 ft); a raised linear mall along one edge offers views and access to exhibits from above. The adjacent Event Hall adds seating capacity of 9,000 (6,000 fixed and 3,000 movable) and serves a wide range of events and activities. Finally, the Conference Center houses a Banquet Hall for 2,000 people, additional larger meeting facilities, smaller meeting rooms, a restaurant and administrative offices – a variety of intimate and colourful areas that contrast the voluminous interiors of the Main Exhibition and Event Halls.

To meet the aggressive completion target and minimize on-site labour, the primary structural elements for both the Main Exhibition and Event Halls were factory pre-assembled, while stepped seating areas in the Event Hall utilize pre-cast concrete parts. However, because of the tight design timeline, not all elements could be pre-planned. The end result was a unique combination of ready-made industrial products with craft work, giving this project a distinct hand-built quality not normally possible at this scale.

In response to the success of phase I and the continuing need for convention space in Japan, a second exhibition hall also designed by Maki was added in 1997, immediately adjacent to the original Makuhari Messe. With its unique catenary tension curve, phase II adds another sculptural roofline to the overall composition, enhancing flexibility for different and larger single events in conjunction with phase I.

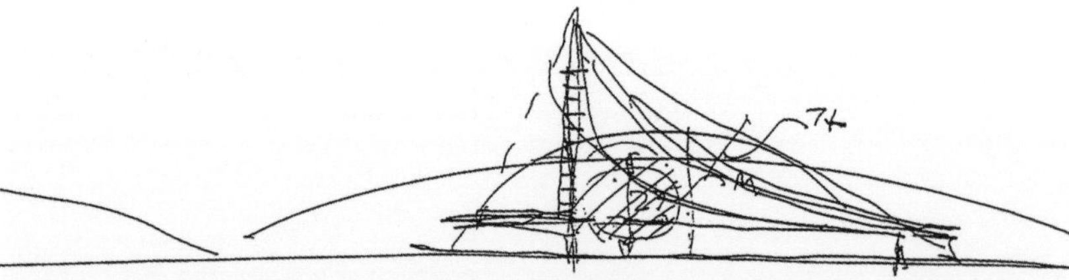

Conceptual sketch of the roof for the North Hall.

Structural model of the roof.

Aerial view of the 540 m (1,772 ft) arching roof of the exhibition hall.

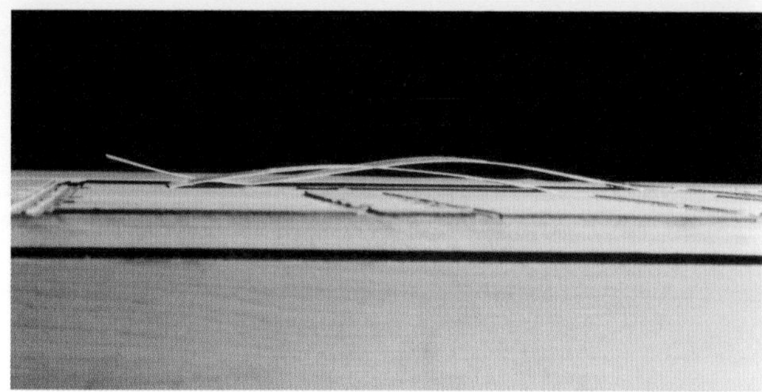

Image model emphasizing the rooflines.

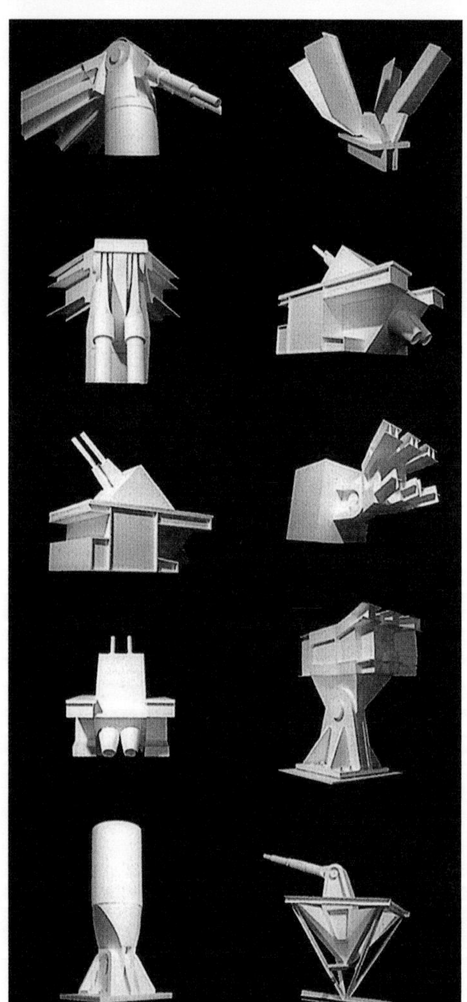

Study models of the joint detail.

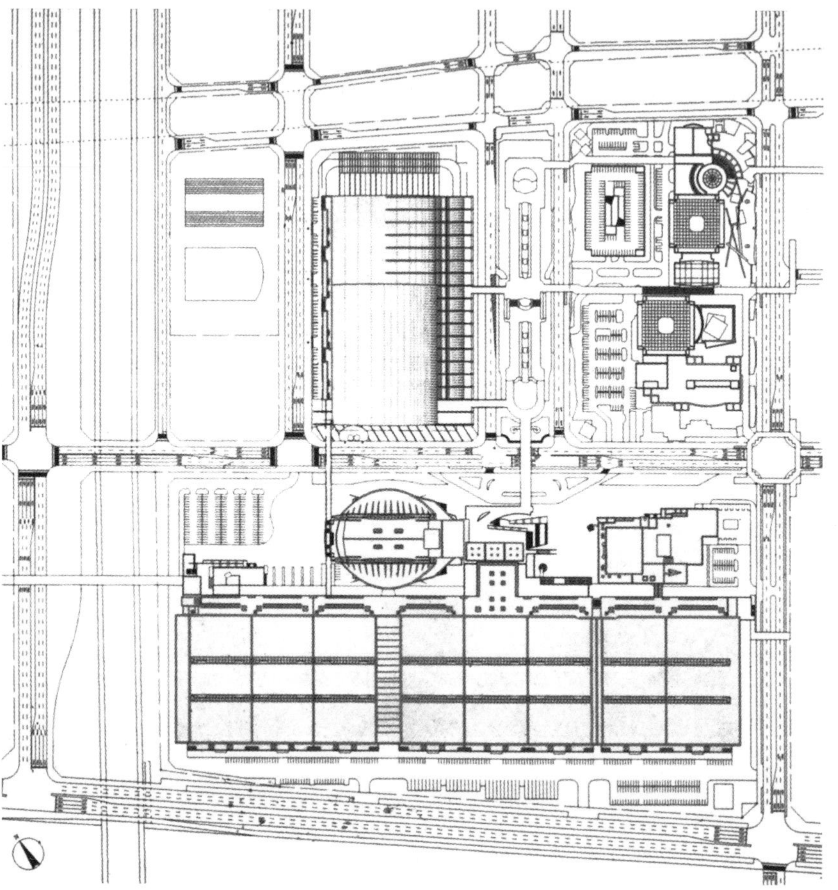

Site plan showing phases I, II and III.

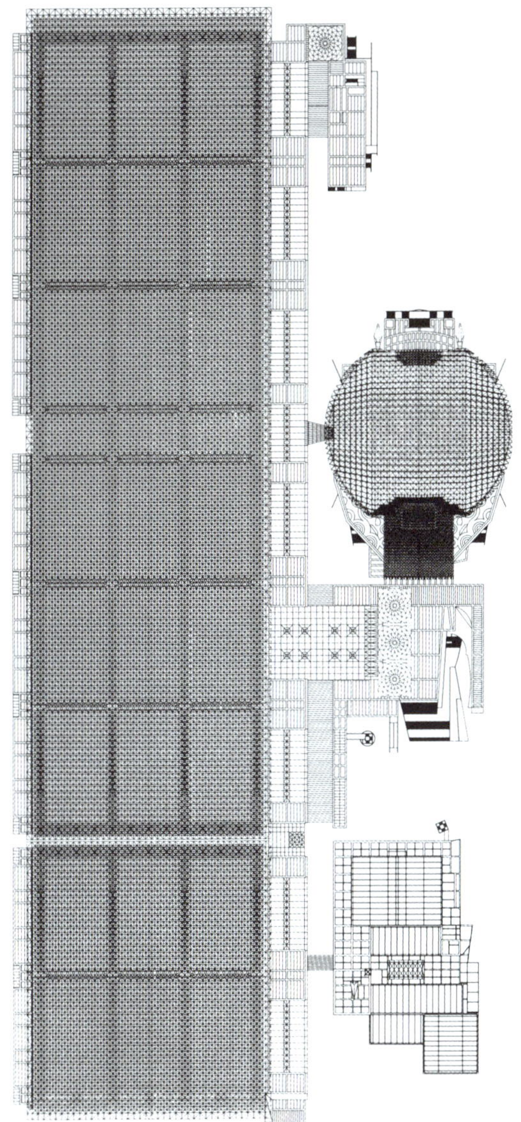

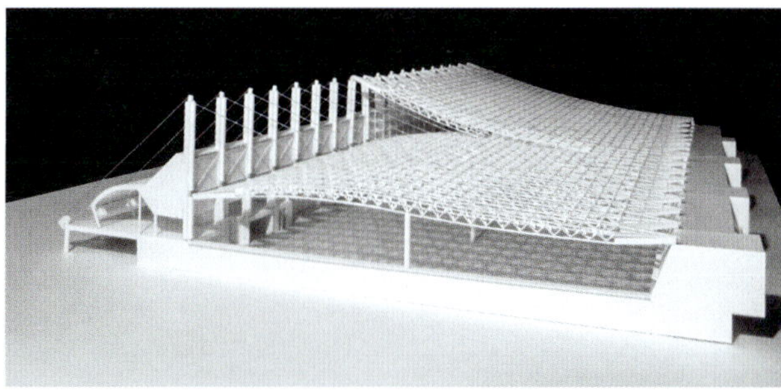

Model of cable-suspended roof of the North Hall.

South elevation of the North Hall (phase II). The glazed elliptical volume contains a conference room.

Roof structure plan.

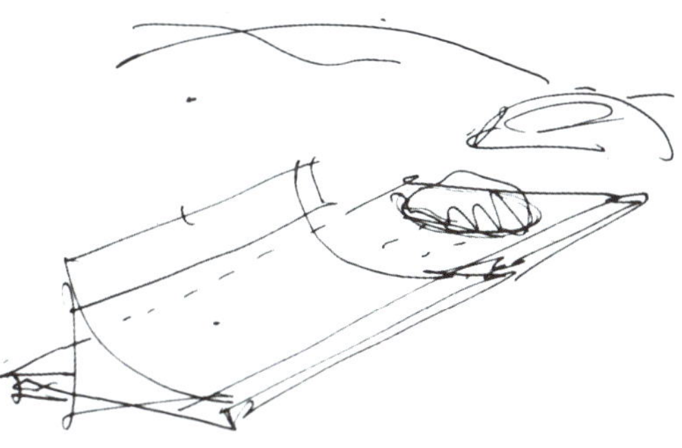

Concept sketch.

Pedestrian bridge towards the main entrance lobby of the Makuhari Messe.

The central mall of the Makuhari Messe connects the entrance to all eight exhibition halls.

Close-up of the roof cladding detail along the primary keel-shaped structural arch.

Interior of the lobby with entrance canopies seen beyond.

Aerial view of Makuhari Messe phases I, II and III, aligned along a straight axis toward Tokyo Bay in Chiba Prefecture.

Detail of the support for the prefabricated truss.

In the North Hall of the Makuhari Messe, the cross-section of the esplanade is modulated in order to create a dramatic entry sequence for the exhibition hall.

In the south wall of the exhibition hall, diffused light enters through the clerestory windows.

9

In Asia

Mediacorp

Location	One-North, Singapore
Status	Completed
Year(s)	2015
Typology	Broadcasting Studios, Offices
Area	118,400 m^2 (1.27m ft^2)

Exterior view of Mediacorp campus where the tapering southern end aligns with the geometry of the curvilinear site boundary.

Mediacorp is a key national institution charged with informing, educating and entertaining Singapore's diverse, multi-lingual populace. With a staff size of over 3,000, the company produces and distributes content across a variety of platforms including television, radio, newspaper, magazines and the internet. In May 2011, Mediacorp launched an international design competition to relocate their headquarters to one-north, a new development area master-planned by Zaha Hadid. Maki and Associates won the competition and the building was completed in 2015.

The design for the new headquarters divides its complex programme into three clear parts: a 1,859-seat broadcast theatre, a broadcast centre and corporate offices. These elements are carefully balanced, forming a gateway to an adjacent park which is also part of the master plan. The gateway features a grand staircase with fifty steps (commemorating Singapore's fiftieth year as an independent nation) and leads to a 'town square' plaza with views over the park. The building's east facade, facing this park, is outfitted with Singapore's largest media wall, streaming Mediacorp content for public viewing. Further civic synergies are created through a media gallery, featuring studio tours, exhibits, interactive displays and live productions of radio, drama, news and variety shows.

Architecturally, the distinctive composition of distended forms, sharp planes and angular profiles create a sculptural and kinetic silhouette in harmony with the master plan geometry. The building's upper levels are clad in bead-blasted stainless steel mirroring the surroundings, the climate and passersby – an ever-changing kaleidoscope of ephemeral reflections in dialogue with the context. At the building's lower levels, the facade is highly transparent and welcoming, maximizing visual connections between inside and outside.

Overall, the impact of the new Mediacorp headquarters goes well beyond simply being an efficient and functional broadcast facility. It actively promotes creative culture by attracting and inspiring visitors, while also creating a civic-scaled entry to the new surrounding development. The building is at once iconic but approachable, appropriate as the leading project for the one-north development.

Mediacorp campus from the main MRT station arrival approach on Stars Avenue.

Site plan of Mediacorp campus.

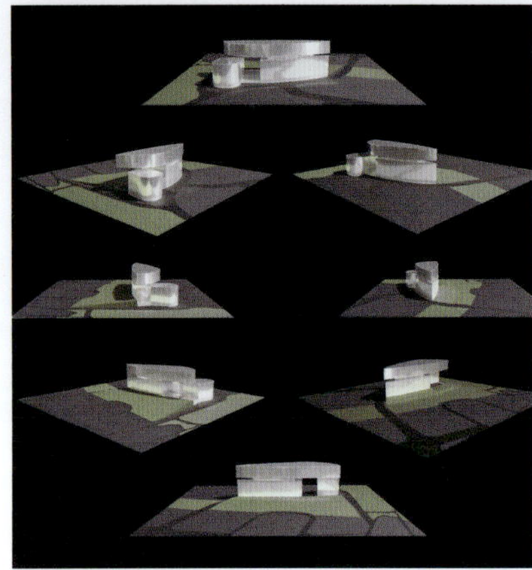

Concept model.

The collaborative workplace wraps around a light-filled, three-storey atrium defined by overhead skylights and a vertical green wall integrated into the central core.

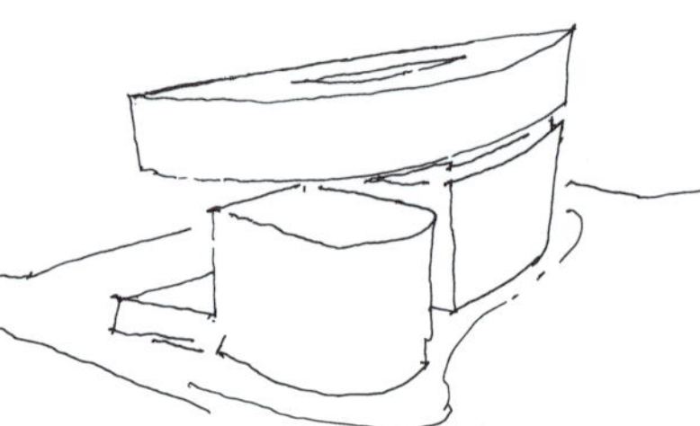

Concept sketch.

Large broadcasting studio with retractable seating.

Bleacher-style collaborative stairs for sitting, learning and interaction.

Theatre foyer.

Lounge and informal meeting area at link bridge.

A 1,549-seat integrated theatre with full broadcasting facilities, organized across three levels – Stalls, Parterre and Tiers 1 & 2 – rising from the stage.

View of east elevation from one-north park.

View toward the Grand Stairway – its fifty steps conceived in tandem with Singapore's fiftieth anniversary of nation building.

A Vanguard Vessel of Media

Heng Chye Kiang

Buildings have a way of 'suddenly' appearing on our landscapes as if by magic. Sometime during the second half of 2015, from the chrysalis of a project under construction emerged, magically, a stunning, shimmering vessel seemingly ready to sail with the traffic along the busy Ayer Rajah Expressway (AYE) in the south of Singapore. From then on, the Mediacorp campus became a beacon for countless motorists on their daily commute.

The Mediacorp campus was officially opened with much fanfare on 8 December 2015 by the Prime Minister Lee Hsien Loong in the presence of some 1,200 guests and staff. At the event, the Chairman of Mediacorp Teo Ming Kian proudly pronounced that the 'Mediacorp Campus will transform the way we work and engage with our audiences, partners and each other' and that 'the new campus would support a collaborative and innovative culture enabling the company to better serve its many stakeholders.'

This is a long-awaited building by Fumihiko Maki in Singapore – the result of a competition-winning entry submitted jointly with DP Architects in 2011; his last major work on the island-state was the Republic Polytechnic (RP) completed in 2007. Whereas the RP distributed its some 200,000 square metres (2.15m ft^2) of floor area in one-and-a-half dozen buildings, the Mediacorp campus packs about half that floor area into in a single building on a challenging compact site. The result is a large twelve-storey structure with four levels of basement.

Mediacorp is a group of commercial media companies with a combined staff of about 3,000. It has business interests in television and radio broadcasting, interactive media, print publishing and filmmaking, and is the largest media broadcaster in Singapore. The brief calls for facilities including a broadcast theatre and studios, technical production facilities, corporate offices as well as public amenities such as cafes, restaurants and a media gallery. The media centre must not only be functional and efficient but also encourage interaction among staff and promote creativity. Instead of a closed facility, it aspires to be publicly oriented, showcasing to visitors the unique operations of its broadcasting centre.

Promise of a Challenging Site

The Mediacorp campus building sits at a critical location within the 200 hectares one-north business park. The park, master-planned by Zaha Hadid in 2001, comprises three main clusters – Biopolis (biomedical R&D hub), Fusionopolis (infocomm, engineering and physical sciences R&D hub) and Mediapolis (digital media industries). This initiative is intended to support Singapore's foray into the knowledge and innovation-driven economy. While much of the construction of the other two clusters has been completed, Mediapolis which takes up 19 hectare (47 acres) of land will house a media ecosystem of diverse media players to help prime Singapore as a future media hub.

Situated on a long curvilinear (almost right-angle) triangular site, 225 × 120 m (738 × 394 ft), the Mediacorp campus is physically and symbolically the vanguard of Mediapolis and has become a veritable landmark for this new cluster of development. Perhaps more importantly, via its design and content, the campus can inspire the industry and help play a catalytic role in developing the media ecosystem.

The 1.5-hectare (3.7-acre) site is bounded on the north by the Stars Avenue, on the west by the one-north Avenue and the east by an elevated linear park raised 7.5 m (24.6 ft) over a parking garage. This awkwardly shaped site has two visually prominent corners – a western corner that faces the built-up section (the 'city') of one-north and the main approach from Ayer Rajah Avenue, and a very sharp southern point that is visible from the AYE.

'Forming' the Vanguard

Being the point building of the media cluster, setting the stage for the erection of future structures beyond the parkland and serving as an interface with the 'city' must have been an important concern in the exercise of collective form making for Maki. If the intent was to create 'unity' with the 'city' and craft a 'built-in link and an implied system of linkage', as he had advocated in his *Investigations on Collective Form* published fifty years earlier, for a segment of the business park that has yet to take shape, then the Mediacorp Campus has succeeded brilliantly.[1]

The complex programme is first translated into three primary groups – the broadcast theatre, the broadcast centre (studios and technical production facilities) and the corporate offices – and expressed architecturally as three distinctive components. These are then artfully assembled – an architectural approach he termed as 'one of making a building out of given components' – to constitute a gateway linking the 'city' to the park and beyond.[2]

Urbanistically and symbolically, this ceremonial gateway or portal fulfils several important roles. Not only does it provide a view corridor in the 250-metre-long (820-ft) west facade, it also allows physical access via a grand staircase from the entrance drop-off to the sheltered 'town square' and the park beyond. The physical link creates a pedestrian spine through the building and an immediate link to the parkland and implies a linkage to the future developments of the media cluster beyond.

Here, the physical connectivity is also layered with symbolism. The fifty steps of the grand staircase commemorate Singapore's fiftieth year as an independent nation when the Mediacorp campus was opened in 2015. Looking up from the 'town square' we see the sky through an alignment of an oculus and a conical skylight in the atrium floor and the ceiling, respectively, of the horizontal corporate offices block that forms the portal six storeys above, perhaps, reminding us of the infinite reach of the all-pervading digital media.

The design solution that assembles the three distinctive component blocks adopts a strategy of complementary contrasts. Volumetrically the blocks are expressed very differently. The theatre block is sculpted as a bulbous form to address the prominent west corner in the axis of approach while the streamlined aileron plan of the corporate offices block hovering over the broadcast centre offers two remarkably sharp points at the northern and southern ends. The result is a building with essentially only two significantly dissimilar long elevations that are masterfully treated to render the constituent components legible. Seen from the Ayer Rajah Expressway, the two elevations converge to a single sharp edge to become the extremely sculpted form that resembles, metaphorically, a refined vessel of media and information.

The Contextual Form

The geometry of the Mediacorp campus's form is highly shaped by the programmatic content as well as the physical and climatic contexts. Facing the business park is a generously articulated western 'city' facade that hugs the curve alignment of road, aptly revealing itself in motion like a strip of moving images. The east elevation is presented as a long, elegantly quiet backdrop to the expansive linear park. Along this facade is also a planted sky terrace with a row of highly ordered trees on the eighth floor, perhaps relating to the parkland below. A timber-decked viewing plateau lined with an extensive, manicured green wall serves the public entrance and eateries along this facade. Social and recreational activities, in addition to Mediacorp weekend events, are held on this deck as well as in the adjoining park. A discerning eye will quickly detect the subtle geometrical articulations that incorporate arcades and awnings necessary in a tropical climate of sudden rains and searing sun.

The same rigour that we see in the controlled palette of materials and forms that gives Maki's buildings such restrained elegance is being extended to the selection and treatment of vegetation on the building. Perhaps given the nature of Singapore's climate a combination of a more luxuriant form of greenery would have enhanced the contrast and yield a new form of tropicalized Maki aesthetics.

Functional Stages

The organization of the programme into the three distinguishable architectural forms is also astutely planned to allow them to function in synergy and independently. Unseen to most, a service road beneath the viewing plateau serves the broadcast theatre, the two major broadcast studios and provides secured vertical access to the broadcast centre and corporate offices above. At least three separate sets of public entrances serve the complex: the first allows controlled access to the broadcast centre and corporate offices; the second to the media gallery; and the third to the broadcast theatre.

Casual visitors and users of the park will be most familiar with the entrance from the viewing plateau to the media gallery where a 'stars cafe' gives them the opportunity to see and mingle with media stars and celebrities. Here, Maki created a stage beyond the formal stage, on which the public and the celebrities are all actors. From here, visitors are led via a discreet tour route to have a glimpse into the production facilities and operations within the broadcast centre and its digital-first integrated newsroom where some 700 journalists produce content for digital, television, radio and print.

To the concert goer, the operation of the broadcast theatre is independent of the other components. Accessible from both the drop-off and the town square, the carefully proportioned double-volume lobby and gallery offer an unimpeded view of the Fusionopolis cluster before one enters the state-of-the-art theatre, integrated with broadcast facilities and a fly tower. The hall can be used for a variety of events including musicals, drama, concerts, variety shows and festivals, although compromises have to be made to accommodate their different needs.

The most spatially spectacular functional aspect is the aileron-plan corporate offices component. Occupying four levels, from floors nine to twelve, this block that hovers above the rest is innovative in many respects. By its sheer size and structural prowess, the corporate offices block is impressive. It stretches the entire length of the site and measures about 65 metres (213 ft) at its widest. One end of the block is cantilevered 66 metres (217 ft) from a super-structural core and floats effortlessly over the theatre block. The other end sits lightly above the broadcast centre block; together, they cut the distinctive silhouette observable from the AYE.

The corporate office spaces are organized around an enormous four-storey central atrium some 120 × 35 m (393.7 × 114.8 ft) and criss-crossed by link bridges and staircases. Five large conical skylights flood this atrium with a soft beautiful light, even while the hot tropical sun blazes outside. This is perhaps Maki's ultimate 'city room', infinitely flexible and shared by some 2,000 corporate citizens.

The link bridges, like the different floor plates that they connect, are similarly carpeted in RGB colours. The visual dynamism of these colourful bridges cutting through the atrium is only surpassed by the straight flight of stairs that directs one's eye diagonally across the height and into the depth of the atrium. While we are reminded of some similar efforts in his earlier buildings, such as the MIT Media Lab, the scale and visual impact of the bridges and stairs in this enormous city room is probably unprecedented in Maki's other works.

The design and configuration of the corporate offices around the city room will perhaps bring about new work practices that will, in Chairman Teo Ming Kian's words, 'transform the way we work and engage with our audiences, partners and each other' and 'support a collaborative and innovative culture enabling the company to better serve its many stakeholders.' These collaborative office spaces are unassigned for hot-desking and encourage interaction, knowledge sharing and creativity among staff. Groups of people gather for discussion on the bridges and in the atrium where a cafe offers snacks and drinks.

Near one end of the atrium, an intimate, tiered gathering space stretches the floor of the atrium to link diagonally to a floor below and, visually, beyond the building to the park. While functionally this little tiered theatre allows for small-scale events, spatially and visually, it is a masterstroke that injected even more spatial interest and variety to the atrium and extends the corporate atrium spatially from the park and parvis to the sky.

As the vanguard in Mediapolis, the Mediacorp campus stands as a leading vessel that exudes an extraordinary presence and permanence, faintly shimmering in its bead-blasted steel cladding and reflecting its surroundings and the changing sky ever so subtly. Maki has created an urban complex that is both 'understandable' and 'imageable'.[3] He has forged remarkable urban strategies and linkages, created delightful interior spaces and established a strong corporate identity for the Mediacorp – a difficult feat given its complex programme on a challenging site that sheer architectural design prowess has turned the liability into an asset.

1 Maki, Fumihiko. *Investigations In Collective Form.* St. Louis: School of Architecture, Washington University, 1964, p19.
2 Ibid., p6.
3 Ibid., p34.

Heng Chye Kiang is the Provost's Professor at the College of Design and Engineering, National University of Singapore, where he was the former Dean of School of Design and Environment (SDE) from 2007 to 2016 and Head of its Department of Architecture prior to his deanship. He teaches and researches urban history, sustainable urban design and planning, and publishes widely in these areas.